EDITED BY

BELINDA WILLIAMS

Closing the Achievement GAP

[A Vision for
Changing Beliefs
and Practices

2nd Edition]

Association for Supervision
and Curriculum Development
Alexandria, Virginia USA

Association for Supervision and Curriculum Development
1703 N. Beauregard St. • Alexandria, VA 22311-1714 USA
Telephone: 800-933-2723 or 703-578-9600 • Fax: 703-575-5400
Web site: http://www.ascd.org • E-mail: member@ascd.org

Gene R. Carter, *Executive Director;* Nancy Modrak, *Director of Publishing;* Julie Houtz, *Director of Book Editing & Production;* Tracey Smith, *Production Manager;* Ernesto Yermoli, *Project Manager;* Georgia McDonald, *Senior Graphic Designer;* BMWW, *Typesetter.*

Printed in the United States of America.

ISBN: 0-87120-838-5   ASCD product no.: 102010
ASCD member price: $20.95 nonmember price: $25.95   s12/03

Library of Congress Cataloging-in-Publication Data
Closing the achievement gap : a vision for changing beliefs and practices / edited by Belinda Williams.—2nd ed.
     p.   cm.
Includes bibliographical references and index.
   ISBN 0-87120-838-5 (alk. paper)
   1. Children with social disabilities—Education—United States. 2. Education, Urban—Social aspects—United States. 3. Academic achievement—United States. 4. Educational change—United States. I. Williams, Belinda. II. Association for Supervision and Curriculum Development.
   LC4091.C56 2004
   370'.91732—dc22   2003020786

13 12 11 10 09 08 07 06 05 04 03   12 11 10 9 8 7 6 5 4 3 2 1

Closing the Achievement Gap

A Vision for Changing Beliefs and Practices

2nd Edition

Introduction

Belinda Williams

*Clearly, issues of power and privilege contribute to the contin-
uation of poor schooling for many children, and the effects of
racism and classism cannot be ignored. Yet, in the course of my
work, I have also come to believe that much of the reason for the
current sorry state of many schools is a genuine lack of understanding on the part of policymakers and practitioners about
what is needed to produce schools that can teach for understanding in the context of a complex pluralistic society.*

—Linda Darling-Hammond (1997, p. xvi)

D espite some evidence of success and strong progress by black, Hispanic, and socioeconomically disadvantaged students from 1970 to
1988, the education reform efforts of the last decade have not en-
abled significant numbers of students to become educationally competitive
or to close the gaps in achievement (D'Amico, 2001; Lee, 2002; National
Center for Education Statistics, 2001; Olson, 1996). The achievement gap is
apparent in a range of educational success indicators (grades, test scores,
dropout rates, college entrance/completion rates, and so forth) and in every
kind of school district and socioeconomic group (D'Amico, 2001).

The Achievement Gap Puzzle:
What's Missing from Current Reforms?

In the following chapters, the authors provide answers to the question,
"What else do we need to know and do to close the achievement gaps
among groups?" The information presented in this book will go beyond

the focus on *urban* education to revisit and update the theory and evidence offered in the first edition (Williams, 1996) in order to

- Elaborate and distinguish between individual and group differences, as well as between the education goals of improving achievement and closing the gaps;
- Analyze the complexity of achievement gaps among groups; and
- Offer integrated strategies to close those gaps.

This research and theory is offered to inform the following groups:

- Legislators responsible for policies and resource allocations
- Educators who make decisions that influence school reform strategies
- Teacher preparation institutions
- Community leaders and parents
- Education researchers

Chapter 1 identifies the indicators and reviews the implications of the gaps in achievement that exist among racial and socioeconomic groups in the United States. It offers a brief historical perspective for the purpose of positioning reform efforts within the social context of education in the United States. A critique of current reform efforts supports the theoretical argument for integration and for revising assumptions about normal human development. Such revisions can help to reframe and inform education proposals. The chapter offers a broad definition of accountability to support and outline the roles and responsibilities of the entire education community.

In Chapter 2, Manning and Kovach identify closing the achievement gap as the major civil rights issue of the 21st century. They identify the following four dimensions of the achievement gap that must be understood to successfully address the complexity of the issue:

- The national drive for excellence in education
- Equity issues related to disparities in the distribution of educational resources
- Organizational features of schools
- The interrelationships between these factors and the larger social context of a society that continues to be deeply divided by race

Issues of equity and race and the standard deviation differences in intellectual patterns and achievement measures continue to impact the education system and practices of sorting. Oakes and Lipton (1999) point out that authorities assume student achievement test performance represents the ability to learn, and they place children in tracks and programs that define their educational experiences, or in other words, what they are taught and expected to learn (see Figure I.1). Other researchers have examined and argued these issues for decades, and this volume will not elaborate them further (Darling-Hammond, 1997; Gould, 1996; Herrnstein & Murray, 1994; Jencks & Phillips, 1998; Jensen, 1969, 1973; Ravitch, 2000). However, as Dickens and Flynn (2001) observe:

> *Some argue that the high heritability of IQ renders purely environmental explanations for large IQ differences between groups implausible. Yet, large environmentally induced IQ gains between generations suggest an important role for environment in shaping IQ.* (p. 346)

FIGURE I.1

Origins of the Achievement Gap and Student Sorting in School

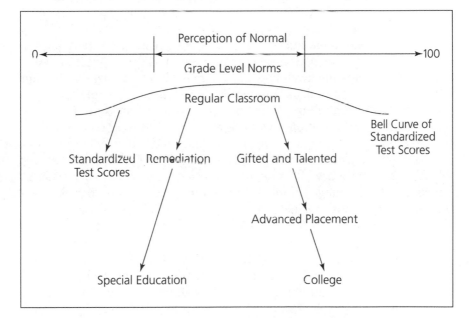

Cognitive psychologists (Gardner, 1983, 1999; Perkins, 1995; Sternberg, 1998) suggest that intelligence is multifaceted and that IQ tests and standardized achievement tests simply measure a limited set of developed or developing abilities, not the intellectual potential for learning. These emerging understandings of cognitive or intellectual development have clear implications for restructuring current systems and practices in schools. For example, decision makers might shift the emphasis of their use of test score data from tracking and placement to identifying ways of strengthening meaningful connections between students' experiences and standards.

Current Understandings of Intelligence and Achievement Gaps Among Groups

In Chapter 3, Marzano considers a major component of what standardized achievement tests and intelligence tests measure—prior knowledge and vocabulary. His review of the literature identifies the role of vocabulary knowledge in developing crystallized intelligence (the abilities to recognize or recall facts, generalizations, and principles, as well as to learn skills). He argues that schools have a powerful opportunity to reverse the dynamic that contributes to achievement gaps by developing students' background knowledge; this will strengthen both language competence and the ability to think in abstract ways.

It is ironic that, amid numerous reports of increasing diversity in public schools in the United States (Berman et al., 1997; Darling-Hammond, 1997) and the growing awareness of gaps in achievement between groups (Haycock, 2001), an in-depth discussion of the implications of diversity is missing. At the beginning of the 21st century, researchers are observing that education reform proposals have avoided a rigorous review and interpretation of the gaps in cognitive and academic achievement patterns, for example, between Japanese or Chinese and white students; among black, Hispanic, and white students; between socioeconomically advantaged and disadvantaged students; and so forth. Such an undertaking offers the best promise for developing a framework to explain and understand normal human development and cultural diversity in the context of learning, and could provide a perspective for scaling up school reforms to close the gaps in achievement. Caine and Caine (1991), in their extensive description and summary of brain research, advise the education community that "Educators do not need another method or approach or model guaranteed to 'save' education." They recommend developing a framework for a more complex form of learning that would help organize and make sense of what is already known.

After many years of examining school reform, Newmann and Wehlage (1995) and Fullan (1999) concur. They urge practitioners and policymakers first to identify "principles of intellectual quality in authentic achievement" in order to avoid fragmentation and incoherence. Identifying principles of intellectual quality must precede the introduction of multiple unconnected innovations that produce what Fullan (quoting Bryk) characterizes as " 'Christmas tree schools'—so many innovations as decorations, superficially adorned."

Schoenfeld (1999), past president of the American Educational Research Association (AERA), recommends "unifying . . . cognitive and social learning . . . and . . . reconceptualizing the discussion of nature versus nurture and social systems." Similarly, citing Piaget and Vygotsky, the National Research Council identifies a critical perspective of the "new science of learning," or in other words, the central role of prior knowledge as elaborated by Marzano (Bransford, Brown, & Cocking, 1999). According to their analysis, all learners come to formal education with a range of prior knowledge, skills, beliefs, and concepts that significantly influence what they notice about the environment and how they organize and interpret it.

Traditionally, educators have described social class influences and experiences as superseding ethnic group effects in such areas as child-rearing practices, educational and occupational aspirations, and achievement motivation. Consequently, it has been a common assumption that providing minorities and the disadvantaged with the experiences of middle-class whites, such as better jobs, housing, preschool, and so forth, will eliminate educational differences. The authors included in this volume recommend that, in addition to social class variables, educational planning must consider culturally different patterns of mental abilities and other behaviors reflecting cultural experience variables (Annenberg Institute for School Reform, 2002).

Culture and Experience in Analyzing and Addressing Achievement Gaps

In Chapter 4, Trumbull, Greenfield, and Quiroz offer a thorough analysis of the nature and dynamics of culture, cultural differences, and language development. They support a broader and deeper understanding of culture (beyond the current attempts of schools to value and celebrate cultural diversity limited to the celebration of heroes, heroines, holidays, and food) as relevant not only to curriculum content (a common starting point for multicultural efforts), but also to the framing of content, such as in the development of performance standards, instruction, assessment, and resource allocation. They review how race, class, length of time in the United

States, and schooling practices all influence the degree to which particular students experience schooling, and they describe successful approaches.

Currently, the limited perspectives of individual researchers whose programs enjoy commercial, popular, or political support are what define and guide education reform proposals (Northwest Regional Educational Laboratory, 1998). Program evaluation criteria have not required coherent, well-defined theoretical foundations for the recommending of particular programs or interventions. Few of these programs, upon intense scrutiny, meet the requirements of good research, such as rigor, appropriateness of fit across theory and other findings, or results with demonstrable equivalent outcomes across diverse, socioeconomically disadvantaged populations (American Institutes for Research, 1999). Oakes and Lipton (1999) characterize the following popular approach to education to illustrate this point:

> Assertive discipline . . . is a commercially hawked scheme to control behavior, and it promotes an authoritarian, anti-community, and less intellectually challenging classroom. Furthermore, it has no support in sound educational research and theory. It is neither honest nor objective to describe popular teaching practices in a neutral manner if they do not stand up to the standards of social justice or education research. (p. xix)

More than 60 years ago, Dewey (1938) emphasized that teaching and learning must be connected with the student's experience. What is that experience, and what cognitive structures developed by that experience enable the individual to both process and make meaning of new knowledge?

Bruer (1997, 1998) cautions the education community to remain skeptical about brain-based educational practice and policy applied to early childhood learning, but encourages the community to look for basic science that is fundamental to the emerging understanding of how neural structures support and implement cognitive functions. Echoing Schoenfeld, Bruer (1997) also urges research programs in education to develop an interactive relationship between cognitive psychology and systems neuroscience. Such a relationship enables educators to discover how current brain research confirms much of what behavioral science already understands about teaching, learning, and cognitive development. Caine and Caine (1991) summarize and recommend a guiding principle for the education community:

> The brain searches for common patterns and connections. . . . Optimizing the use of the human brain means using the brain's infinite capacity to make connections—and understanding what conditions maximize this process. In essence, students learn from their entire ongoing experience. In many ways,

content is inseparable from context. . . . Every complex event embeds information in the brain and links what is being learned to the rest of the learner's current experiences, past knowledge, and future behavior. The primary focus for educators, therefore, should be on expanding the quantity and quality of ways in which a learner is exposed to content and context. (pp. 5–6, 128)

Content of Professional Development for Educators to Close Achievement Gaps

In Chapter 5, Zeichner outlines professional development requirements for expanding the quantity and quality of ways in which a learner is exposed to content and context. He challenges the education community to recognize that "no approach to curriculum and instruction can close this achievement gap without corresponding changes in teacher education." In this chapter, he describes culturally responsive instruction and the kinds of teachers, curriculum, and classroom environments that enable all students to achieve high standards.

The role of culture in human development and learning, described by Vygotsky and Piaget, bears a close affinity to Dewey's ideas concerning the role of experience in learning. Cole (1996) describes forms of "social capital." According to Cole, language, tools, number systems, the alphabet, vocabulary, art, relationships, and so forth facilitate the learner's engagement and success in school. Cole, and more recently Goodlad (2002), both critically acknowledge that if school reform continues to ignore these aspects of cultural experience, it is doomed to fail.

With so many well-recognized theorists according culture this central position, why have explanations of human development excluded or marginalized the role of culture? As Betancourt and Lopez (1993) observed:

Despite the historical and contemporary awareness concerning the importance of culture among a number of scholars, the study of culture and related variables occupies at best a secondary place in American (mainstream) psychology. It appears to be the domain of cross-cultural psychology and is often associated with the study of ethnic minorities, which is as segregated from mainstream psychology as is cross-cultural research. There seems to be a widespread assumption that the study of culture or ethnicity contributes little to the understanding of basic psychological processes or to the practice of psychology in the United States. (p. 629)

More recently, Greeno, Collins, and Resnick (1996) offered the following assessment of current trends in education research:

We believe that educational research is undergoing a major advance that will further deepen our theoretical understanding of fundamental processes of cognition, learning, and teaching and further strengthen our abilities to contribute to educational practice. This advance is leading toward a psychology of cognition and learning that includes individual, social, and environmental factors in a coherent theoretical and practical understanding. Accomplishing this change will require merging and extending concepts and methods that, until recently, have developed relatively separately in cognitive science, in ecological psychology, and in ethnographic anthropology and sociology. (p. 15)

Understanding Human Development and Learning: Making the Connections

The Annie E. Casey Foundation (2000) calls for a "connections framework" that recognizes another important component in human development—"Successful, happy, healthy kids need families that are strong—families that not only love them, but also provide for, nurture, support, and teach [them]." It has long been understood that families and parents are the first teachers and that resilience, or the ability to cope with stress, develops when individuals experience caring, support, a sense of purpose, and high expectations (Benard, 1996; Rutter, 1987; Werner & Smith, 1992; Winfield, 1991).

Werner and Smith (1992) offer their own research as well as that of their American and European colleagues as evidence and identification of enabling caregivers. They suggest that if parents are incapacitated or unavailable, other persons in a youngster's life—such as grandparents, older siblings, caring neighbors, family day care providers, teachers, or ministers—can play an enabling role. In Chapter 6, Benard introduces evidence supporting the role of *resilience* in human development and its implications for education reform to close the achievement gaps. She describes turnaround teachers and schools and the transformative power of teachers to tip the scale from risk (including factors such as poverty, dysfunctional families, drugs, crime, and abuse) to resilience.

When students are placed at risk, teachers often have a heightened perception of students as helpless, emotionally stressed, and unable to do schoolwork. Stevens examines opportunity-to-learn standards in Chapter 7. In addition to supports for school and family structures, she categorizes the following variables related to students' academic achievement:

- Content coverage
- Content exposure

- Content emphasis
- Quality of instructional delivery

Stevens describes recent research results that identify outcomes in schools where opportunity-to-learn standards have been introduced. In addition, she highlights the crucial role of the principal in assuring the implementation of opportunity-to-learn standards.

To create the kinds of schools recommended by the authors represented in this volume requires attention to school management, organization, structures, and practices. In Chapter 8, Louis and Ingram challenge the education community and education reformers to create schools where all teachers, as well as students, are learners. They identify socio-economic, political, and organizational conditions that reformers must address to close the achievement gaps between groups. Identifying leadership roles and describing successful schools, the authors define and illustrate required forms of teacher engagement, such as with the school as a social unit, with students, with academic achievement, and with a body of knowledge.

Chapter 9 provides a framework of both theory and evidence to support reform proposals and efforts to close the achievement gaps among groups. Elements of this framework include

- Integrating cross-disciplinary knowledge (biology, sociology, and psychology) of normal human development in varied cultural contexts;
- Embedding the current knowledge of normal human development in comprehensive reform and professional development to focus on teaching and learning;
- Transforming school organization, management, resources, and practices for engaging the community and family; and
- Aligning political policy and support to facilitate the transition from fragmentation to complex, comprehensive reform.

To address these broad categories, the chapter outlines the roles of all segments of the education community, including those of federal, state, and local governments; higher education; educators; and community organizations, agencies, and parents.

References

American Institutes for Research. (1999). *An educators' guide to schoolwide reform*. Washington, DC: Pelavin Research Center.

Annenberg Institute for School Reform. (2002). *School communities that work: A National Task Force on the future of urban districts* [Online]. Providence, RI: Brown University. Available: http://www.schoolcommunities.org/gaptl.html

Annie E. Casey Foundation. (2000). *Kids count data book*. Baltimore, MD: Author.

Benard, B. (1996). Fostering resiliency in urban schools. In B. Williams (Ed.), *Closing the achievement gap: A vision for changing beliefs and practices* (pp. 69–119). Alexandria, VA: Association for Supervision and Curriculum Development.

Berman, P., McLaughlin, B., McLeod, B., Minicucci, C., Nelson, B., & Woodworth, K. (1997). *School reform and student diversity*. Washington, DC: U.S. Department of Education.

Betancourt, H., & Lopez, S. R. (1993). The study of culture, ethnicity, and race in American psychology. *American Psychologist, 48*(6), 629–637.

Bransford, J. D., Brown, A. L., & Cocking, R. R. (Eds.). (1999). *How people learn: Brain, mind, experience, and school*. Washington, DC: National Academy Press.

Bruer, J. T. (1997). Education and the brain. *Educational Researcher, 26*(8), 4–16.

Bruer, J. T. (1998). Brain science, brain fiction. *Educational Leadership, 56*(3), 14–18.

Caine, R. N., & Caine, G. (1991). *Making connections: Teaching and the human brain*. Menlo Park, CA: Addison-Wesley.

Cole, M. (1996). *Cultural psychology: A once and future discipline*. Cambridge, MA: The Belknap Press of Harvard University Press.

D'Amico, J. J. (2001). A closer look at the minority achievement gap. *ERS Spectrum, 19*(2), 4–10.

Darling-Hammond, L. (1997). *The right to learn: A blueprint for creating schools that work*. San Francisco: Jossey-Bass.

Dickens, W. T., & Flynn, J. R. (2001). Heritability estimates versus large environmental effects: The IQ paradox resolved. *Psychological Review, 108*(2), 346–369.

Dewey, J. (1938). *Experience and education*. New York: Collier Books.

Fullan, M. (1999). *Change forces: The sequel*. New York: The Falmer Press.

Gardner, H. (1983). *Frames of mind: The theory of multiple intelligences*. New York: Basic Books.

Gardner, H. (1999). *Intelligence reframed: Multiple intelligences for the 21st century*. New York: Basic Books.

Goodlad, J. I. (2002). Kudzu, rabbits, and school reform. *Phi Delta Kappan, 84*(1), 16–23.

Gould, S. J. (1996). *The mismeasure of man*. New York: W.W. Norton & Company.

Greeno, J. G., Collins, A. M., & Resnick, L. B. (1996). Cognition and learning. In D. C. Berliner & R. C. Calfee (Eds.), *Handbook of educational psychology* (pp. 14–46). New York: Macmillan.

Haycock, K. (2001). Closing the achievement gap. *Educational Leadership, 58*(6), 6–11.

Herrnstein, R., & Murray, C. (1994). *The bell curve: Intelligence and class structure in American life*. New York: Free Press.

Jencks, C., & Phillips, M. (1998). *The black-white test score gap*. Washington, DC: Brookings Institution Press.

Jensen, A. (1969). How much can we boost IQ and scholastic achievement? *Harvard Educational Review, 39*(2), 1–123.

Jensen, A. (1973). *Educability and group differences*. New York: Harper & Row.

Lee, J. (2002). Racial and ethnic achievement gap trends: Reversing the progress toward equity? *Educational Researcher, 31*(1), 3–12.

National Center for Education Statistics. (2001). *NAEP summary data tables* [Online]. Washington, DC: U.S. Department of Education. Available: http://nces.ed.gov/nationsreportcard

Newmann, F. M., & Wehlage, G. G. (1995). *Successful school restructuring: A report to the public and educators*. Washington, DC: The American Federation of Teachers.

Northwest Regional Educational Laboratory. (1998). *Catalog of school reform models* (1st ed.). Portland, OR: Author.

Oakes, J., & Lipton, M. (1999). *Teaching to change the world*. New York: McGraw-Hill College.

Olson, L. (1996). Achievement gap widening, study reports: Progress of minority students has stalled. *Education Week, XVI*(14), 31.

Perkins, D. N. (1995). *Outsmarting IQ: The emerging science of learnable intelligence*. New York: Free Press.

Ravitch, D. (2000). *Left back: A century of failed school reforms*. New York: Simon & Schuster.

Rutter, M. (1987). Psychosocial resilience and protective mechanisms. *American Journal of Orthopsychiatry, 57*, 316–331.

Schoenfeld, A. H. (1999). Looking toward the 21st century: Challenges of educational theory and practice. *Educational Researcher, 28*(7), 4–14.

Sternberg, R. J. (1998). Abilities are forms of developing expertise. *Educational Researcher, 27*(3), 11–20.

Werner, W. E., & Smith, R. S. (1992). *Overcoming the odds: High risk children from birth to adulthood*. Ithaca, NY: Cornell University Press.

Williams, B. (1996). *Closing the achievement gap: A vision for changing beliefs and practices*. Alexandria, VA: Association for Supervision and Curriculum Development.

Winfield, L. (1991). Resilience, schooling, and development in African American youth: A conceptual framework. *Education and Urban Society, 24*(1), 5–14.

1

What Else Do We
Need to Know and Do?

Belinda Williams

*[The No Child Left Behind Act expresses] my deep belief in our
public schools and their mission to build the mind and character
of every child, from every background, in every part of America.*

—President George W. Bush, January 2001

In order to close the achievement gap, states, districts, and schools
serving socioeconomically disadvantaged and culturally diverse students must implement the reforms referred to by President Bush and
delineated in the No Child Left Behind Act of 2001 (NCLB Act). The sober-
ing statistics reported by the Education Trust (2001) reveal the magnitude
of this task and the extent of the achievement gaps among groups (see
Figure 1.1 and Haycock, 2001, for expanded analysis):

- Of every 100 Asian kindergartners, 94 will graduate from high
  school, 80 will complete some college, and 49 will obtain at least a
  bachelor's degree.
- Of every 100 black kindergartners, 87 will graduate from high
  school, 54 will complete at least some college, and 16 will earn a
  bachelor's degree.
- Of every 100 Latino kindergartners, 62 will graduate from high
  school, 29 will complete some college, and 6 will obtain a bachelor's degree.
- Of every 100 white kindergartners, 91 will graduate from high
  school, 62 will complete at least some college, and 30 will obtain at
  least a bachelor's degree.

FIGURE 1.1

Highest Educational Attainment for Every 100 Kindergartners

24-Year-Olds	Blacks	Asians	Latinos	Whites
Graduated from high school	87	94	62	91
Completed at least some college	54	80	29	62
Obtained at least a bachelor's degree	16	49	6	30

Source: U.S. Bureau of the Census (2000).

In addition, current trends predict that when these white kindergartners are 17, over 95 percent will be in high school reading at a 12th grade level while 25 percent of their black peers will have dropped out or, if still in school, will read at an 8th grade level (D'Amico, 2001). Ample evidence shows that these disparities predict not only educational but economic prospects for America's minority populations.

In a commentary responding to United States and international achievement comparisons, Bracey (2002), remarks, "We [in the United States] don't have a 'public school system as we know it.' We have two. One is for poor and minority students, the other is for the rest of us." Will the NCLB Act be sufficient to address the varied gaps Bracey has characterized (urban, rural, suburban, racial, socioeconomic), or is the limited emphasis on standards and accountability that targets schools, teachers, and students a simplistic variation of the "one-size-fits-all" factory model introduced in the early 1900s?

According to Darling-Hammond (1997), despite numerous reform efforts, current structures of schools still reflect the mechanistic factory model/assembly line concept and the influence of behaviorism. The factory metaphor identifies the parallels between education and the "tough-minded" management practices of industry, or in other words, the use of scientific efficiency that allows for "few individual judgments and little variability" in order to obtain short-range profitability (Oakes & Lipton, 1999). Current reforms seem to echo the observations of a parent who, in the 1920s, described schools as similar to an assembly line "of uncompleted Ford cars in the factory, moving always on, with a screw put in or a burr tightened as they pass—standardized, mechanical, pitiful" (Haley, 1924, quoted in Darling-Hammond, 1997, p. 41).

Federal efforts to educate all children, initiated by the 1965 Elementary and Secondary Education Act (ESEA) with the imposition of desegregation plans, were heightened by the landmark education reform report from the

National Commission on Excellence in Education, *A Nation at Risk: The Imperative for Educational Reform* (1983). *A Nation at Risk*, in contrast to reports from the national commissions in the 1930s and 1940s, introduced a major shift in the overarching goal of education, namely, to educate all children, not just provide a differentiated education that sorts children by their likely occupations (Ravitch, 2000). *A Nation at Risk* alerted the general public and the education community to this significant shift in the following way:

> *Individuals in our society who do not possess the levels of skill, literacy, and training essential to this new era [the information age] will be effectively disenfranchised, not simply from the material rewards that accompany competent performance, but also from the chance to participate fully in our national life. A high level of shared education is essential to a free, democratic society and to the fostering of a common culture, especially in a country that prides itself on pluralism and individual freedom.* (p. 7)

Despite this warning, issued two decades ago, every major national report since then has revealed, with grim statistics, the limited progress made in the United States toward attaining the high level of shared education required for the information age. The "one-size-fits-all" strategy governing the current structures of schools ignores the complexity of the dynamics influencing the gaps among groups. Narrow theories of how individuals learn limit progress and engender narrow, simplistic strategies for closing the gaps among groups (see Figure 1.2). Jencks and Phillips (1998) observe:

> *This individualistic framework is not designed to capture the impact of relational, organizational, and collective processes that embody the social structure of inequality. . . . Since organizational, relational and collective processes are omitted, the individualistic framework is unable to specify fully the mechanisms by which certain individual attributes produce certain social outcomes, or spell out how and why these attributes result in individuals being sorted into different social positions.* (p. 508)

Several reports (College Entrance Examination Board, 1999; D'Amico, 2001; Viadero, 2000a, 2000b) identify the complex dimensions and issues related to achievement gaps. The most widely accepted explanations for the achievement gaps include assumptions about such issues as poverty; academic coursework and instruction; peer pressure; student attendance and mobility rates; disparities in resources; parenting; preschool; teacher quality and attitudes; stereotype threat; teacher expectations; television; test bias; and genetics.

FIGURE 1.2

Individual Differences vs. Group Differences

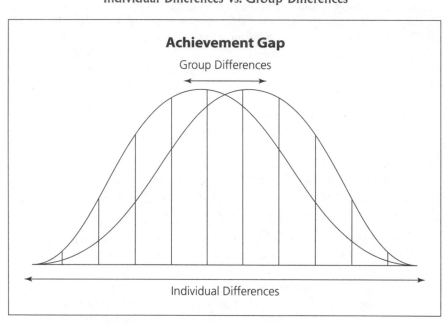

Given this complexity, Lee (2002) criticizes the tendency to offer unexamined explanations of achievement gaps among groups. Interventions attributed to the narrowing of the racial and ethnic achievement gap, observed between 1970 and 1988, reflect the assumption that the effects of certain factors on student achievement are constant across groups. However, assumptions about effects across time periods and groups fall short of explaining the current widening gap phenomenon. What the situation now calls for is a new framework for empirical research that will include all racial and ethnic groups at all achievement levels.

Lee offers a challenge to the education and research communities to reconsider their assumptions and to give a better account of the complexities of studying and analyzing achievement gaps. What assumptions inform current reform proposals? In addition to the reform strategies noted in the NCLB Act (such as privatization, vouchers, and so forth), current reform debates include professionalizing teaching and teacher education (Cochran-Smith & Fries, 2001), establishing a knowledge base for the teaching profession (Hiebert, Gallimore, & Stigler, 2002), and deregulating teacher preparation (with such approaches as alternative routes and teacher tests). Are these strategies and assumptions sufficient to address the magnitude of the complex change required?

The Current Federal Reform Strategy

Since the passage of the ESEA, nearly $200 billion in federal spending failed to impact the enormous achievement gaps that exist in the United States. To readdress this failure, the 2001 NCLB Act incorporates the following principles and strategies:

- Increased accountability for districts and schools
- More choices for parents and students
- Greater flexibility for states, districts, and schools
- Putting reading first

Increased accountability for school districts and schools requires monitoring and evaluation of assessment results. *More choices for parents and students* will give students the opportunity to obtain supplemental services and attend a better public school or charter school within the school's district. *Greater flexibility for states, school districts, and schools* gives states and local education agencies (LEAs) the option of transferring up to 50 percent of their funding under major state grant programs to any one of the programs, or to Title I, that is, Teacher Quality State Grants, Educational Technology, Innovative Programs, and Safe and Drug-Free Schools. *Putting reading first* ensures increased federal investment in scientifically based reading instruction programs in the early grades and professional development for K–3 teachers in the essential components of reading instruction.

Professionalizing Teaching: Establishing a Knowledge Base

In this book, the authors synthesize a significant emerging body of knowledge to elaborate the currently understood complexities of group differences in achievement. Current understanding offers support for a *framework* that may define, integrate, and inform implementation strategies. The definitions and strategies challenge all levels of the education community to take responsibility and accountability for closing the achievement gaps, including federal, state, and local governments; higher education; state, district, and school administrators; and community and parent groups. The framework these authors offer promises success in addressing what Bracey (2002) characterizes as the "dual system" now in place in U.S. public schools and can ensure the "high level of shared education" essential to individual freedom. Specifically, the authors provide theory and evidence to show that current reform strategies are

- Superficial and fragmented,
- Limited to improving individual achievement while perpetuating gaps between groups,
- Lacking in theoretical coherence, and
- Inadequate to define or address the persistent challenge.

Finally, the authors define a knowledge base, identify evidence, and describe practices that go beyond improving achievement to actually closing the gaps.

The earlier edition of this book (Williams, 1996) offered a synthesis of available research and theory and a critique of education reform. Much of that synthesis and critique recommended an examination of prevailing assumptions and a rejection of the *deficit hypothesis* that defines many reform proposals. For example, many reform approaches assume the problem is located in and limited to a lack in the culture, in abilities, in motivation, or in coping skills of children and their families (Williams & Newcombe, 1994) (see Figure 1.3). Astuto, Clark, Read, McGree, and Fernandez (1993) identified the prevalence of similar narrow assumptions that lie beneath past and current reforms and limit the scope of change recommended for schools. Astuto and her colleagues assert:

> The insidious effect of taken-for-granted assumptions is the way they interconnect with and reify one another in a seemingly logical set of relationships. If one assumes that the maintenance of the social, economic, and political order be a priority for education, then attempts by schools to counteract the fragmentary effects of diversity through the support and promotion of a common cultural tradition is appropriate. . . . Subscribing to a deficit model of cultural, parental, and community resources and values further limits the allies educators believe they can call upon for support. . . . If, on the other hand, educators began with a belief in the transformative role of education, the value of accessing diversity, a faith in the potential success of every student, a commitment to collaborative and political linkages with parents and communities, then mustering the inventiveness to create new ways of organizing on behalf of children would be the logical, moral, and just thing to do. (p. 41)

Will current reform proposals, which address standards, accountability, and the professionalizing of teaching, contribute to the *transformative* role

FIGURE 1.3

Toward a New Vision of Low-Performing Learners

Current View	A New Vision
Deprived	Culturally different
Failing/low achieving	Unrecognized abilities/underdeveloped potential
Unmotivated	Engaged/self-motivated/effortful
At risk	Resilient

Source: Williams and Newcombe (1994).

of education that Astuto and her colleagues recommend? Missing from current reform proposals is specific attention to the value of accessing diversity, a faith in the potential of every student, and a commitment to collaborative and political linkages with parents and communities that *create new ways of organizing on behalf of children.*

Describing the nature of the *urban* achievement gap, the previous edition of this book introduced and synthesized research and theory that support four major themes:

- Calls for paradigm shifts in understanding the role of social interaction, values, and standards in human development in urban contexts
- Caution against views of intervention in urban schools that reduce the focus to curriculum, instruction, and assessment
- Challenges to current deficit and at-risk characterizations of urban students
- Reconceptualizations of teacher preparation along with support for organizational change in schools and classrooms

Significant evidence exists showing that generic restructuring frameworks and designs will not sufficiently change urban, rural, or suburban schools to close achievement gaps. Generic frameworks and designs do not pay sufficient attention to the unique issues and complex conditions schools with existing achievement gaps must confront every day. In spite of significant evidence to the contrary, many educators continue to seek the single program, fragmented strategies, or an approach to "good teaching" that will improve all students' achievement (Haberman, 1991).

Limitations of Fragmented
Reform Approaches and Programs

Isolated and fragmented approaches and programs reflect the narrow assumptions Astuto and her colleagues identified (1993):

- Implementing standards and accountability assumes that *all* educators have the knowledge, skills, and *will* required to teach *all* students to high standards.
- Funding vouchers and charter schools assumes the use of new knowledge and skills to educate *all* students.
- Reducing class size assumes teachers will know what to do differently in classrooms with fewer students.
- Decentralization (site-based management) assumes educators in schools have knowledge, skills, and resources not available to central office educators.

These assumptions ignore abundant and mounting evidence about the complexity of existing achievement gaps between black and white, Asian and white, white and Hispanic, and high- and low-income students. In addition, gaps once assumed to be limited to urban or rural schools and schools serving disadvantaged students are now being identified in suburban communities and schools (D'Amico, 2001). Continued failure to formulate reform strategies supported by a thorough analysis and synthesis of *all* available evidence leaves to chance the possibility of closing the gaps among groups.

Researchers at the Consortium for Policy Research on Education conducted such an analysis. Following 15 years of research in scores of schools and districts in several states around the country, these researchers conclude, "A stronger focus on instructional improvement and on appropriate professional development is required for a larger payoff in student achievement" (Cohen & Lowenberg Ball, 2001). The following summary of their findings elaborates the crucial dynamics of the teaching and learning process:

> *If instruction is interaction, it must be dynamic. The active elements include teachers' and students' perceptions and use of one another, of the academic tasks in which they engage, and of their environments. Students' learning practices—how they go about the work of learning—shape the enactment of tasks, the teacher's role, and the influence of environments. Teachers' teaching practices—how they frame and use academic tasks, acquaint themselves with*

*what students know and can do, enact the instructional discourse, and medi-
ate the environment—also influence how teaching and learning unfold and
hence the opportunities for learning that students have and can use.* (p. 75)

Additional evidence supports these research-based recommendations
and observations. John H. Johnson, the National Director of Education for
the National Association for the Advancement of Colored People asserts,
"Standards reform has been created in a vacuum. . . . It assumes that
everyone is equal, but it's clear that there are inequities" (Borja, 2001).
Similarly, authors of a 1996 *ASCD Infobrief* conclude, "In the search for
solutions, policymakers are exploring new arrangements for financing and
governing urban schools. Equally important are two factors that more directly affect the day-to-day experiences of students: provisions to person-
alize . . . schools, and professional development for educators."

A review of the literature underscores the insights of Dewey (1938),
who describes the factors that directly affect the day-to-day experiences of
students and teachers. Dewey asserts that educators must be familiar with
the conditions of the local community—physical, historical, economic,
occupational, and so forth—and must utilize these physical and social sur-
roundings to contribute to building learning experiences. Dewey suggests
that this connection between the knowledge of experience and the *content*
of new knowledge is meaningful and worthwhile learning.

Theoretical Integration to Define Normal Human Development

Dewey's assumptions about the role of *experience* in teaching and learning elaborate those of other cognitive theorists defining the *new science of
learning*, which constitutes a focus on the process of knowing (Bransford,
Brown, and Cocking, 1999). Vygotsky's (1929, 1981) elaboration of the
role of culture and social context in learning (Glassman, 2001), as well as
Piaget's description of the role of schemes in perception and the process
of learning (the individual's codification of experience) (Piaget, 1969), provide a basis for exploring and developing the following:

- An integrated theory of normal human development in varied
  contexts
- A theoretical foundation for teaching and learning
- A comprehensive definition of school reform to educate all children
  (see Figure 1.4)

FIGURE 1.4

Toward Theoretical Integration: The Foundation for a Theory
of Learning and Teaching Connections

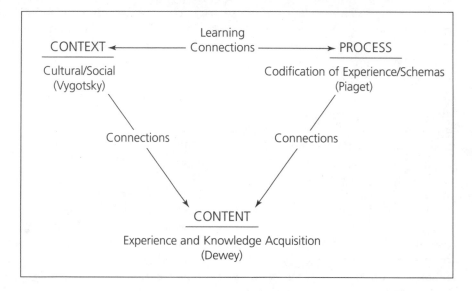

A theoretical framework of normal human development (how learning occurs), supported by evidence, holds promise for closing gaps in achievement for all groups of children. This would include both those for whom existing educational systems and structures have been successful, and those diverse populations for whom traditional education has failed (blacks, Native Americans, Hispanic Americans, urban and rural populations, and the socioeconomically disadvantaged). The major task may not be to present new knowledge but to offer, in a more provocative way, theory and research that has until now been ignored by education theorists, researchers, policymakers, the education community, and education reformers.

References

Association for Supervision and Curriculum Development. (1996). Urban education: Policies of promise. *An Infobrief Synopsis (5)*.

Astuto, T., Clark, D. L., Read, A., McGree, K., & Fernandez, L. P. (1993). *Challenges to dominant assumptions controlling educational reform*. Andover, MA:

The Regional Laboratory for Educational Improvement of the Northeast and Islands.

Borja, R. R. (2001). Black state lawmakers target 'gap.' *Education Week, 21*(14), 27.

Bracey, G. W. (2002). International comparisons: An excuse to avoid meaningful educational reform. *Education Week, 21*(19), 30–32.

Bransford, J. D., Brown, A. L., & Cocking, R. R. (Eds.). (1999). *How people learn: Brain, mind, experience, and school.* Washington, DC: National Academy Press.

Cochran-Smith, M., & Fries, M. (2001). Sticks, stones, and ideology: The discourse of reform in teacher education. *Educational Researcher, 30*(8), 3–15.

Cohen, D., & Lowenberg Ball, D. L. (2001). Making change: Instruction and its improvement. *Phi Delta Kappan, 83*(1), 73–77.

College Entrance Examination Board. (1999). *Reaching the top: A report of the National Task Force on Minority High Achievement.* New York: Author.

D'Amico, J. J. (2001). A closer look at the minority achievement gap. *ERS Spectrum, 19*(2), 4–10.

Darling-Hammond, L. (1997). *The right to learn: A blueprint for creating schools that work.* San Francisco: Jossey-Bass.

Dewey, J. (1938). *Experience and education.* New York: Collier Books.

Education Trust. (2001). Highest educational attainment for every 100 kindergartners. *Achievement in America 2001.* Washington, DC: Author.

Glassman, M. (2001). Dewey and Vygotsky: Society, experience, and inquiry in educational practice. *Educational Researcher, 30*(4), 3–14.

Haberman, M. (1991). The pedagogy of poverty versus good teaching. *Phi Delta Kappan, 73*(4), 290–294.

Haycock, K. (2001). Closing the achievement gap. *Educational Leadership, 58*(6), 6–11.

Hiebert, J., Gallimore, R., & Stigler, J. W. (2002). A knowledge base for the teaching profession: What would it look like and how can we get one? *Educational Researcher, 31*(5), 3–15.

Jencks, C., & Phillips, M. (1998). *The black-white test score gap.* Washington, DC: Brookings Institution Press.

Lee, J. (2002). Racial and ethnic achievement gap trends: Reversing the progress toward equity? *Educational Researcher, 31*(1), 3–12.

National Commission on Excellence in Education. (1983). *A nation at risk: The imperative for educational reform.* Washington, DC: U.S. Government Printing Office.

Oakes, J., & Lipton, M. (1999). *Teaching to change the world.* New York: McGraw-Hill College.

Piaget, J. (1969). *The mechanisms of perception.* New York: Basic Books, Inc.

Ravitch, D. (2000). *Left back: A century of failed school reforms.* New York: Simon & Schuster.

U.S. Bureau of the Census. (2000, March). *Current population reports, educational attainment in the United States.* Washington, DC: Author.

Viadero, D. (2000a). Lags in minority achievement defy traditional explanations. *Education Week, 19*(28), 1.

Viadero, D. (2000b). Minority gaps smaller in some pentagon schools. *Education Week, 19*(29), 1.

Vygotsky, L. S. (1929). The problem of the cultural development of the child, II. *Journal of Genetic Psychology, 36*, 414–434.

Vygotsky, L. S. (1981). The development of higher forms of attention in childhood. In J. V. Wertsch (Ed.), *The concept of activity in Soviet psychology* (pp. 189–240). Armonk, NY: M. E. Sharpe.

Williams, B. (1996). *Closing the achievement gap*. Alexandria, VA: Association for Supervision and Curriculum Development.

Williams, B., & Newcombe, E. (1994). Building on the strengths of urban learners. *Educational Leadership, 51*(8), 75–78.

2

The Continuing Challenges of Excellence and Equity

JoAnn B. Manning and John A. Kovach

The persistence of the achievement gap between black and white students in grades K–12 is cause for concern among researchers and social policy analysts. The gap is especially problematic because of its role in continued social and economic inequality in the United States. For several decades now, the civil rights movement has identified the gap as a major issue. Although the black and white achievement gap was actually cut by 50 percent in reading and by about 33 percent in mathematics between 1970 and 1990 (National Center for Education Statistics, 2001), it has been widening each year since. Overall, efforts to close the gap have made little progress (Gordon, 2001; U.S. Department of Education, 2001).

In the 21st century, discussion on raising the academic achievement of minority students has broadened to include other ethnic groups; the gap now exists between students who are white and Asian American and those who are black, Hispanic, and Native American. The following four elements are key to the discussion:

- The national drive for excellence in education
- Equity issues related to disparities in the distribution of educational resources
- Organizational features of schools related to tracking, remediation, and special education
- The interrelationship among all of these factors and the larger context of a society that continues to be deeply divided by race

This chapter explores the roots and nature of the achievement gap and some of its dimensions, including expectations of excellence, data from the National Assessment of Educational Progress (NAEP), and inequity in resources. It presents case studies that reflect successful attempts to decrease the gap. It also includes recommendations for changes in curriculum and instruction, grouping and tracking, retention and remediation, and school district policy. Finally, it examines implications for curricular, schoolwide, district, and community strategies for more equitable education.

The Roots of the Gap

The minority achievement gap is seen as early as kindergarten, persists through secondary levels, and is reflected in differential Scholastic Assessment Test (SAT) scores for black and white youth (U.S. Department of Education, 2001). Even within the *same* schools and when social class holds constant, the minority gap exists, and it continues beyond postsecondary education, when minority college youth are twice as likely to drop out after their freshman year of college as their white counterparts (National Center for Education Statistics, 2001). These dimensions of the gap are important to grasp. They show themselves at a young age, tend to persist, and grow worse the longer a minority child is in school.

Further, while the achievement gap formally appears as early as kindergarten, assessments have shown that a sizable achievement gap can be found in young children *before* they start school (Kober, 2001). Does this mean that schooling cannot do much to close the gap that seems to originate in the differing social and cultural conditions racial groups experience in the United States? Or does this appearance of the gap at such a young age suggest the need for early intervention for those groups that are more likely to fall behind academically? Some have interpreted the early appearance of the achievement gap to mean that schooling cannot do much to close the gap (U.S. Department of Education, 2001). It is important to note, however, that a more critical interpretation might simply suggest the causes of the gap lie beyond the walls of schools.

The Nature of the Gap

It is essential to understand two important aspects of the contemporary achievement gap in order to assimilate the educational initiatives that have been effective in closing the gap.

First, the gap is not simply an urban or educational problem. During the past decade, many educational researchers tended to focus on the urban nature of the gap (Daniels, 2002; Wang & Kovach, 1996; Wang & Reynolds, 1995). To be sure, it was more blatant in urban areas having high concentrations of poor and minority students, and these studies were valuable in understanding the roots of the achievement gap. However, to respond effectively to the achievement gap between different racial groups in the United States today, it is important to understand that the dimensions of the gap transcend the conditions found in urban schools. On average, minority students—with the exception of Asian Americans—are doing worse than their white counterparts on standardized tests (National Task Force on Minority High Achievement, 1999).

Second, the achievement gap transcends social class. Even within the same schools, middle-class black students tend to score lower on achievement tests than whites. This aspect is particularly critical in the current era of high-stakes testing, with implications that extend to college and beyond.

Certainly, the achievement gap is a complex phenomenon. Therefore, educators need to grasp the following dimensions:

- Minorities are growing in number in U.S. public schools, having increased from 22 percent to 30 percent between 1972 and 1998 (U.S. Census Bureau, 2001);
- Economic inequality is linked to race and class in the United States; and
- Access to educational resources is differential.

Understanding the reciprocal relationship between schooling and these causes is important, because the relationship helps explain growing evidence from schools across the nation that shows poverty and race do not have to be impediments to high achievement. Many schools having high percentages of poor and minority youth have indeed closed the achievement gap.

Expectations of Excellence and the Racial Divide

Standards-based reforms, which demand that all students succeed, provide for accountability testing. This testing has made the achievement gap much more visible over the past decade. With the social pressure that high-stakes testing has put on schools to foster achievement in increasingly diverse student populations, the achievement gap has become more troubling and politicized, and emotions of individuals representing the various interest groups have become highly charged. Thus, research must look at the effects of accountability testing on minority students—to identify negative trends in the relationship between high-stakes testing and increased dropout rates, effects on average students, and patterns in grade retention (Langenfeld, Thurlow, & Scott, 1996).

27

As noted, reading and mathematics achievement for blacks and Latinos showed improvement through the 1970s and 1980s. This trend in narrowing the gap continued until about 1990 for blacks and until 1992 for Latinos (National Center for Education Statistics, 2001), when the achievement gap began to worsen. In basic skills areas, where mastery is a prerequisite even for unskilled jobs, data from the National Center for Education Statistics (2001) show that over 50 percent of all minority high school students exhibit deficiencies:

- Only 1 percent of black 17-year-olds can comprehend information from a specialized text, such as the science section of a daily newspaper. This compares with just over 8 percent of white youth of the same age.
- Only 20 percent of black high school students can comprehend a less specialized text that over 50 percent of whites understand.
- In elementary algebra, which is considered a gateway course for college preparation, only 1 percent of black students can successfully solve a problem involving more than one basic step in its solution; 10 percent of white students can solve such a problem.
- Although 70 percent of white high school students have mastered computation with fractions, only 3 percent of black students have done so.
- By the time they graduate from high school, black and Latino students are reading on the same level as white 8th graders.

These differential levels of secondary achievement equate to the following results: Minorities have lower high school graduation rates and General Education Degree attainment rates; their SAT scores are, on average, lower; and fewer go to college. Ultimately, young blacks are half as likely as whites to earn a bachelor's degree. If there is no intervention by educational institutions, the achievement gap that shows itself as early as kindergarten will diminish the chances that a minority youth will graduate from high school, attend and remain in college through graduation, and achieve relative economic success.

NAEP Data and the Achievement Gap

Data from the NAEP reveal some of the important intricacies of the achievement gap. Many researchers emphasize that the gap merely reflects racial bias built into the development and norming of standardized tests (Camara & Schmidt, 1999; Jencks & Phillips, 1998; Koretz, 2000).

Other researchers point to the obvious class bias in standardized tests—for example, the direct correlation between SAT scores and income that holds for all racial and ethnic groups except Asian Americans.

By the time poor and minority youth reach 8th grade, they are, on average, about three grade levels behind other students. If race and income were stronger determinants of test achievement than school policy and practice, the NAEP scores for minority and poor children could be expected to be fairly similar across all states, but this does not hold true. For example, Latino 8th graders in Indiana and Montana are only two grade levels behind whites, while those in Tennessee are five years behind. These data suggest that the differing state strategies and school structures do make a difference (Haycock, 2001). While some states have raised achievement for minority students, they continue to show a large and widening black-white gap. Other states, such as Virginia and North Dakota, have closed the gap, according to NAEP data, while attaining higher achievement levels for all students. Quite simply, what goes on in schools does matter.

One important study of the achievement gap using NAEP data compared schools with high concentrations of minority students to those with lower concentrations (Stull & Wang, 2001). The study investigated school organizational factors and teacher practices as they impact minority and nonminority achievement in reading. Figure 2.1 shows some common characteristics of schools serving high concentrations of minority students. The study concluded that schools that serve predominantly minority populations are different.

FIGURE 2.1

Characteristics of Schools Serving Predominantly Minority Populations

- Larger
- More special education classes
- Greater student mobility
- More poor children
- Lower per-pupil expenditures
- More likely to use tracking or ability grouping

Source: Stull and Wang (2001).

The study further concluded that schools with high concentrations of high-achieving minority students appeared almost identical to schools with high concentrations of high-achieving nonminority students, with the exception of the percentage of students eligible for free or reduced lunch and per-pupil discretionary dollars. Teachers in the high-achieving schools were more likely to have an advanced degree, were more experienced, and graded papers more on organization and coherence than on the length of the written assignment. They also devoted less time to reading assessments and reading activities and routinely used fewer reading resources. These findings make it apparent that the way schools are organized and the types of strategies and assessments teachers use in the classroom do matter.

Inequity in Resources

During the 20th century, educators and policymakers constructed multiple categories, homogeneous groupings, and remedial practices to address diverse student needs arising from inequitable learning outcomes. In the 1960s, the federal government turned to special categorical programs as its principal way of guaranteeing education for all U.S. students. The Elementary and Secondary Education Act provided categorical funding for "educationally deprived" students. The Individuals with Disabilities Education Act provided funds to support special education programs for students classified with physical and neurological problems when it appeared they could not be accommodated in regular programs.

Although the original intent of these initiatives was to promote educational equity, numerous studies have found minimal effects for most forms of ability grouping and tracking (Gamoran, 2001; Kulik, 2001; Oakes & Lipton, 2001); grade retention and remediation (Alexander, Entwisle, & Dauber, 2001; Jimerson, 2001; Temple, Reynolds, & Ou, 2001); and special education (Finn, Rotherman, & Hokanson, 2001; Wang & Reynolds, 1995; Winfield, Johnson, & Manning, 1993). A major issue is whether students in these categories, groupings, and tracks have equal access to high-quality curriculum, teachers, and learning experiences. More often than not, racial and ethnic minorities and students from lower socioeconomic backgrounds are overrepresented in the lower or non-college-bound groups and assigned the least qualified teachers.

In order to close the achievement gap for all children, it is necessary for states, school districts, and schools to address inequities in resources and in students' opportunities to learn. Indeed, major disparities exist in the allocation and use of resources in schools with achievement gaps between minorities and white and Asian American students. How then can education providers best use their resources and talents to serve every student most effectively and efficiently? They must acknowledge and develop strategies to address academic gaps between minority and nonminority students (Goertz, 1999). Studies have identified resources that could affect the achievement gap. As high-stakes assessments measure more rigorous content, students need access to challenging curricula and instruction (Ferguson, 2000; Green, 2001); high-quality teachers who have the content knowledge, pedagogy, and high expectations required to teach challenging content to a diverse group of learners (Arroyo, Rhoad, & Drew, 1999; The College Board, 1999); and necessary extra supports to ensure student success (James, Jurich, & Estes, 2001). Figure 2.2 summarizes these needs.

FIGURE 2.2

What Students Need: Resources for Closing the Gap

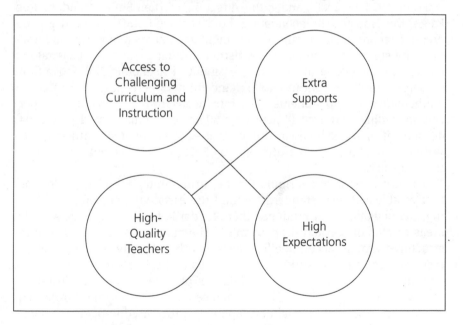

Case Examples of Closing the Achievement Gap

A key to closing the achievement gap is to realize there is no "magic bullet." It would certainly be convenient if reformers could concentrate their efforts on one single area to get guaranteed results in boosting minority achievement. The truth is, the achievement gap is a complex, multilayered phenomenon that requires an ongoing, sustained, multifaceted approach. To close the gap effectively, educators and social policy decision makers must use available data to develop strategies that involve change in schools, as well as initiatives that have an impact on families and the community.

Even in all of its complexity, the task at hand is not overwhelming. States like Connecticut, Delaware, North Carolina, Rhode Island, and Texas have made improvements by concentrating efforts on teacher quality, accountability measures that are tied to subgroup achievement, and rigorous initiatives that provide sustained support for minority students. The following case examples highlight some of the initiatives.

Accountability Measures Link People to Results: The Houston Independent School District

From 1994 to 2000, under the direction of then-Superintendent Rod Paige, the Houston Independent School District (HISD) showed an impressive record in closing the achievement gap between minority and non-minority students throughout the district. In that period, the pass rate of black students taking the Texas Assessment of Academic Skills rose from 61 percent to 82 percent in reading, and from 45 percent to 75 percent in mathematics. Latino students' pass rates went from 60 percent to 77 percent in reading, and from 44 percent to 80 percent in mathematics. In 1994, 40 percent of the schools in this district—the nation's seventh largest—were classified as "low performing." By 2000, only 7 percent remained in that category.

There was no secret formula for the turnaround of the HISD. The district established high standards around the essential skills areas of reading, mathematics, and writing. Other standards focused on targets in the areas of attendance and dropout rates. The entire school district was restructured around accountability measures that directly linked people to results. It tied cash incentives for principals and schools to desired results and targets. In addition, the school district provided "targeted assistance" to low-performing schools. This assistance included everything from help in planning and professional development to increased budgets for books and instructional materials. The district had to develop its own reading program, and it provided extensive professional development to math teachers to equip them with the content knowledge they needed. Finally, the HISD gave teachers in targeted core academic areas the opportunity to share best practices and successful teaching strategies. All of these changes occurred within a large, bureaucratically organized, urban school district that was assumed to be ungovernable and impossible to change (Cawelti & Protheroe, 2001).

Whole School Reform: Harriet Baldwin Elementary School, Boston Public Schools

The case of Harriet Baldwin Elementary School is particularly interesting because of the 283 students served: 72 percent were Asian American, 17 percent were black, 7 percent were white, and 4 percent were Latino. The SAT-9 reading and mathematics test scores improved considerably from 1996 to 1998; the school's scores are well above the national median, and substantially higher than the scores for other elementary schools in the district (Johnson & Asera, 1999). On the 1996 math test, 66 percent of 3rd graders at the school scored at Level 1 or 2 (little or no mastery of basic knowledge and skills/partial mastery). By 1998, 100 percent of the students scored at Level 3 or 4 (solid academic performance/superior performance beyond grade-level mastery).

Baldwin Elementary adopted a whole school reform model that included changing the school climate in ways that staff and students noticed immediately. The principal made herself highly visible, moving around the schoolyard and halls at times when students were arriving or changing classes. There was a strong focus on changing academic instruction and adopting classroom strategies best suited to the high percentage of English as a Second Language (ESL) students in the school. The school invested in professional development related to ESL strategies in order to implement a successful whole school literacy initiative. In addition, the school forged new relationships with parents and community groups, including 40 college students who acted as tutors and mentors to Baldwin students during and after school. Finally, when Baldwin became part of the first cohort of schools in the 21st Century Program, it instituted widespread organizational changes that included a coordinated curriculum, primary and elementary instructional leadership teams, and regularly scheduled meetings.

The Baldwin Elementary case reinforces the idea that whole school reform is not rocket science. The school set clear goals, focusing on academic standards, developing sustained supports for teachers and leaders, committing to the maintenance of a climate conducive to learning, and increasing parent and community connections. Most important in this case is the effort to develop reform measures focused on the specific needs of the high ESL population. Whole school reform measures cannot simply be seen as generic categories that can be dropped into any school without tailoring the reforms to the specific school's organizational structure and student population needs. It is critical that all attempts to close the achievement gap in a school or school district must, at all levels and stages of the reform process, be data-driven in order to be successful.

Equity in School Funding: The State of Michigan

Funding disparities between districts serving predominantly minority populations and more affluent districts serving nonminority students constitute a persistent problem tied to the achievement gap (Walker & Gutmore, 2000). The efforts of the state of Michigan to deal with this problem are particularly noteworthy because of the accompanying gains seen in closing the achievement gap. Even with statewide gains, however, Michigan currently recognizes that more focused reform efforts are necessary in order to address the minority achievement gap more fully.

In 1993, the state of Michigan abolished local property taxes as a base for school funding and offset the loss in revenue with increased state funding. This change meant that per-pupil spending in the lowest districts almost doubled during the four-year period from 1994 to 1998. This attempt to bring equity to school funding and resources, coupled with a statewide initiative targeting chronically underperforming schools, resulted in raising the status of Michigan education as measured by American College Test (ACT), SAT, NAEP, and the Third International Math and Science Study (TIMSS) results. Since 1996, the percentage of seniors taking the ACT and SAT exams has increased, and average scores of state students are significantly higher than national averages. Michigan scores on the NAEP in 4th and 8th grade mathematics are also well above the national average. Improved test scores have been seen at all grade levels, with only five states scoring higher than Michigan's 4th graders and only four states scoring higher than its 8th graders. Last April, Michigan placed first in the nation in mathematics and science achievement on TIMSS (Michigan Department of Education, 2001).

Even with statewide improvements in test scores, the achievement gap, as measured by NAEP scores, persists in Michigan. It is clear that funding equity alone has not transformed educational performance for all students, as noted in New Jersey's Abbott Schools, where it was found that equalizing funding to school districts alone was not enough to raise performance in the lowest-performing schools. In order to directly address the achievement gap in Michigan, the state adopted five strategies to effect substantial and meaningful academic improvement in low-performing, predominantly urban and minority schools (Michigan State Board of Education,

2001). These strategy areas, listed in Figure 2.3, have each been assigned to a task force for the development of sets of workable proposals and benchmarks to measure levels of implementation.

The lessons in Michigan are especially important for two reasons: (1) there is a national trend of fierce competition among municipalities for taxable business property; and (2) zoning practices result in de facto segregation by race and class where expensive homes and new commercial developments are separated from neighborhoods housing the poor. Although equity in school funding alone is not enough to close the gap, these state-level funding initiatives—combined with whole school reform measures and increased access to educational resources for schools serving minority students—are a powerful base from which to launch an attack on the achievement gap.

FIGURE 2.3

Strategies for Effecting Academic Improvement in Low-Performing Schools

* Ensuring excellent educators
* Elevating educational leadership
* Embracing the information age
* Improving early childhood literacy
* Integrating communities and schools

Source: Michigan State Board of Education (2001).

It will be interesting to watch future changes in Michigan, however, because overall school funding has been reduced recently through state reductions in taxes that have significant portions earmarked for the school appropriations fund. Lawmakers, with the good intention of lowering constituents' tax burden, inadvertently reduced the growth potential of school appropriations (Drake, 2002), and the effect this reduction will have on the achievement gap is not yet known.

Organizational Features of Schools

The overall assumption about the achievement gap is that schools can indeed do much to close the gap, even if the gap originates in social factors beyond the control of schools. The case studies presented here offer proof of this. They show the critical importance of high standards and expectations of high achievement for all students, the need for a challenging curriculum with a strong focus on an academic core, and professional development and other supports for teachers and school leaders.

Further, as the NAEP data show, the ways in which schools are organized and deliver instruction do matter in the struggle to close the gap. A well-defined organizational support structure can narrow the achievement gap by maximizing academic learning time (Lewis & McDonald, 2001; Zimmerman, 2001); encouraging school staff to create a climate for improvement by organizing staff into teams to develop shared responsibility for decision making (Katzenbach & Smith, 1993); coordinating services (Darling-Hammond, 1997); and reducing the size of classes or schools (Howley, 2001; North Carolina Department of Public Instruction, 2000; Pritchard, 1999; Steifel, Berne, Iatarola, & Fruchter, 2000).

Many of our schools continue to base their understanding and teaching on student differences. It is evident that the way schools are organized perpetuates these practices and understandings, providing policymakers and educators with a way to "solve" an array of problems attributed to the growing diversity of students (Oakes & Lipton, 2001). Reports, including those from Darling-Hammond (1997) and Finn and colleagues (2001), reveal the following findings:

- Millions of students are improperly identified as "learning disabled" when they simply have not been properly taught to read at a young age.
- Race is a key factor in determining who is enrolled in special education.
- Blacks, particularly boys, are disproportionately identified as having attention deficit hyperactivity disorder and are underrepresented in programs for the gifted.
- Standards-based reforms are prompting some schools to assign more students to special education classes so as to exclude them from participating in proficiency tests.

Clearly, the content of professional interactions remains largely focused on student—rather than curricular or systemic—deficits (Pugach & Warger, 1993). It is necessary, therefore, to provide recommendations on how schools and districts can organize to ensure curricular equity by changing practices in the areas of curriculum and instruction, grouping and tracking, retention and remediation, and district policy.

Curriculum and Instruction

Teachers and principals need to receive training that helps them address diversity in learning rates and styles. Very few teachers believe they were adequately trained to handle the many responsibilities of teaching. Many teacher-education curricula focus on subject-area content and not on evaluating and effectively teaching to student cultural experiences. This leads to a body of teachers who do not know how to evaluate their students and meet each individual learner's needs.

Too often, newer, less experienced teachers are assigned to teach students most at risk for retention or dropout. Instead, schools should assign the most experienced and capable teachers, who have already successfully demonstrated their ability in the classroom.

Schools should also explore more flexible curricula. For example, a shift from a lecture and test-taking approach to instruction focused on interest-based learning could be beneficial to all students (instead of only those who are college bound). In this format, high school students would be exposed to career-based or project-based education that would be applicable in "the real world."

Grouping and Tracking

Many critics of ability grouping suggest that the instructional experience of minority and poor students is often limited to rote drill of basic skills. All grouping should include high expectations, rigorous curriculum, and equitable access to high-quality instruction. Educators should encourage even the lower ability groups to reach their potential. Schools should insist on the highest quality of teachers and high-quality course material for all as steps in the right direction.

Schools and districts should also encourage flexible grouping. Grouping different-age students of similar ability can be more effective than grouping by age or grade. Multi-age classrooms enrich children's learning and development.

Also, students should have a say in their placement. Students who feel they have a voice in the path of their education are more invested in the learning process. Educators should help them develop goals and action plans to meet those goals. Teachers should hold conferences with the students to evaluate progress toward their goals.

Retention and Remediation

Early childhood education is the key to preventing retention. The earlier children begin attending school, the better their chances of academic success. High-quality preschool can provide the opportunity for children who are academically behind to catch up with their peers before entering kindergarten. Mandatory, full-day kindergarten has been shown to reduce the risk of students being retained in later grades. This is especially important in light of research that links retention after the 1st grade to the high school dropout rate.

When remediation is needed, it is vital that it be proportional to a student's academic needs. Retention aside, students who are below grade level need remediation. Many adults operate under the misunderstanding that retention by itself is remediation. This is often not the case. Students may benefit more from staying with their peer group and receiving supplemental remediation or assistance than from being retained.

School District Policy

Our current educational system is based on the categorization of students. Given that each student is unique, it is important to move away from a "one-size-fits-all" mentality and encourage innovation and flexibility in the provision of services. Instead of offering standard services for the various categories of students, schools must adopt a more individualized approach that addresses the particular needs of each student. This will shift the focus from the classification of students to adapting and implementing standards-based instructional strategies tailored to the needs of each student.

Districts can align resources with standards, curriculum, test content, and professional development as a straightforward and effective way to begin closing the gap. If they take a systemic approach, schools and school districts will institutionalize changes in a relatively short period of time. These changes can transform the structure and functioning of school systems serving minority students to resemble those of systems serving primarily nonminority high-performing students.

Implications for Eliminating the Achievement Gap

Finding effective ways to eliminate the achievement gap in schools has become a more explicit focus of current school restructuring efforts. Academic achievement gains will not improve significantly unless schools also restructure to support students' learning (Rossman & Morley, 1995; Wehlage, Smith, & Lipman, 1992). Accordingly, principals, teachers, school district administrators, researchers, policymakers, parents, and community members must all reconceptualize how schools and the community should enhance mutual goals to increase student success (Corcoran, Fuhrman, & Belcher, 2001; Epstein, 2001; Honig & Jehl, 2000; Smylie & Crowson, 1996; Smylie, Crowson, Chou, & Levin, 1994; Wehlage, Smith, & Lipman, 1992). Restructuring that takes a critical look at all the conditions of learning—including leadership, curriculum and instruction, organization and management, and family and community—is most likely to lead to improved student achievement (Merseth, Schorr, & Elmore, 2000). Being effective, as demonstrated in the case studies, requires using appropriate data to address these critical areas.

Focus on Curriculum and Instruction

The primary task of the school is to focus on successfully meeting the academic needs and related services required to ensure schooling success for every student. Schools that are doing well with poor and minority students possess a clear and unfettered focus on intellectual matters (Elmore, 2000; Haycock, 1998). They also concentrate resources and efforts on providing students with challenging curriculum and high-quality instruction (U.S. Department of Education, 1998).

A central idea in the current view of learning is that students do not simply receive and store information. Rather, they transform it, link it to knowledge they already hold, and use it to build a coherent interpretation of the world and its events. School curriculum and instruction must therefore incorporate the following:

- New definitions of human intelligence
- More sophisticated methods of assessment
- An increased emphasis on collaborative learning
- Greater use of innovative and adaptive instructional strategies
- A focus on solving real-world problems using concepts and skills from multiple subject areas

Schoolwide Organizational Support

School implementation of a challenging curriculum is often unsuccessful when a clear mission and a well-defined organizational structure that optimize the use of time and resources for student learning are lacking.

Increasingly, evidence shows that the spread and sustainability of new and improved approaches to teaching and learning require new professional and social norms and normative structures that are currently foreign to many schools. The goal of every school should be to establish and maintain schoolwide organizational supports that ensure optimal opportunities for the learning success of all students. Below are descriptions of several areas on which to focus.

Strong and effective leadership. Principals are key to the success of any school but are especially important in schools focused on eliminating the achievement gap. Effective principals are strong instructional leaders who focus on teaching and learning. They create the strategic framework to improve curriculum and instruction while fulfilling other responsibilities, such as budgeting and management. Successful principals recognize that these other tasks help improve the ultimate mission of the school: student academic success.

Collaborative decision making and problem solving. Implementation of school teaming requires the delegation and distribution of formal decision-making authority among school personnel who share resources and responsibilities for all of the students in the school. The principal must provide leadership that incorporates clear statements of where the school is going; an understanding of how to create an atmosphere of learning, collegiality, and leadership for all; and a commitment to a vision of excellence and equity (Barth, 1990). School staff need to learn how to generate and analyze data about student achievement and the way schools function.

Adaptive and personalized environments. The most effective schools develop learning communities that are responsive to a wide range of student needs. Many elementary schools have reduced class size in early grades to increase academic success. Secondary schools are reducing the size of schools by creating academies, teams, and smaller units (Howley, 2001; Pritchard, 1999; Steifel, Berne, Iatarola, & Fruchter, 2000).

Efficient and effective use of time. Researchers suggest that a considerable decrease in the achievement gap is made possible by creating flexible structuring and maximizing academic learning time (Lewis & McDonald, 2001; Zimmerman, 2001). One common way to accomplish this is to add time to the school day or school year by adding supplemental before- and after-school programs. The institution of summer programs and flexible schedules can also increase academic learning time.

Ongoing data-based professional development. Teachers in schools experiencing an achievement gap require continuous opportunities to develop expertise and renewal. Schools should build professional development into the school day and calendar and sustain it, align it with the content of curriculum, and focus it on improving instruction with activities centered on the classroom. The schools that are most successful in concentrating professional development resources and time match the needs of educators and students in each school, as determined by current data analysis, and engage teachers in learning about the materials they teach and the skills they need to improve classroom instruction (U.S. Department of Education, 1998).

School District Approaches

With new state standards for achievement, most school districts serving high percentages of minority, poor, or at-risk children have come under great pressure to close the gap between their students' abilities and state standards. A strong chorus of critics has correctly pointed out that such high-stakes testing alone will not close the achievement gap (Jencks & Phillips, 1998; Kober, 2001). In fact, an overemphasis on testing may detract from overall educational quality if teachers are simply "teaching the test" at the expense of emphasizing a broad array of critical thinking and writing skills. But even critics of the testing craze would agree that the intense focus on testing does raise the bar of expectations to an equal level for all children. This measure of high expectations, even if only found in a few narrowly defined academic areas, is one important ingredient in all high-performing learning communities.

One study (Cawelti & Protheroe, 2001) found that six school districts with significant percentages of at-risk children did manage to close the achievement gap by transforming themselves from a set of low-performing schools into high-performing learning communities. The researchers found that the districts had test-driven elements to define actions for districts, schools, and classroom teachers, along with data-driven plans for improvement in student learning. Test scores for all students improved through a plan that included the following:

- Extensive efforts to align instruction with test content
- Detailed analysis of student responses to tests or assessments designed to be similar to the high-stakes tests
- Provision of immediate remediation and instruction for individual students as indicated by analysis of individual student assessment data

The schools studied were also found to have well-established support networks for teachers and leaders that included appropriate professional development, an understanding of the need to nurture, a climate conducive to learning, and strong accountability for performance.

Family, Community, and Social Service Connections

Although schools are the designated institutions for providing formal education during children's formative years, all members of today's society must recognize they have a stake in children's education. Adults need to view education as a community responsibility to support future citizens who will embody creative spirit, critical thinking, and high standards. To encourage this view, local communities must embrace their children, families, and schools. School-community connections must be aimed at improving student learning and addressing both barriers to learning and the factors that enable it. The forging of working connections with multiple groups and agencies, including higher education institutions and health, social, recreational, and other support services, is essential to the success of children in school.

Conversely, schools need to understand the dynamics of the neighborhoods in which they are located and the opportunities and challenges presented by changing conditions. The schools must continuously determine what kinds of additional supports, services, and opportunities are available to sustain students' learning and development (Manning & Rodriguez, 2000; Wang & Boyd, 2000). In one instance, the superintendent of a poor district with the highest rate of pregnancy in the state approached the president of a community hospital to address the issue. A partnership resulted in a restructuring of the middle school, a state-of-the-art clinic, and alternative options for students to complete high school.

Schools need to be able to depend on their community to be strong, cohesive, and capable of providing resources outside the schools as the need arises (Merseth, Schorr, & Elmore, 2000). Teachers and administrators must be prepared to create effective partnership programs to ensure good schools and successful students (Epstein, 2001). To enhance academic and social learning within a community context, schools should identify specific goals and ways of altering parent, teacher, and student behaviors that affect learning. Schools should then educate and persuade each member of the community to behave in the desired manner (Etzioni, 1991; Redding, 2001; Sergiovanni, 1993). For example, review, maintenance, and enrichment activities can supplement the extra help given in school classes before students take achievement tests. Members of the community can carry out these activities in community centers, housing projects, local libraries, or school buildings. Funds to support the maintenance of these services can come from public and private sources.

Conclusion

The case examples highlight the idea that efforts to close the achievement gap must center on several fundamental elements that can act as catalysts for real and substantial academic improvement in schools serving minority students. The literature shows that when the conditions are right, what schools do relative to instruction does make a difference. It is also evident that schools must be organized around clear goals focused on academic standards that include high expectations for performance by *all* students. These high standards must become a guide for comprehensive reform and capacity-building in supports for teachers and leaders, as well as for strengthening school-community connections. The way in which schools institute these reforms must be guided by data, sustained, and not fragmented. If whole school reform is the focus of transformation efforts and if achievement for *all* students is the goal, those students at the bottom will benefit most from such changes.

Because the achievement gap appears even before minority youth reach kindergarten, any holistic approach to closing the gap must include high-quality preschool and parent education programs. Reform measures must use data to prescribe appropriate supplemental educational opportunities for students who are low-achieving, and must focus attention on ensuring that these are high-quality interventions. In the end, these changes in school conditions and functioning, coupled with accountability measures in the form of some sort of periodic "report card," can help educational professionals become communities of learners committed to making significant strides in closing the achievement gap.

A closing caveat is pertinent to forecasting the success that educational professionals will have in their scaling-up efforts to close the achievement gap. Ultimately, the achievement gap is rooted in the larger context of a society that continues to be deeply divided by social class and race. The dynamics of racism in our society are tied to a system of grossly unequal economic rewards. As economic inequality worsens and competition for good educational opportunities—such as scholarships, internships, and good jobs—increases, racial discrimination and inequities based on race will be heightened. Given projections by economists that the U.S. economy is in a deep recession, the challenges of the achievement gap will most likely remain as part of the educational landscape in this country for some time to come. Educational reformers need to remember this caveat not as an excuse for inaction, but as a component of a call to action that is guided by an "optimism of the heart," and stems from a deep understanding of positive accomplishments achieved to date in closing the gap.

References

Alexander, K. L., Entwisle, D. R., & Dauber, S. L. (2001). Dropout in relation to grade retention: An accounting from the beginning school study. *The CEIC Review, 10*(5), 3–4, 12.

Arroyo, A., Rhoad, R., & Drew, P. (1999). Meeting diverse student needs in urban schools: Research-based recommendations for school personnel. *Preventing School Failure, 43*(4), 145–153.

Barth, R. S. (1990). *Improving schools from within: Teachers, parents, and principals can make the difference.* San Francisco: Jossey-Bass.

Camara, W. J., & Schmidt, E. (1999). *Group differences in standardized testing and social stratification* (College Board Rep. No. 99-5). New York: College Entrance Examination Board.

Cawelti, G., & Protheroe, N. (2001). *High student achievement: How six school districts changed into high-performance systems.* Arlington, VA: Educational Research Service.

College Entrance Examination Board. (1999). *Reaching the top: A report of the National Task Force on Minority High Achievement.* New York: Author.

Corcoran, T., Fuhrman, S. H., & Belcher, C. L. (2001). The district role in instructional improvement. *Phi Delta Kappan, 83*(1), 78–84.

Daniels, L. A. (Ed.). (2002). *The state of Black America 2002.* New York: National Urban League.

Darling-Hammond, L. (1997). *The right to learn: A blueprint for creating schools that work.* San Francisco: Jossey-Bass.

Drake, D. C. (2002). *A review and analysis of Michigan tax policies impacting K–12 finances.* Lansing, MI: Michigan Association of School Administrators.

Elmore, R. F. (2000). *Building a new structure for school leadership.* Washington, DC: Albert Shanker Institute.

Epstein, J. L. (2001). *School, family, and community partnership: Preparing educators and improving schools.* Boulder, CO: Westview Press.

Etzioni, A. (1991). *A responsive society.* San Francisco: Jossey-Bass.

Ferguson, R. (2000). *Cultivating new routines that foster high achievement for all students: Frameworks and ideas for collaborating to reduce racial achievement gaps.* Cambridge, MA: Harvard University, John F. Kennedy School of Government, Wiener Center for Social Policy.

Finn, C. E., Rotherman, A. J., & Hokanson, C. R. (Eds.). (2001). *Rethinking special education for a new century.* Washington, DC: Thomas B. Fordham Foundation and the Progressive Policy Institute.

Gamoran, A. (2001). Classroom organization and instructional quality: An examination of tracking and de-tracking. *The CEIC Review, 10*(5), 15–16, 23.

Goertz, M. E. (1999). *Implementing standards-based reform: Challenges for state policy* [Online]. Retrieved December 14, 2001. Available: http://www.c-b-e.org/PDF/ws1999goertz.pdf

Gordon, E. (2001). Affirmative development of academic abilities: Developing human capital in the twenty-first century. *The CEIC Review, 10*(4), 3–4.

Green, R. (2001). Closing the achievement gap: Lessons learned and challenges ahead. *Teaching and Change, 8*(2), 215–224.

Haycock, K. (1998). Good teaching matters . . . a lot. *Thinking K–16, 3*(2), 3–14.

Haycock, K. (2001). Closing the achievement gap. *Educational Leadership, 58*(6), 6–11.

Honig, M. I., & Jehl, D. J. (2000). Enhancing federal support for connecting educational improvement strategies and collaborative services. In M. C. Wang & W. L. Boyd (Eds.), *Improving results for children and families: Linking collaborative services with school reform efforts* (pp. 175–197). Greenwich, CT: Information Age Publishing.

Howley, C. (2001). *Research on smaller school size: What education leaders need to know to make better decisions.* Arlington, VA: Educational Research Service.

James, D. W., Jurich, S., & Estes, S. (2001). *Raising minority academic achievement: A compendium of education programs and practices.* Washington, DC: American Youth Policy Forum.

Jencks, C., & Phillips, M. (1998). *The black–white test score gap.* Washington, DC: Brookings Institution Press.

Jimerson, S. (2001). Meta-analysis of the effects of grade retention, 1990–1999: A basis for moving beyond grade retention and social promotion. *The CEIC Review, 10*(5), 7–8, 21.

Johnson, J., & Asera, R. (1999). *Hope for urban education: A study of nine high-performing, high-poverty urban elementary schools.* Austin, TX: University of Texas, Charles A. Dana Center.

Katzenbach, J. R., & Smith, D. K. (1993). *The wisdom of teams: Creating the high-performance organization.* New York: HarperCollins.

Kober, N. (2001). *It takes more than testing: Closing the achievement gap.* Washington, DC: Center on Education Policy.

Koretz, D. (2000). The impact of score differences on the admission of minority students: An illustration. *NBETPP Statements, 1*(5), 1–15.

Kulik, J. (2001). Tracking, de-tracking, and skill grouping: Conclusions from experimental, ethnographic, and regression studies. *The CEIC Review, 10*(5), 17–18, 23.

Langenfeld, K. L., Thurlow, M. L., & Scott, D. L. (1996). *High stakes testing for students: Unanswered questions and implications for students with disabilities* (Synthesis Report No. 26) [Online]. Retrieved November 30, 2001. Available: http://www.coled.umn.edu/nceo/Online Pubs/Synthesis26.htm

Lewis, D., & McDonald, J. (2001). How one school went to a year-round calendar. *Principal, 80*(3), 22–25.

Manning, J. B., & Rodriguez, L. (2000). Community for learning: Connections with community services. In M. C. Wang & W. L. Boyd (Eds.), *Improving results for children and families: Linking collaborative services with school reform efforts* (pp. 19–32). Greenwich, CT: Information Age Publishing.

Merseth, K. K., Schorr, L. B., & Elmore, R. F. (2000). Schools, community-based interventions, and children's learning and development: What's the connection? In M. C. Wang & W. L. Boyd (Eds.), *Improving results for children and families: Linking collaborative services with school reform efforts* (pp. 35–52). Greenwich, CT: Information Age Publishing.

Michigan Department of Education. (2001, August 28). *Status of Michigan education continues to improve: State hits grand slam with ACT, SAT, NAEP, TIMSS results* [Press release]. Lansing, MI: Author.

Michigan State Board of Education. (2001, June 12). *State board adopts quality improvement strategies: Goal to improve academic achievement in underperforming schools* [Press release]. Lansing, MI: Author.

National Center for Education Statistics. (2001). *NAEP summary data tables.* Washington, DC: U.S. Department of Education.

North Carolina Department of Public Instruction. (2000). *The role of district level staff in closing the gap* [Online]. Retrieved January 24, 2002. Available: http://www.dpi.state.nc.us/closingthegap/staff.html

Oakes, J., & Lipton, M. (2001). Can unlike children learn together? A question that goes to the heart of democratic public schooling. *The CEIC Review, 10*(5), 9–10, 21–22.

Pritchard, I. (1999). *Reducing class size: What do we know?* Washington, DC: U.S. Department of Education.

Pugach, M. C., & Warger, C. L. (1993). Curriculum considerations. In J. Goodlad & T. Lovitt (Eds.), *Integrating general and special education* (pp. 125–148). New York: Merrill-Macmillan.

Redding, S. (2001). The community of the school. In S. Redding & L. G. Thomas (Eds.), *The community of the school* (pp. 1–25). Lincoln, IL: Academic Development Institute.

Rossman, S. B., & Morley, E. (1995). *The national evaluation in cities in schools: Executive summary.* Washington, DC: The Urban Institute.

Sergiovanni, T. J. (1993). *Building community in schools.* San Francisco: Jossey-Bass.

Smylie, M. A., & Crowson, R. L. (1996). Working with the scripts: Building an institutional infrastructure for children's services coordination in schools. *Educational Policy, 10*(1), 3–18.

Smylie, M. A., Crowson, R. L., Chou, V. T., & Levin, R. K. (1994). The principal and community-school connections in Chicago's radical reform. *Educational Administration Quarterly, 30,* 342–364.

Steifel, L., Berne, R., Iatarola, P., & Fruchter, N. (2000, Spring). High school size: Effects on budgets and performance in New York City. *Educational Evaluation and Policy Analysis, 22*(1), 27–39.

Stull, J., & Wang, M. C. (2001, April). *The determinants of achievement: Minority students compared to non-minority students.* Paper presented at the annual meeting of the American Educational Research Association, Seattle, WA.

Temple, J., Reynolds, A., & Ou, S. R. (2001). Grade retention and school dropout: Another look at the evidence. *The CEIC Review, 10*(5), 5 6, 21.

U.S. Census Bureau. (2001). *Overview of race and Hispanic origin: Census 2000 brief.* Washington, DC: U.S. Department of Commerce.

U.S. Department of Education. (1998). *Guidance on the Comprehensive School Reform Demonstration program.* Washington, DC: Author.

U.S. Department of Education. (2001). *Educational achievement and black–white inequality.* Washington, DC: Author.

Walker, E., & Gutmore, D. (2000). *The quest for equity and excellence in education: A study of whole school reform in New Jersey special needs districts.* South Orange, NJ: Seton Hall University, Center for Urban Leadership, Renewal, and Research.

Wang, M. C., & Boyd, W. L. (Eds.). (2000). *Improving results for children and families: Linking collaborative services with school reform efforts.* Greenwich, CT: Information Age Publishing.

Wang, M. C., & Kovach, J. (1996). Bridging the achievement gap in urban schools: Reducing educational segregation and advancing resilience-promoting strategies. In B. Williams (Ed.), *Closing the achievement gap: A vision for changing beliefs and practices* (pp. 10–36). Alexandria, VA: Association for Supervision and Curriculum Development.

Wang, M. C., & Reynolds, M. (1995). *Making a difference for students at risk: Trends and alternatives.* Thousand Oaks, CA: Corwin Press.

Wehlage, G., Smith, E. G., & Lipman, P. (1992). Restructuring urban schools: The New Futures experience. *American Educational Research Journal, 29*, 55–96.

Winfield, L., Johnson, R., & Manning, J. (1993). Managing instructional diversity. In P. B. Forsyth & M. Tallerico (Eds.), *City schools: Leading the way* (pp. 97 130). Thousand Oaks, CA: Corwin Press.

Zimmerman, J. (2001). How much does time affect learning? *Principal, 80*(3), 7–11.

3

Direct Vocabulary Instruction: An Idea Whose Time Has Come

Robert J. Marzano

One of the perceived "truisms" in education has been that a student's intelligence or aptitude accounts for the lion's share of the variation in student achievement. For example, the strong relationship between intelligence and achievement was one of the more salient findings in the seminal research of Coleman and colleagues (1966) and Jencks and colleagues (1972). More recently, Jensen (1980) and Herrnstein and Murray (1994) have argued that aptitude is not only the strongest predictor of academic achievement, but that it is a genetically determined, immutable characteristic. Of course, if one accepts this position, it paints a bleak picture for certain students and even certain socioeconomic groups.

In contrast, the basic premise of this chapter is that what was previously thought to be unchangeable is, in fact, quite malleable. When one carefully examines the research on intelligence or aptitude, the conclusion can be drawn that at least some of those aspects of intelligence that are most closely associated with academic achievement can, in fact, be altered by direct interventions taken by schools. In addition, these interventions have been known for years, although they have been severely underutilized, particularly in the last two decades.

A first step is to consider the research linking aptitude to achievement. Some discussions of this issue make a distinction between intelligence and aptitude (Anastasi, 1982; Snow & Lohman, 1989). However useful, the distinction is a fairly technical one and does not serve the purposes of this discussion. Consequently, throughout this chapter the terms intelligence and aptitude are used interchangeably.

Intelligence and Academic Achievement

The relationship between intelligence and academic achievement has an intuitively valid ring to it. The more intelligence one has, the easier it is to learn, and school is certainly about learning. Indeed, numerous studies have documented a statistically significant relationship between intelligence and academic achievement (Bloom, 1984a, 1984b; Dochy, Segers, & Buehl, 1999; Fraser, Walberg, Welch, & Hattie, 1987; Walberg, 1984). If one assumes, as do Jensen, Herrnstein, and Murray, that intelligence is a fixed, immutable characteristic, then there is little hope that schools can alter the impact of aptitude on achievement. However, an examination of the nature of aptitude provides a quite different perspective. Specifically, if one makes a distinction between two types of intelligence, then the potential intervening role for schools becomes evident.

A basic distinction between two types of intelligence was first proposed by Cattell (1971/1987) and further developed by Ackerman (1996). Within this theory base, intelligence is seen as consisting of two constructs: intelligence as knowledge, or *crystallized intelligence*, and intelligence as cognitive processes, or *fluid intelligence*. Crystallized intelligence is exemplified by the ability to recognize or recall facts, generalizations, and principles, along with the ability to learn and execute domain-specific skills and processes, such as multiplying and dividing. Fluid intelligence is exemplified by procedures such as abstract reasoning ability, working memory capacity, and working memory efficiency. Where fluid intelligence is assumed to be innate and not subject to alteration from environment factors, crystallized intelligence is thought to be learned. It is also assumed that fluid intelligence is instrumental in the development of crystallized intelligence. That is, the more efficient a person is at the cognitive processes involved in fluid intelligence, the more easily he will acquire crystallized intelligence as he interacts with the world.

A question pertinent to the present discussion is which type of intelligence—crystallized or fluid—is more strongly related to academic achievement? Rolfhus and Ackerman (1999) conducted one of the most extensive studies of the relationship among crystallized intelligence, fluid intelligence, and academic achievement. They administered intelligence tests to 141 adults, along with tests of knowledge in 20 different subject areas. They then examined the relationship between scores on the tests of subject matter knowledge and fluid versus crystallized intelligence. They found little relationship between academic knowledge and fluid intelligence but noted a strong relationship between academic knowledge and crystallized intelligence. As Rolfhus and Ackerman (1999) state, these findings suggest that academic "knowledge is more highly associated with [crystallized] abilities than with [fluid] abilities" (p. 520). These findings are quite consistent with those reported by Madaus, Kellaghan, Rakow, and King (1979), who found that the correlation between measures of fluid intelligence and achievement was relatively small when controlled for the home environment of students and characteristics of the school.

The strong correlation between crystallized intelligence and achievement goes a long way in explaining the strong relationship between prior knowledge and achievement. In fact, the research finding that prior knowledge is strongly correlated with academic achievement is as ubiquitous as the research finding that aptitude is strongly correlated with academic achievement (Alexander & Judy, 1988; Alexander, Kulikowich, & Schulze, 1994; Bloom, 1976; Boulanger, 1981; Dochy et al., 1999; Schiefele & Krapp, 1996; Tamir, 1996; Tobias, 1994). One of the most extensive investigations of the relationship between prior knowledge and academic achievement was conducted by Dochy and colleagues (1999). In their analysis of 183 studies, they found that 91.5 percent of the studies demonstrated positive effects of prior knowledge on learning, and those that did not measured prior knowledge in ways that were indirect, questionable, or even invalid.

If one considers the research on intelligence and academic achievement and the research on prior knowledge and academic achievement as a set, some clear generalizations emerge. First, the research supports the notion that crystallized intelligence or learned intelligence, as opposed to fluid or innate intelligence, is the stronger correlate of academic achievement. Second, it is a small step to go from crystallized intelligence to prior knowledge. In fact, for all practical purposes, they might be considered identical. Crystallized intelligence is learned knowledge about the world; prior knowledge is learned knowledge about a specific domain. One might say, then, that enhancing a student's background knowledge is akin to enhancing his crystallized intelligence, which is one of the strongest determiners of academic achievement. This fact strongly suggests that schools can directly influence the type of intelligence most closely associated with academic achievement. The task for schools is simply that of enhancing the background knowledge of students.

The most direct way of enhancing student background knowledge is to increase their access to a wide variety of experiences such as cultural field trips, prolonged contact with families who have a wide variety of resources, and the like. Programs that take this approach have great potential (Scheerens & Bosker, 1997; Teddlie & Reynolds, 2000). However, such programs require extraordinary resources in terms of time, energy, and finances. Fortunately, an indirect way of enhancing the general background knowledge of students is through direct vocabulary instruction. In short, the central thesis of this chapter is that direct vocabulary instruction is a time-honored but underutilized technique for enhancing the background knowledge and, consequently, crystallized intelligence of students and can be particularly useful with those students who have limited access to a broad experiential base.

Before an examination of the rationale for and validity of direct vocabulary instruction, it is useful to clarify the relationships among fluid intelligence, crystallized intelligence, and achievement. It is certainly true that students who have high fluid intelligence *and* access to a variety of experiences will quite naturally acquire substantial crystallized intelligence. It is not the case, however, that an individual with low crystallized intelligence has low fluid intelligence. Indeed, a person with high fluid intelligence who does not have access to a variety of experiences will also have low crystallized intelligence simply because of lack of opportunity to acquire it. The person with low fluid intelligence and limited access to a wide experiential base is in a double bind. Such a person not only suffers from reduced ability to acquire crystallized intelligence but also has limited access to the experiential base to build that type of intelligence. Direct vocabulary instruction, then, can greatly serve any students who do not have access to a wide experiential base, whether they have moderate to high fluid intelligence or low fluid intelligence.

Crystallized Intelligence and Vocabulary Learning

Although crystallized intelligence is not synonymous with vocabulary development, a large vocabulary is one of the best general indicators of intelligence (Chall, 1987). Indeed, Coleman and colleagues (1966) used verbal ability measured primarily by vocabulary knowledge as their primary dependent measure (Madaus et al., 1979). Not surprisingly, the relationship between vocabulary knowledge and academic achievement is also well-established. For example, as early as 1941, researchers estimated that for students in grades 4 through 12, there was about a 6,000-word gap between students at the 25th and 50th percentiles on standardized tests (Nagy & Herman, 1984). Using a more advanced method of calculating vocabulary size, Nagy and Herman (1984) estimated the difference to be anywhere between 4,500 and 5,400 words for low- versus high-achieving students.

What is there about vocabulary that makes it such a strong proxy measure for crystallized intelligence and such a strong correlate of academic achievement? There are at least two perspectives that provide an answer to this question: (1) the nature of memory, and (2) the relationship between language and thought.

The Nature of Memory

Permanent memory is the repository for everything learned—all knowledge and skill. A common model for the manner in which information is represented in permanent memory is that it is organized in modular form. Anderson (1995) refers to these modules as memory "records." Tulving (1972) further explains that memory records come in two basic forms: episodic and semantic. Episodic memory records are of actual experiences. For example, if a foreign student who has never seen a football game attends the Super Bowl, she will store that event in permanent memory as an episodic record. Semantic records are derived from episodic records. They contain decontextualized information. In the case of our foreign student, she would organize information about football games (in general) from her episodic record of direct experience. It is our semantic records that allow us to make inferences about new knowledge and link new knowledge to old knowledge.

In terms of the discussion in this chapter, a key feature of semantic records is that they have a "label" or a "tag" associated with them. In the case of our foreign student, that label or tag would probably be *football games*. In fact, a vocabulary term can be defined as a word or phrase that is used as a "tag" for a given semantic memory record. This sheds light on the strong link between vocabulary knowledge and crystallized intelligence. As students have new experiences, they store these experiences as memory records. Fully formed memory records have an associated tag or label. The more records one has with their accompanying tags, the more crystallized intelligence.

This also explains the strong relationship between vocabulary knowledge and socioeconomic status (SES). For example, Nagy and Herman (1984) found a consistent difference in vocabulary development between groups at different SES. They estimated a 4,700-word difference in vocabulary knowledge between high- and low-SES students. Similarly, they estimated that mid-SES 1st graders know about 50 percent more words than do low-SES 1st graders. Graves and Slater (1987) found that 1st graders from higher-income backgrounds had about double the vocabulary size of those from lower-income backgrounds. Although different researchers use slightly different estimates, all seem to agree that there are huge variations in the size of vocabulary between students from different backgrounds.

The Relationship Between Language and Thought

It is probably safe to say that Chomsky was one of the first linguists to provide a compelling argument that language and thought are inextricably linked. This argument was made in his book *Syntactic Structures* (1957) and then expanded in *Aspects of a Theory of Syntax* (1965). Pinker has described more recent advancements in *The Language Instinct* (1994).

The initial insight Chomsky elucidated in *Syntactic Structures* was that sentences must be characterized by two structural descriptions, not one, as is the case with grammar systems designed prior to Chomsky's work (the traditional grammar that is commonly taught in school). The "deep structure" of language deals with the underlying semantic and syntactic nature of language. The "surface structure" of language deals with the actual use of language. The necessity for the two forms is most easily seen with imperatives. The surface structure *go away* is understood by ordinary speakers as a realization of the underlying form or deep structure *you will go away*. Where the surface structure of language is the observable expression of language, it is the deep structure that depicts the basic "thought" underlying language.

The actual format of deep structure language has been the subject of much discussion. The most popular model for describing the basic unit of linguistic thought is the proposition. The construct of a proposition has a rich history in both psychology and linguistics (Frederiksen, 1977; Kintsch, 1974; Norman & Rumelhart, 1975). In simple terms, "a proposition is the smallest unit about which it makes sense to make the judgment true or false" (Anderson, 1990b, p. 123). Clark and Clark (1977) have noted that there is a finite set of the types of propositions used to express linguistic thought. Some of the basic types of propositions are exemplified by the following:

- Birds fly.
- Birds are pretty.
- Birds eat fruit.
- Birds live in trees.
- Birds have a purpose in the ecosystem.

What we call thinking—particularly abstract thinking—is a matter of stringing together basic propositions like those above into complex semantic networks (Kintsch, 1974, 1979). The ability of a person to think in complex ways, then, is a function of his ability to express experiences in propositional format. This illuminates the importance of vocabulary. Where the proposition is the basic unit of linguistic thought, vocabulary terms are the building blocks of propositions. In other words, without knowledge of the vocabulary terms that describe an experience, an individual has no way to express the experience semantically. A limited vocabulary inhibits one's ability to store experiences in abstract ways—as semantic records. Enhancing vocabulary knowledge, then, might be viewed as a direct path to enhancing students' language competence and their ability to think in abstract ways.

Myths and Realities of Vocabulary Instruction

The research on direct vocabulary instruction provides a final and practical validation for the arguments presented in this chapter. Indeed, this literature indicates that direct vocabulary instruction has a well-documented effect on student achievement (Stahl & Fairbanks, 1986). In fact, some researchers have concluded that employing direct vocabulary instruction is one of the most important instructional interventions, particularly with students who have little access to a rich experiential base (Becker, 1977). In spite of this, practicing direct vocabulary instruction at the school level is somewhat rare in U.S. schools (McKeown & Curtis, 1987). This unfortunate situation is due, in part, to an argument that direct vocabulary instruction is a futile or, at best, low-yield endeavor in terms of student learning. The research of Nagy and Anderson (1984) has fueled this conclusion; they have estimated that the number of words in "printed school English" (that is, those words students in grades 3 through 9 will encounter in print) is about 85,000. Obviously, it would be impossible to teach this many words one at a time. Stahl and Fairbanks (1986) summarize this position in the following way:

> Since vocabulary teaching programs typically teach 10 to 12 words a week or about 400 words per year, of which perhaps 75 percent or 300 are learned, vocabulary instruction is not adequate to cope with the volume of new words that children need to learn and do learn without instruction. (p. 100)

Nagy and Herman (1987) offer an alternative to direct vocabulary instruction: wide reading. Simply stated, this is the practice of encouraging students to read a variety of subjects, themes, and types of literature. They argue as follows:

> If students were to spend 25 minutes a day reading at a rate of 200 words per minute for 200 days out of the year, they would encounter a million words of text annually. According to our estimates, with this amount of reading, children would encounter between 15,000 and 30,000 unfamiliar words. If 1 in 20 of these is learned, the yearly gain in vocabulary will be between 750 and 1,500 words. (p. 26)

If one subscribes to this position, then direct vocabulary instruction is not only unadvisable but downright foolish. However, this argument is not entirely accurate. In fact, an analysis of the extant research provides a strong counterargument for direct vocabulary instruction.

Five Principles of Direct Vocabulary Instruction

The discussion below organizes the research on vocabulary learning around five principles. These form the basis for the design of a systematic approach to enhancing students' crystallized intelligence through direct vocabulary instruction.

Principle #1: Students must encounter words in context more than once to learn them. Nagy and Herman (1987) base their conclusion about the utility of wide reading, in part, on the assumption that students will learn some, albeit few, of the new words they encounter in their reading. Still, if students read enough (for example, 25 minutes per day, 200 days a year), then the few words they learn will add up to a substantial number (between 750 and 1,500 words per year, as noted previously). However, wide reading might not add new words to students' vocabularies as easily as the argument above implies.

A study by Jenkins, Stein, and Wysocki (1984) dramatically demonstrates this point. They found that to learn a new word in context (without instruction), students must be exposed to the word about six times before they have enough experience with it to ascertain and remember its meaning. Also interesting is that beyond six exposures to a new word, the increase in learning was negligible. These findings are consistent with those reported by Stahl and Fairbanks (1986), who found that multiple exposures to words produced a significantly better understanding of those words (although Stahl and Fairbanks did not identify an optimal number of exposures).

These conclusions seriously undermine the logic of the "wide reading" approach to vocabulary development as the sole vehicle for vocabulary development. Again, the working principle underlying the approach is that students will figure out the meaning of and remember a portion, albeit small, of the new words they encounter in their reading. However, this argument fails to acknowledge that students will encounter the vast majority of these words only a few times. Indeed, word frequency studies indicate that most words appear very infrequently in written material. More than 90 percent of the words students will encounter while reading occur less than once in a million words of text; about half occur less than once in a billion words (Nagy & Anderson, 1984). Thus, the encounters students have with new words in their reading are, for the most part, isolated, single encounters that will not produce enough exposure for them to learn the new words.

Principle #2: Direct instruction in new words enhances the learning of words in context. Perhaps one of the most useful findings from the Jenkins and colleagues study (1984) is that even superficial instruction of words greatly enhances the probability that students will learn the words from context when they encounter them in their reading. Specifically, students who had prior instruction on words they encountered in context exhibited one-third (that is, about 33 percent) more achievement relative to their understanding of the words encountered than did those students who had no prior instruction.

Perhaps most significant about these findings is that the prior instruction was minimal. In fact, it amounted simply to providing students with a sheet that contained definitions of the new words along with an example of each word used in a sentence. Students were allowed to read the sheet, but they received no help from the teacher. In addition, students had only about 40 seconds to study each word—certainly not enough time to digest the information about the new words in any depth. Yet this superficial instruction produced an average of one-third higher performance scores on a test of word knowledge after students encountered the words in context.

Principle #3: Generating imagery representations enhances recall of vocabulary. One of the best ways to stimulate recall of newly learned vocabulary terms is to have students generate imagery representations of the meaning of new words. For example, a student has been presented with the information that the term *mode*, from mathematics, refers to "the most frequent number in a set of numbers." To elaborate on this, the student might form a mental picture of a set of numbers, with one number appearing many more times than any other number. Figure 3.1 depicts this kind of set.

Numerous studies support the powerful effects on learning that the creation of mental representations or symbolic representations have for a student (Paivio, 1990). For example, in an analysis of 11 controlled studies, Powell (1980) found that instruction techniques employing the use of

FIGURE 3.1

Student's Mental Picture Depicting *Mode*

2 2 2 3 4 4 4 4 4 4 4 4 4 4 5 5 6 6 6 7 7

imagery produced achievement gains in word knowledge that were 34 percentage points higher than techniques that did not use imagery.

Principle #4: Instruction in content-specific words produces greater learning. There is a distinct difference between the effects of instruction in words from generalized vocabulary lists and words that are specific to a given topic. Many vocabulary development programs use vocabulary lists of high-frequency words—words that commonly appear in the written language (Carroll, Davies, & Richman, 1971; Harris & Jacobson, 1972). However, these high-frequency lists typically do not focus on the written material students encounter in school. When coupled with the research by Stahl and Fairbanks (1986), this fact becomes significant.

In their meta-analysis, Stahl and Fairbanks found that instruction in general words, like those found in high-frequency word lists, enhanced students' ability to understand new content by 12 percentage points. By way of illustration, assume that two students of equal ability are asked to read and understand new information. Student A is in a program that teaches about 10 to 12 words each week from one of the high-frequency word lists. Student B does not receive this instruction. Now assume that students A and B take a test on the new content, and that student B achieves a score in the 50th percentile. All else being equal, student A will receive a score at the 62nd percentile on that same test, simply from having received systematic vocabulary instruction. This is certainly a significant gain.

However, the effects of direct vocabulary instruction are even more powerful when the words taught are those that students will most likely encounter in the new content they are learning. To illustrate, again consider students A and B who have been asked to read and understand new content. Student B, who has not received direct vocabulary instruction, receives a score on the test at the 50th percentile. Student A, who has received direct instruction *on words that have been specifically selected because they are important to the new content*, will obtain a score at the 83rd percentile.

Principle #5: You do not have to know a word in depth for it to be useful. The final premise derived from the research on vocabulary instruction is that students do not have to know words in depth to find them useful. E. D. Hirsch made this point salient in his 1988 book *Cultural Literacy: What Every American Needs to Know*, wherein Hirsch identified 4,546 terms and phrases that every student should know to be "culturally literate." He referred to his list as a "national vocabulary." Although I believe Hirsch's list of terms and phrases is biased and not an accurate accounting of what students should know (for a detailed discussion of the criticisms of Hirsch's list, see Marzano, Kendall, & Gaddy, 1999), I do agree with his contention that students need not know terms in depth. A surface level knowledge of terms that form the basis for general understanding of a subject area is sufficient to provide students with a solid platform on which they can build more sophisticated understandings.

To validate his position, Hirsch elaborates on a retrieval theory he characterizes as schema theory. He notes that when one reads or hears a word, memory activates a hierarchical array of information about that term. He refers to that activated information as schema. As described by Hirsch, those pieces of information an individual associates with a word or phrase comprise that person's schema for that term. Thus, Hirsch's notion of schema is akin to the description of a memory record. A key aspect of schema is that the information is stored in a hierarchic fashion, with the more common knowledge at the upper, most accessible levels. To exemplify this idea, Hirsch relates the findings of a study by Collins and Quillian (1969). Collins and Quillian posited that an individual's schema for the word "canary" might appear in a hierarchic fashion such as the following:

canary	can sing
	is yellow
	has wings
bird	can fly
	has feathers
	has skin
animal	can move around
	eats
	breathes

If it is true that the information closest to the top of the hierarchy is the most available, then people should remember the top-level information more quickly than the bottom-level information. Collins and Quillian's study tested this hypothesis by providing subjects with sentences such as these:

- Canaries can move around.
- Canaries are yellow.
- Canaries can fly.

Collins and Quillian asked subjects to determine whether each sentence was true or false. According to schema theory, people should be able to verify the accuracy of sentences that draw upon information from the higher levels of the schema more quickly than sentences that draw upon information from the lower levels of the schema. The study findings supported the hierarchic schema hypothesis. Hirsch (1988) made the following comments about the findings:

> Collins' and Quillian's observations suggest that the top portion of the schema is the important part to know. The schema canary can yield an indefinite number of facts and association[s] by remote inference from knowledge of the world: canaries have backbones; canaries have their own special pattern of DNA; canaries are descended from reptiles; canaries must drink water; canaries mate; canaries die. One could go on this way for a long time with specifications not only from biology, but from physical knowledge: canaries obey the law of gravity and the laws of motion, and so on. But this secondary information about canaries is not important in communicating with fellow human beings. What is functional in reading, writing, and conversation is the distinctive system of traits in the schema we use—the traits that differentiate canaries from other birds: their smallness, yellowness, ability to sing, use in human culture, being kept in cages, and so on. We need to know the primary traits commonly associated with [the schema] canary in our culture in order to deploy the associations rapidly when we encounter the word canary in reading. (pp. 58–59)

Since the Collins and Quillian experiment, a number of other studies have demonstrated the hierarchic nature of human knowledge. (For reviews see Anderson, 1990a, 1990b, 1995.)

Based on research evidence that top-level schema information is necessary and sufficient for general literacy purposes, Hirsch (1988) reasoned that schools should address the learning of his national vocabulary with a great deal of latitude and should hold students accountable for only general knowledge of his 4,546 terms and phrases. As he observed:

> The nature of this world knowledge as it exists in the minds of literate adults is typically elementary and incomplete. People reliably share just a few associations about canaries, such as yellow, sing, kept in cages, but not much more. Literate people know who Falstaff is, that he is fat, likes to eat and drink, but they can't reliably name the Shakespeare play in which he appears. They know who Eisenhower was, and might recognize "military-industrial complex," but they can't be counted on to state anything else about Eisenhower's Farewell Address. In short, the information that literate people

dependably share is extensive, but limited—a characteristic central to this discussion. (p. 127)

To reiterate, although I find many problems with Hirsch's "national vocabulary" list, I support the notion that it is possible to approach vocabulary terms and phrases legitimately from a top-level schema perspective— that students do not have to know a word's precise meaning for the word to aid them in their learning. This is not to say that students should not learn content in depth. Indeed, knowing words at a surface level provides the basis upon which students can develop an in-depth understanding at a later time.

In summary, it is possible to organize the research on vocabulary around five principles. Taken together, these principles provide a picture of how a highly effective vocabulary development program might look. Such a program could directly impact the background knowledge or crystallized intelligence of students, as well as their language competence and their ability to generate abstract semantic memory records. Specifically, these principles imply the following:

- Students should receive direct instruction on words and phrases that are critical to their understanding of content.
- As part of this instruction, students should be exposed to new words multiple times—preferably about six times.
- Students should be encouraged to represent their understanding of new words using mental images, pictures, symbols, and the like whenever possible.
- The goal of vocabulary instruction should not necessarily be an in-depth understanding of new words, but rather an accurate, albeit surface, knowledge of new words that will form the basis for greater understanding of content.

Identifying the Critical Subject Matter Terms

The principles above imply that the beginning point in designing a vocabulary program to enhance students' crystallized intelligence or academic background knowledge is to identify those terms that are central to academic learning. As mentioned previously, word lists that have typically been used as the basis for direct instruction in vocabulary are derived from general word frequency counts of words. Consequently, they do not focus on academic content students encounter in school.

Recently, researchers at Mid-continent Research for Education and Learning (McREL) identified 6,700 terms that are critical to the understanding of 14 different subject areas (Marzano et al., 1999). As an illustration of the nature of those words, the following are a few mathematical terms and phrases within the general category of probability that are appropriate for students in grades 6–8:

- Experiment
- Odds
- Theoretical probability
- Tree diagram
- Simulation
- Experimental probability

Based on the earlier discussion in this chapter, one can conclude that an understanding of these terms at the top schema level would provide students with a firm foundation on which to build more detailed and deeper understandings of probability.

There are at least two significant aspects of the McREL academic vocabulary list. First, the number of terms is small enough to make direct instruction feasible. If students were to receive instruction in about 18 words per week over the course of their K–12 schooling, they would be exposed to all 6,700 terms covering 14 subject areas. Of course, it would be possible to greatly reduce the number of terms directly taught to students if selected subjects are targeted (for example, mathematics, science, language arts, and social studies). Second, by definition, these terms are the ones students will most probably encounter in their subject matter classes. As already noted, Stahl and Fairbanks (1986) found that instruction in words encountered in reading produced a 33 percentage point gain in comprehension. Therefore, lists of subject matter terms, such as those produced by McREL, provide a new foundation for vocabulary development with the potential of directly affecting students' academic background knowledge.

A Process for Vocabulary Development

With a viable list of academic terms finally in place, it is possible to undertake a systematic approach to enhancing students' academic background knowledge. Specifically, schools can directly teach students the terms they will encounter in their subject areas, and they can do so easily if subject matter teachers systematically teach these terms as a regular part of classroom instruction. It is important to coordinate this effort from teacher to teacher and grade level to grade level. To ensure that students receive instruction in all the critical terms at appropriate times, the school must do cross-grade planning to determine which words are taught at specific grade levels for specific subjects.

Along with a correlated effort to directly teach the subject matter words, the research implies a sequential process for the learning of these academic terms. This process involves the following six steps:

1. Students receive a brief, informal explanation, description, or demonstration of the term.
2. Students receive an imagery-based representation of the new term.
3. Students describe or explain the term in their own words.
4. Students create their own imagery-based representations for the term.
5. Students elaborate on the term by making connections with other words.
6. Over time, teachers ask students to add new information to their understanding of terms and delete or alter erroneous information.

To illustrate the use of this process, consider the term *area model* from mathematics. The first step in the process involves providing students with a brief informal explanation, description, or demonstration of the target term. It is important to emphasize that a "description" or "explanation" is not the same as a definition. The intent of this process is to develop top-level schema knowledge for academic terms, not an in-depth knowledge. Given this freedom, the first step can be relatively simple and short. For example, the teacher might say, "*Area model*: A technique mathematicians use to represent the chances of something occurring. For example, I might create an area model to represent your chances of becoming a millionaire if you graduate from high school and another area model depicting your chances of becoming a millionaire if you graduate from college."

The second step in the process involves presenting students with an imagery-based representation of the term. In this case, the teacher might present students with the representation depicted in Figure 3.2.

The third step in the process is the point at which students begin to actually use the information provided in the first two steps. Here students construct their own meaning of the term by formulating a description or explanation. Again, because the goal is top-level schema development, the students' descriptions can be quite nontechnical and stated in ways that are meaningful to the student only. The basic criterion for the students' explanations is that they represent an accurate understanding of the top-level information about the term.

FIGURE 3.2

Teacher's Representation of *Area Model*

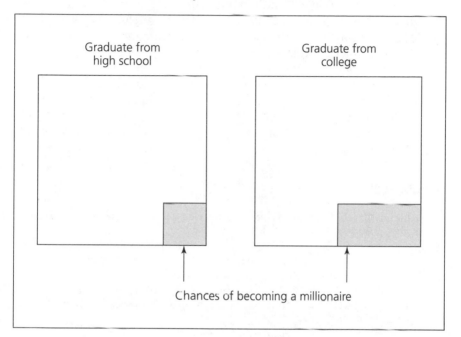

The fourth step in the process requires students to construct an imagery-based representation of the term. Again, these representations can be quite idiosyncratic to individual students as long as they convey accurate information. A student might draw a picture or symbol representing the term. The critical aspect of this step is to facilitate the translation of the information about the term into an imagery-based memory record.

The fifth step requires students to make connections. Here they might compare or contrast the new term with known terms. The emphasis in this step is on having the students elaborate on the information about the new term.

The final step in the process involves students revising their understanding of the term over time. If the students keep the terms in a vocabulary booklet, they can easily facilitate this. Occasionally, the teacher might ask students to review the words in their vocabulary notebooks with an eye toward adding new information or altering information that has proved to be less than totally accurate over time.

Conclusions

This chapter has presented the rationale and design for a systematic approach to enhancing the crystallized, learnable intelligence of students through direct vocabulary instruction. Both research and theory strongly support the viability of this endeavor. Such an approach has the potential for bringing about dramatic gains in academic achievement, particularly for those students who suffer from low crystallized intelligence for a variety of reasons. Because such students are traditionally the underserved minority, one might legitimately conclude that an implementation and trial of the approach described in this chapter is of paramount importance in K–12 education.

References

Ackerman, P. L. (1996). A theory of adult intellectual development: Process, personality, interests, and knowledge. *Intelligence, 22*, 227–257.

Alexander, P. A., & Judy, J. E. (1988). The interaction of domain-specific and strategic knowledge in academic performance. *Review of Educational Research, 58*(4), 375–404.

Alexander, P. A., Kulikowich, J. M., & Schulze, S. K. (1994). How subject-matter knowledge affects recall and interest. *American Educational Research Journal, 31*(2), 313–337.

Anastasi, A. (1982). *Psychological testing* (5th ed.). New York: Macmillan.

Anderson, J. R. (1990a). *The adaptive character of thought.* Hillsdale, NJ: Lawrence Erlbaum and Associates.

Anderson, J. R. (1990b). *Cognitive psychology and its implications* (3rd ed.). New York: W. H. Freeman.

Anderson, J. R. (1995). *Learning and memory: An integrated approach.* New York: John Wiley & Sons.

Becker, W. C. (1977). Teaching reading and language to the disadvantaged— What we have learned from field research. *Harvard Educational Review, 47*, 518–543.

Bloom, B. S. (1976). *Human characteristics and school learning.* New York: McGraw-Hill.

Bloom, B. S. (1984a). The search for methods of group instruction as effective as one-to-one tutoring. *Educational Leadership, 41*(8), 4–18.

Bloom, B. S. (1984b). The 2 Sigma problem: The search for methods of instruction as effective as one-to-one tutoring. *Educational Researcher, 13*(6), 4–16.

Boulanger, D. F. (1981). Ability and science learning. *Journal of Research in Science Teaching, 18*(2), 113–121.

Carroll, J., Davies, P., & Richman, B. (1971). *The American Heritage word frequency book.* Boston: Houghton Mifflin.

Cattell, R. B. (1971, 1987). *Intelligence: Its structure, growth, and action* (Rev. ed.). Amsterdam: North Holland Press. (Original work published 1971)

Chall, J. S. (1987). Two vocabularies for reading: Recognition and meaning. In M. G. McKeown & M. E. Curtis (Eds.), *The nature of vocabulary acquisition* (pp. 7–17). Hillsdale, NJ: Lawrence Erlbaum Associates.

Chomsky, N. (1957). *Syntactic structures.* The Hague: Moutan.

Chomsky, N. (1965). *Aspects of a theory of syntax.* Cambridge, MA: MIT Press.

Clark, H. H., & Clark, E. V. (1977). *Psychology and language.* San Diego, CA: Harcourt Brace Jovanovich.

Coleman, J. S., Campbell, E. Q., Hobson, C. J., McPartland, J., Mood, A. M., Weinfield, F. D., & York, R. L. (1966). *Equality of educational opportunity.* Washington, DC: U.S. Government Printing Office.

Collins, A. M., & Quillian, M. R. (1969). Retrieval time for semantic memory. *Journal of Verbal Learning and Verbal Behavior, 8,* 240–247.

Dochy, F., Segers, M., & Buehl, M. M. (1999). The relationship between assessment practices and outcomes of studies: The case of research on prior knowledge. *Review of Educational Research, 69*(2), 145–186.

Fraser, B. J., Walberg, H. J., Welch, W. W., & Hattie, J. A. (1987). Synthesis of educational productivity research. *Journal of Educational Research, 11*(2), 145–252.

Frederiksen, C. H. (1977). Semantic processing units in understanding text. In R. O. Freedle (Ed.) *Discourse production and comprehension: Volume 1.* (pp. 58–88). Norwood, NJ: Ablex.

Graves, M. F., & Slater, W. H. (1987, April). *Development of reading vocabularies on rural disadvantaged students, inner-city disadvantaged students and middle class suburban students.* Paper presented at the American Educational Research Association conference, Washington, DC.

Harris, A., & Jacobson, M. (1972). *Basic elementary reading vocabulary.* New York: Macmillan.

Herrnstein, R. J., & Murray, C. (1994). *The bell curve: Intelligence and class structure in American life.* New York: The Free Press.

Hirsch, E. D., Jr. (1988). *Cultural literacy: What every American needs to know.* With an updated appendix. New York: Vintage Books.

Jencks, C., Smith, M. S., Ackland, H., Bane, M. J., Cohen, D., Grintlis, H., Heynes, B., & Michelson, S. (1972). *Inequality: A reassessment of the effect of family and schooling in America.* New York: Basic Books.

Jenkins, J. R., Stein, M. L., & Wysocki, K. (1984). Learning vocabulary through reading. *American Educational Research Journal, 21*(4), 767–787.

Jensen, A. R. (1980). *Bias in mental testing.* New York: The Free Press.

Kintsch, W. (1974). *The representation of meaning in memory.* Hillsdale, NJ: Lawrence Erlbaum Associates.

Kintsch, W. (1979). On modeling comprehension. *Educational Psychologist, 1,* 3–14.

Madaus, G. F., Kellaghan, T., Rakow, E. A., & King, D. (1979). The sensitivity of measures of school effectiveness. *Harvard Educational Review, 49*(2), 207–230.

Marzano, R. J., Kendall, J. S., & Gaddy, B. B. (1999). *Essential knowledge: The debate over what American students should know.* Aurora, CO: McREL.

McKeown, M. G., & Curtis, M. E. (Eds.). (1987). *The nature of vocabulary acquisition.* Hillsdale, NJ: Lawrence Erlbaum Associates.

Nagy, W. E., & Anderson, R. C. (1984). How many words are there in printed school English? *Reading Research Quarterly, 19*(3), 304–330.

Nagy, W. E., & Herman, P. A. (1984). *Limitations of vocabulary instruction* (Tech. Rep. No. 326). Urbana, IL: University of Illinois, Center for the Study of Reading. (ERIC Document Reproduction Service No. ED 248 498)

Nagy, W. E., & Herman, P. A. (1987). Breadth and depth of vocabulary knowledge: Implications for acquisition and instruction. In M. G. McKeown & M. E. Curtis (Eds.), *The nature of vocabulary instruction* (pp. 19–36). Hillsdale, NJ: Lawrence Erlbaum Associates.

Norman, D. A., & Rumelhart, D. E. (1975). *Explanations in cognition.* New York: W. H. Freeman and Company.

Paivio, A. (1990). *Mental representations: A dual coding approach.* New York: Oxford University Press.

Pinker, S. (1994). *The language instinct: How the mind creates language.* New York: Harper Perennial.

Powell, G. (1980, December). *A meta-analysis of the effects of "imposed" and "induced" imagery upon word recall.* Paper presented at the annual meeting of the National Reading Conference, San Diego, CA. (ERIC Document Reproduction Service No. ED 199 644)

Rolfhus, E. L., & Ackerman, P. L. (1999). Assessing individual differences in knowledge: Knowledge, intelligence, and related traits. *Journal of Educational Psychology, 91*(3), 511–526.

Scheerens, J., & Bosker, R. (1997). *The foundations of educational effectiveness.* New York: Elsevier Science Ltd.

Schiefele, U., & Krapp, A. (1996). Topics of interest and free recall of expository text. *Learning and Individual Differences, 8*(2), 141–160.

Snow, R. E., & Lohman, D. F. (1989). Implications of cognitive psychology for educational measurement. In R. Linn (Ed.), *Educational measurement* (3rd ed.) (pp. 263–331). London: Collier Macmillan Publishers.

Stahl, S. A., & Fairbanks, M. M. (1986). The effects of vocabulary instruction: A model-based meta-analysis. *Review of Educational Research, 56*(1), 72–110.

Tamir, P. (1996). Science assessment. In M. Birenbaum & F. J. R. C. Dochy (Eds.), *Alternatives in assessment of achievements, learning processes, and prior knowledge* (pp. 93–129). Boston: Kluwer.

Teddlie, C., & Reynolds, D. (Eds.) (2000). *The international handbook of school effectiveness research.* London: Falmer Press.

Tobias, S. (1994). Interest, prior knowledge, and learning. *Review of Educational Research, 64*(1), 37–54.

Tulving, E. (1972). Episodic and semantic memory. In E. Tulving & W. Donaldson (Eds.), *Organization of memory* (pp. 185–191). New York: Academic Press.

Walberg, H. J. (1984). Improving the productivity of America's schools. *Educational Leadership, 41*(8), 19–27.

4

Cultural Values in Learning and Education

Elise Trumbull, Patricia Marks Greenfield, and Blanca Quiroz

In a 2nd grade classroom, the teacher is conducting a discussion, calling on students for answers to her questions:

> *The children are whispering answers among themselves after one student is called on to respond to the teacher. The teacher then announces to the classroom, "I have heard people whispering, and I really don't like it because why? They need to learn by themselves, and you really aren't helping them learn."* (Isaac, 1999, p. 34)

In a 3rd grade classroom in the same school district, the following discussion is also going on:

> *Seven students are sitting on the rug, discussing the material they have just read. The teacher notices that one child seems to be answering most of the questions. She encourages him to whisper the answer to a friend so that another child can answer.* (Adapted from Rothstein-Fisch, Trumbull, Isaac, Daley, & Pérez, 2003)

What's going on? Here are two elementary teachers with very different notions of what is appropriate in a discussion. In one classroom, whispering answers to another student is thought to interfere with learning; in the other, it is apparently thought to foster learning. The first teacher's response to students helping each other reflects the view that learning is an individual matter, while the second teacher's response reflects the view that learning is a group matter. In an interview, the second teacher stated that her practice of allowing students to whisper answers to each other "lets both children feel successful and work cooperatively" (Rothstein-Fisch et al., 2003).

In fact, these slivers of life in two classrooms point to some essential but usually invisible differences in ways of thinking about knowledge, learning, and teaching. Not incidentally, these differences are associated with unconscious assumptions about what teachers will reward and punish. The fundamental difference between the two teacher approaches is based on the distinction between individualistic and collectivistic value systems (Greenfield, 1994; Markus & Kitayama, 1991).

Schools in the United States emphasize individualism and independence as a goal of development. Many classroom interactions and activities aim for individual achievement, encourage autonomous choice and initiative, and focus on logical-rational cognitive skills over social development (Delgado-Gaitan, 1993, 1994). Unless it is part of socially structured and identified collaborative activities, cooperation in school activities is called "cheating" (Cizek, 1999). Schools evaluate students on the basis of independent work, and teachers may discourage and label as cheating even the most informal efforts by students to help each other (Correa-Chávez, 1999; Isaac, 1999). What generally goes unrecognized is that the definition of cheating is quite culturally variable. Students from minority[1] cultures may have internalized very different definitions from those of their teachers (Rothstein-Fisch et al., 2003).

The theme of this chapter is that a broader understanding of the cultural value systems in which children grow up is necessary to improve the education of minority students. If school reforms are to close the achievement gap, they must recognize the role of culture in schooling and the relationships between home culture views of child development and those implicit in schooling practices. By the time children enter school, most of them have mastered modes of interpersonal engagement through interactions with their families and communities. Yet families and communities are culturally diverse throughout the United States, and the customary modes of activity and interaction of many families differ from those favored by the mainstream European American culture represented in

---

[1] The term "minority" is objectionable to many; it can be taken as disparaging, though the authors clearly do not intend it as such here. Because it so commonly appears in the literature to which the authors refer and is simpler than terms like "nondominant cultures/communities," we sometimes use it. Minorities/nondominant groups are those whose values the mainstream/dominant culture either does not recognize or actively devalues. The authors use the term "mainstream" interchangeably with "dominant" to refer to those who share a set of values that are normative in major societal institutions such as schools and government. Where possible, we refer to groups by the names they use to characterize themselves (Latino, Mexican American, European American, African American, Pueblo, etc.).

public schools. Should children listen quietly to adults in order to learn best? Should they raise questions and contribute actively and competitively to classroom discussions? The answers to these questions depend in large measure on one's cultural background.

This chapter offers new understandings of culture and how its role in schooling and human development can help teachers to be more successful with their diverse groups of students. It presents concrete examples of the kind of cross-cultural conflict that occurs when children of collectivistic cultures encounter individualism in U.S. schools. It offers potential solutions to such conflict in the form of teacher innovations documented in Bridging Cultures, a collaborative action research project with teachers. It also considers how the histories of various groups influence their relationship with the dominant European American culture and affect social and educational outcomes for students. The chapter ends with implications for schools and a theory of multicultural development.

Human Development in Cultural Contexts

To understand how far and where our education system needs to go to adopt a culture-based approach to human development and schooling, it is necessary to consider the dominant approach to development in the 20th century. Most teachers and teacher educators were schooled in a Piagetian approach to developmental psychology, which saw development as primarily an individual rather than a social matter (Piaget, 1932/1965). The alternative paradigm focuses more on how varying social interactions affect development (Greenfield, 1984; Rogoff, 1990; Vygotsky, 1978). According to this view, children develop competencies through social interactions, especially with more competent members of the group (family, peers, and so forth). These social interactions, in turn, reflect cultural values and standards for appropriate behavior. In other words, children's social interactions are culturally constituted.

This social perspective recognizes that development will take different paths, depending on the goals of child rearing in a particular community (Greenfield, 1994; Greenfield & Suzuki, 1998). More research is clearly needed on how cultural values shape development and which dimensions of culture may be particularly salient for children from nondominant cultures in U.S. schools. In the meantime, U.S. classrooms continue to reflect the individual orientation to development, considering achievement a personal matter and paying less attention to how the social environment of the school and students' home communities influence it (Graue, Kroeger, & Prager, 2001).

Child Development and Cultural History

Vygotsky highlighted the importance of cultural history as a dimension in understanding individual development within various groups (Scribner, 1985). Research on various ethnic and cultural groups up to now has focused mostly on the contact (dominant) culture, or how children adapt to the expectations of that culture; it has paid less attention to the cultures of origin (Berry, 1987) and how values associated with those cultures may persist across generations, influencing development. However, both aspects of cultural history are a central component of the development of children from nondominant groups.

Different ethnic groups have different perspectives on the role of ancestral cultural history. These perspectives vary with a group's traditions and the time and manner in which the group becomes incorporated into a dominant society. For example, Japanese culture places so much importance on ancestral history that it clearly identifies distinctions among generations since emigration from Japan (*issei* for first generation, *nisei* for second generation, and so forth). For African Americans, the significance of African roots is more controversial. Some hold that the experience of slavery and subsequent discrimination entirely wiped out a distinctive African American culture. Sudarkasa (1988) acknowledges the historical influence of slavery, but posits that the prior culture of Africans who adapted to and survived slavery affected the nature of their adaptation. Others point to numerous practices from African cultures that remain. For instance, African American handclapping games are practically identical to games played in West Africa (Merrill-Mirsky, 1991). It is likely that the sophisticated language play of African American dialect (for example, "playing the dozens" and "signifyin'") has its origins in African cultures as well (Smitherman, 1981).

Value Orientations: A Key Aspect of Cultural History

Development and socialization take place as people adapt to different ecological[2] and economic conditions (Berry, 1967, 1987; Draper & Cashdan, 1988). This adaptation accounts for what has been called the

---

[2] "Ecology" in sociological terms refers to the study of the social environment, particularly with regard to the relations among people and their social institutions, including systems for ensuring that children acquire the skills they will need to be successful adults within the particular group. The implication is that educators need to examine particular cultures' approaches to child rearing and schooling with reference to the particular environment of the group and not with reference to another group's goals, values, or practices.

"material" side of culture. However, human beings have an intrinsic need to create meaning from their experiences (Bruner, 1990). How they do so becomes reflected and rationalized in different value orientations. This is the "symbolic" side of culture. These two sides come together in a view of culture as a collective way to attach meaning to ecological conditions (Kim, 1991).

The social ecology and economic circumstances of children from minority cultures in the United States (or in other Western countries) often differ from those of children growing up in the societies of their ancestral origin. The ways in which these children adapt to ecological conditions (the material side of culture) are less likely to demonstrate their ancestral cultural roots than are their value orientations (an aspect of symbolic culture). Value orientations are the major source of ancestral continuity in minority children's development. For instance, while it may not be economically necessary for a family to cook together or share child rearing, such practices may persist over generations because of a continuing value of group cohesion.

Viewing behavior and thought processes from a values perspective makes it possible to go beyond the mere identification of cultural or other group differences. It clarifies the adaptive function and the *meaning* of cultural differences for the groups involved (Kim & Choi, 1994). In this way, it is possible to move beyond a focus on surface artifacts and behaviors to the motivations for them.

The Acquisition of Culture

As children develop, they construct modes of appropriate behavior by participating in a variety of social interactions that reflect a group's value orientation. Interaction in each setting is based on and reflects an "invisible culture" (Philips, 1972), or what Small calls "a lacy film that ingratiates itself into every crevice of behavior, silently but powerfully influencing what people do" (1998, p. 50). Invisible culture involves the implicit communication of values, norms, and aspirations through social interaction and everyday routines (Cazden, 1988). "[I]n *every* culture, parents unconsciously transmit the rules, the structure, and the goals of that society to their children" (Small, 1998, p. 47).

Individualism and Collectivism

Recent theory and research have distinguished the cultural value orientations of individualism and collectivism (Greenfield & Cocking, 1994;

Kagitcibasi, 1989; Triandis, 1989).[3] Harking back to its Anglo-Saxon and northern European immigrant origins, mainstream culture in the United States is generally individualistic (Hofstede, 1983; Lebra, 1994). It encourages independence and individual achievement as important goals of development (Markus & Kitayama, 1991). The public school system is one cultural-institutional setting that highlights these aspects of individualism. In contrast, many immigrant and minority groups living in the United States have a cultural history of collectivism.

Collectivism is a cultural value orientation that emphasizes interdependence, as well as the preservation and permanence of prescribed relationships that are hierarchically structured around family roles and multiple generations. A collectivistic history is part of the cultural and cross-cultural roots of Native American Indians, Native Hawaiians, Native Alaskans, Latin Americans, Africans, Asians, and Arabs (Greenfield & Cocking, 1994; Barakat, 1993).

Children are socialized to certain values from birth, values that influence their fundamental orientation towards their roles within the family, within society, and as learners. For example, conceptualizations of intelligence in individualistic and collectivistic cultures differ. In U.S. dominant culture, an intelligent child is one who is aggressive and competitive. In a collectivistic culture, an intelligent child may be one who knows how to complete chores for the family (Small, 1998).

In collectivistic cultures, infants spend most of their time with other human beings. The value of physical objects is primarily that they mediate social relationships (Greenfield, Brazelton, & Childs, 1989). For example, a toy would be of little value outside its role in an interaction with another person.

Individualistic cultures, on the other hand, tend to emphasize technological knowledge of the physical world as a way of facilitating independence. Parents are likely to hope and believe their children will be verbally competent and able to construct knowledge of the physical world from

---

[3] While there are common core values across societies that could be characterized as collectivistic, there is great variation among these societies in terms of how the values are manifested. In addition, there is great variation within any given society in the degree to which an individual espouses and acts on the values that tend to characterize that society. Anthropologists, in particular, often object to the individualism/collectivism construct because they are wary of categorical systems that lump groups of cultures together. In their view, each culture is unique (Strauss, 2000). The authors understand these objections and the dangers of dichotomous categories. Nevertheless, we find this construct a useful starting point for understanding the conflicts many immigrant and other minority students experience when participating in schooling in the United States.

observing and manipulating toys that stimulate independence and technological mastery. To that end, a parent in the United States might provide a baby with toys so that the baby will amuse himself while developing skill in manipulating objects. Similarly, parents in individualistic cultures tend to emphasize distal modes of communication through linguistic means, as opposed to proximal modes of communication such as touching and holding (Greenfield, 1994).

Schools by and large define children's early cognitive development in terms of their knowledge of the physical world and linguistic communication skills parents from independence-oriented, individualistic cultures place a high value on. In contrast, parents from interdependence-oriented cultures are likely to promote their children's social intelligence. Most teachers today are grounded in Piagetian notions of child development, which represent a Western European view of the world. Piagetian theory, like the Western scientist, emphasizes the development of knowledge of the physical world apart from social goals. This corresponds to an ethnotheory of development in which cognitive knowledge is valued for its own sake, apart from the social uses to which it is put.[4] As a result, this difference in emphasis can lead to conflicts in the classroom for students from minority cultures.

Many characteristics of schooling contrast with the collectivistic traditions of numerous minority and immigrant cultures. The ancestral cultures of collectivistic groups emphasize interpersonal relationships, respect for elders and tradition, responsibility for others, and cooperation (Blake, 1993, 1994; Delgado-Gaitan, 1993, 1994; Kim & Choi, 1994; Suina & Smolkin, 1994). Those values, though not absent in the culture of schooling, are emphasized less than those mentioned earlier. The following section demonstrates where and how conflicts based on differences in values tend to develop.

Achievement Orientation

Encouraging children's individual achievements in school can stimulate an independent sense of self that undermines the child's social affiliation and responsibility for others. The hierarchical relationships and respect for elders and authority important in collectivistic cultures (Triandis, 1989) present a contrast to the individualistic view of egalitarianism. However, the development of critical thinking requires children to articulate and

---

[4] An ethnotheory is a theory espoused by a particular cultural group.

even argue their views with older family members and others on a relatively egalitarian basis (Delgado-Gaitan, 1993, 1994).

This practice can become a source of conflict between the two value orientations because schools are likely to evaluate negatively the academic performance of children who are not vocal and adept at logical-rational modes of argumentation (Okagaki & Sternberg, 1993). At home, a child may be disciplined for the same behaviors that are expected in school—in this case, arguing or debating with parents or other elders (Delgado-Gaitan, 1994).

Rather than valuing the knowledge and wisdom of older family members, the impersonal text is the basic source of learning in U.S. schools. As a contrasting example, in the Pueblo Indian worldview, parents and grandparents are the repositories of knowledge, providing a social connection between the generations. The introduction of encyclopedias, reference books, and the like undermines "the very fiber of the connectedness" (Suina, 1991, p. 153). Along with teachers, such books displace family elders as the authorities for knowledge.

Collectivistic or interdependence-oriented societies, such as those in Japan and China, adhere to collectivistic practices in their classrooms, including learning from other children and teaching the whole class rather than attending to individual students (Stigler & Perry, 1988). These practices moderate the individualistic bias intrinsic to school-based formal education in the United States. However, it is also clear that the spread of formal education and urbanization, as well as the development of commercial economies, are moving these societies in more individualistic directions.

The following example of conflict between individualism and collectivism demonstrates the struggle Latino immigrant families go through as they try to reconcile their collectivistic home cultures with the individualistic orientation of the public schools. In this case, the issues relate to achievement, group versus individual success, and what counts as a good student:

An "Outstanding" Student

Erica tells her mother that she got the highest grade in the class on her math test. She says she is really proud of herself for doing so well and for doing the best in the class. She says she guesses she is really smart. When asked how the mother should respond, a teacher said, "Agree emphatically that yes, she certainly is smart and that the test proves she is capable of doing virtually anything if she applies herself. Erica has done well and needs the appropriate recognition. It will obviously enhance self-esteem and increase her chances of success in life." In contrast, a Latino immigrant mother answered,

"She should congratulate her, but tell her not to praise herse
should not think so much of herself." Moreover, this mother worr
much praise could make the student see other children as less worthy.

This example demonstrates the teacher's view of the child as a self-contained, independent achiever. As far as the teacher is concerned, there is no conflict in this scenario because if the student did her best on the test, she is entitled to feel proud of herself. However, the mother perceived a conflict: The student deserved credit for doing well, but she should not separate her achievement from her relationship to the group.

Differing Discourse Norms: The Role of Social Knowledge

During one of our observations of a Los Angeles prekindergarten class made up of mostly Latino children, the teacher was showing a real chicken egg that would soon hatch (Greenfield, Raeff, & Quiroz, 1996). She asked children to describe eggs by thinking about the times they had cooked and eaten them. One child tried three times to talk about how she cooked eggs with her grandmother, but the teacher disregarded these comments in favor of a child who explained that the insides of eggs are white and yellow. A Latina member of our research team noted that the first child's answer was typical of the associations that her invisible home culture encourages. That is, objects are most meaningful when they mediate social interactions. But in this case, the teacher expected students to describe eggs as isolated physical entities. Eggs as mediators of social relationships and social behavior were irrelevant.

This incident has a number of implications for teaching. First, because she did not recognize the invisible culture that generated the description of cooking eggs with grandmother, the teacher devalued the child's contribution and, implicitly, the value orientation it reflected. Second, because she didn't consider the collectivistic value orientation, she didn't realize her question was ambiguous. Children who shared the teacher's value orientation would assume she was interested in the physical properties of eggs, even though she had not explicitly said so. Children who didn't share the teacher's value orientation would make a different assumption.

In a culturally sensitive school environment, the teacher both validates the social relationships of children from collectivistic backgrounds by showing interest in their family experiences, and is explicit about her expectations for a topic of study. This approach facilitates a process of bidirectional cultural exchange at school, wherein some collectivistic values become part of the classroom while at the same time children from collectivistic cultures get practice in the cognitive operations necessary for school success (Gutiérrez, Baquedano-López, & Tejeda, 1999).

The different value placed on cognitive and social development was illustrated during conferences between a 4th grade teacher and the Latino immigrant parents of her students (Greenfield, Quiroz, & Raeff, 2000). To the teacher, the conference was a forum for discussing the academic performance of the children as independent achievers with unique capabilities and potential. In contrast, parents wanted to talk about their children's social behavior and role in the family. The result was miscommunication and frustration on both sides. Neither party seemed aware, however, that the frustration and dissatisfaction stemmed from fundamental differences in their views of the children themselves. That is, the teacher saw the children as independent learners, but to parents they were family members. Mutual understanding of invisible cultures could open up dialogue about both cultural views.

The following vignette is based on a real-life incident from a preschool in Los Angeles.

Whose Blocks?

Kevin, a European American preschooler, is playing with some blocks. Jasmine, the daughter of Mexican immigrant parents, takes a few of the blocks he is not currently using. The boy hits her. The teacher tells Jasmine that she should not take other children's things. Mrs. Rios, Jasmine's mother, who happens to be visiting the classroom that day, becomes upset that the teacher does not reprimand the boy for his act of aggression. After all, in her extended family, material objects are shared. Possession or personal property is a negative concept akin to selfishness. Her interpretation of the incident comes from her collectivistic view: The boy showed selfishness in refusing to share the toy with her daughter, and then he compounded his undesirable behavior with physical aggression.

In contrast to the mother's response, the teacher's reaction is consonant with individualistic values of independence. Objects are the property of a single individual, even if only temporarily, as in school. Hence, the teacher treats the girl as the primary transgressor because she took away a toy "belonging" to another child. It is clear that not all teachers from the mainstream U.S. culture would respond as this teacher did. Many would focus on the undesirability of physical aggression. Nevertheless, most would probably see the boy as the original victim and the girl as the first encroacher. Because the girl would not be seen as a victim of the boy's selfishness, her own legitimate need for rectification would go unrecognized.

A teacher in Los Angeles described a situation in which Latino students formed groups at every opportunity, despite the teacher's insistence that students work alone. The primary purpose of these groups was not necessarily to work on the task together but simply to be together and to talk while working. However, from the teacher's point of view, this social interaction was a problem, if not outright cheating.

Discussion of the Bridging Cultures Project below traces the thread of students' group orientation across many of the innovations teachers created.

A Need to Make Values Explicit

As is evident, there are several potential sources of conflict between individualism and collectivism in school settings. Because the cultures are invisible, such conflicts may not rise to consciousness, and when they do they are often not recognized as cultural.

Teachers also may inadvertently criticize parents for adhering to a different set of ideals about children, families, and parenting—either explicitly or implicitly through the content of parent education courses provided by the school. For instance, by teaching parents that homework is to be done in a quiet place where the child is undisturbed by others, teachers may undercut the cooperative arrangements of the home. Often such arrangements charge older siblings with helping younger ones complete tasks (Delgado-Gaitan, 1994). Working alone, apart from the rest of the family, is not automatically an understandable and acceptable strategy for homework completion. Teachers may conscientiously try to create culturally sensitive environments for their students (for example, through multicultural displays and activities) while simultaneously structuring classroom and home-school interaction patterns that violate invisible cultural norms of various minority groups.

If the teacher and the parent were familiar with each other's value systems, dialogue and compromise on how to respond to instances of conflict, such as the one described in the "Whose Blocks?" vignette, would be possible. However, with no understanding of each other's value systems, teacher and parent may experience misunderstanding and frustration. When such conflicts remain hidden and unaddressed, children are forced to struggle with mixed messages about social behavior. The implication for education is that teachers and parents need to understand and respect each other's value systems, and they should seek ways to harmonize them for the benefit of children, families, classrooms, and communities.

The Bridging Cultures Project:
Creating Culturally Responsive Classrooms

The Bridging Cultures Project was founded to address the goal of making classroom practices more harmonious with students' cultural values. Bridging Cultures is a teacher's professional development and research project. Through this project, the authors have guided educators to understand the two value systems of individualism and collectivism and to use this understanding to improve schooling for Latino immigrant students in California, most of whom have come from rural areas of Mexico.

Seven bilingual Spanish-English elementary teachers from the greater Los Angeles area have participated in the project since fall 1996.[5] After a series of three workshops on culture, they became researchers in their own classrooms and schools, sharing their observations and innovations with each other and staff researchers over a period of more than five years. Several publications have documented their creative practices (Rothstein-Fisch, Greenfield, & Trumbull, 1999; Trumbull, Rothstein-Fisch, & Greenfield, 2000; Trumbull, Rothstein-Fisch, Greenfield, & Quiroz, 2001). Based on the individualism-collectivism framework, the teachers made changes primarily in three areas: relationships with parents and family, classroom management and organization, and curriculum/instruction/ assessment.

Relationships with Parents

All of the Bridging Cultures teachers devoted considerable energies toward developing good relationships with parents prior to participation in the project, yet they reported that seeing themselves and parents through "cultural eyes" had an immediate and positive impact.

Teachers began to see parents not simply as uneducated, but as possessing knowledge from a different values perspective. Kindergarten teacher Kathryn Eyler said:

> *"[I realized that] I have a culture, too, and it dictates what I do. It's not just, 'Oh well, the Latino parents do this and that because that is their culture.' I*

---

[5] Teacher participants in the Bridging Cultures Project are Marie Altchech, Catherine Daley, Elvia Hernandez, Kathryn Eyler, Giancarlo Mercado, Amada Pérez, and Pearl Saitzyk. The professional researchers are Patricia Greenfield, University of California, Los Angeles (UCLA); Blanca Quiroz, UCLA (now Harvard); Carrie Rothstein-Fisch, California State University, Northridge; and Elise Trumbull, WestEd.

do what I do because of my culture. And this is the first time that I really had an understanding of that. And not, you know, just thinking, 'Well, yes, you read to your children, and that's a universal right idea.' No, that's from my culture." (Rothstein-Fisch, Trumbull, Quiroz, & Greenfield, 1997)

Teachers used the concepts of individualism and collectivism to begin to see things from parents' perspectives. This shift allowed them to forge mutuality in working toward student success. They became more comfortable in talking with parents to learn about their backgrounds, values, and goals for their children. In short, information flowed not just from teacher to parent, but in the other direction as well.

In line with the importance of face-to-face social relationships in the collectivistic system, teacher-parent relationships became more personal, with teachers attending out-of-school family events. Picking up on a perceived parental preference, some teachers increased opportunities to interact with parents informally on the school grounds before and after school. Said 2nd grade teacher Catherine Daley:

"One of our school rules directs the teachers to accompany their students to the exit gate and to remain there until the parents arrive or until the gate is closed. I take this opportunity to have mini-conferences with the parents. These conversations may never even deal with the child. They may touch on the weather or any other social topic. It may even be just a simple greeting. Yet I find that these interactions foster a closer bond with the parents." (Trumbull, Rothstein-Fisch, Greenfield, & Quiroz, 2001, p. 77)

Teachers made changes in parent-teacher conferences, which both parents and teachers had previously experienced as uncomfortable. In line with the cultural focus on groups rather than the individual, several teachers experimented with small-group conferences; these worked extremely well in some classrooms (Quiroz, Greenfield, & Altchech, 1999). Parents seemed more comfortable talking in the group and focusing on the progress of a group of students rather than on their own individual children. Fifth grade teacher Marie Altchech commented:

"I found the group conferencing to be relaxing for the parents. It was a less threatening environment than the individual conferencing style, with support and company lent by the other parents. This format elicited a group voice from the parents rather than an individual voice. It also represented a shift in the balance of power." (Trumbull, Rothstein-Fisch, Greenfield, & Quiroz, 2001, p. 69)

In addition, teachers consciously respected parents' concern for children's social development by allowing that to be a primary topic, rather than emphasizing the cognitive and academic over the social.

Teachers discovered that the parents' desire to help their children (and teachers) was an excellent resource they could use to solve a multitude of problems. Mrs. Eyler approached parents about a school attendance problem; in response, mothers came up with a strategy to help each other get children to school when a kindergartner's sibling was ill and the parent needed to stay home. First grade teacher Pearl Saitzyk engaged parents as partners in helping children practice reading at home, and saw a surge in end-of-year reading scores on Spanish language tests. She explained how her new cultural understanding allowed her to approach parents in this way:

> "Although I had a basic connection with the culture of my students in that I majored in Spanish and I, too, come from a family of immigrants, it was the Bridging Cultures focus that made me aware of where and how I was holding back and holding onto my views, even without wanting to. It was this awareness and willingness to open to another view that made last year my most successful school year academically and interpersonally (parent involvement-wise). Last year I feel the students, parents, and I were a real team." (Trumbull, Rothstein-Fisch, Greenfield, & Quiroz, 2001, p. 82)

Classroom Management and Organization

Third grade teacher Amada Pérez commented on how eager students were to help with classroom tasks, to the degree that she often found herself saying, "You can help tomorrow." Much to their surprise, Bridging Cultures teachers came to realize they were restricting helpful behavior, highly valued in their children's home environments. They wanted each classroom job carried out by a single individual, however, when they recognized that this mode of helping had cultural roots in the values of individual responsibility, they began to let their students express their own cultural values by helping each other with classroom jobs. Mrs. Eyler assigned children to work in pairs to organize the classroom library, take attendance, clean the blackboard, and serve as monitors (for example, to help the group line up for an assembly). Fourth grade teacher Giancarlo Mercado went to a "no monitor" system: All students now take care of what needs to be done, without individual assignments.

Other changes affected both classroom organization and academics. For instance, Mrs. Pérez set up a "homework club," where students helped each other prepare to complete their homework. They were not allowed to actually *do* the homework in the group; it had to be completed individually. Nevertheless, the group support led to a near-100 percent homework completion rate. The vignette below also shows students' group, rather than individual, orientation to classroom success.

The Star Chart

Mrs. Pérez noticed that her use of a classroom chart to record students' mastery of the times tables didn't seem as motivating as it was intended to be. The chart had all the students' names on it, with a box for each number in the times tables (2, 3, 4, etc.). Students were to recite the tables to her individually and get a star for each box in turn, as they mastered the tables. She asked students how it could be used, and they suggested a class goal of filling in all the boxes with stars. They would help each other reach the goal. They wouldn't rest until everyone had succeeded. The students themselves transformed the activity from an individual to a collective one. In addition, all of these 3rd graders achieved at a higher level than their grade standard prescribed. (Rothstein-Fisch et al., 2003)

Comparative observations in a Bridging Cultures and a non-Bridging Cultures classroom of Latino immigrant 2nd graders in Los Angeles showed the Bridging Cultures teacher encouraging students to help each other with their work and the children enthusiastically doing so (Isaac, 1999). In stark contrast, observations in the non-Bridging Cultures classroom revealed inner conflict between the children's desires to help each other with their work and their teacher's rules against mutual aid. For example, one student showed knowledge of the teacher's rule by telling a particular classmate not to help another. Yet when the teacher was not looking, this same student tried to help the child himself. It was apparent that conflicting values at home and school were translating into internal confusion and conflict. The encouragement of helping at clearly specified times in the Bridging Cultures classroom shows respect for the children's culture, reinforces their parents' developmental goals and socialization, and reduces the children's inner conflict between warring value systems.

Bridging Cultures classrooms consider sharing, like helping, as a strength to be capitalized on in both learning and social development. Latino immigrant parents strongly value sharing over personal property (Raeff, Greenfield, & Quiroz, 2000). As the "Whose Blocks?" vignette shows, students in schools where the individualistic value system is the norm will likely treat classroom items as private property, even if only temporarily. In Bridging Cultures classrooms, students share nearly everything. Materials like pencils, pens, rulers, and markers are likely to be kept in baskets that can be set out for small groups rather than kept individually in desks. Mrs. Eyler describes her previous approach to community property in the classroom and how she has modified it as follows: "There is one propeller in the Legos. I used to say, 'He had it first,' and then tell them to take turns. Now I say, 'You need to find a way to share it'" (Trumbull, Diaz-Meza, Hasan, & Rothstein-Fisch, 2001, p. 22).

Curriculum, Instruction, and Assessment

As mentioned earlier, some cultures see the social and cognitive aspects of human development as integrated, while others see them as separate strands of development. In keeping with the latter perspective, teachers in the United States usually expect students to focus classroom talk on academic topics during a lesson. In contrast, students from the collectivistic Latino immigrant culture are likely to integrate academic and social topics. Students from Bridging Cultures classrooms often respond to a question like, "What do we know about birds that live in our habitat?" with stories about activities involving family members (much like the earlier story of the kindergartner responding to a question about eggs). Bridging Cultures teachers positively value this kind of discourse, and they *also* show their students how to use the alternative approach they will be expected to master in school.

Figure 4.1 shows a strategy Mrs. Altchech used to help her students map their own discourse to "scientific discourse." She used a T-chart, writing a short summary of students' contributions to a science lesson discussion on the left side; on the right side she wrote science facts taken from their stories with her assistance.

Teachers in U.S. classrooms often become impatient with students' "stories." Students from Latino immigrant families may eventually get the idea that their cultural modes of thinking and using language are less valid, and eventually stop participating so enthusiastically (Trumbull, Diaz-Meza, & Hasan, 2000). With the understanding of *why* students use language in particular ways, teachers are likely to respond more constructively, respecting and using the culture of the home. Indeed, students' use of language in the classroom always reflects particular sociocultural values and perspectives (Gutiérrez, 1993; Miramontes & Commins, 1991).

The vignette below illustrates how K–2 teacher Elvia Hernandez recognized a student's family-oriented discourse.

FIGURE 4.1

Sample T-Chart Based on a Science Lesson

Student Experience	Scientific Information
Carolina's Story "I was playing in the garden with my grandmother. I saw a hummingbird near the cherry tree. It was really pretty." "The bird stood in the air. I tried to go close to it, but it kept flying away—this way and that way. Its wings moved so fast, I couldn't see them."	*Hummingbird* Brownish with bright iridescent green and red coloring around head and neck. Birds can hover and fly in any direction, wings beat rapidly. Has to eat frequently because of using so much energy in its movements (high metabolism).* *Content introduced by Mrs. Altchech.

Source: Adapted from Trumbull, Diaz-Meza, and Hasan (2000).

Grandmother's Clock

"I tr[y] to listen to everybody and not discourage them from relating family experiences as they related to the concepts being taught. I started to teach time this week, and one of the kindergartners raised her hand and said, 'We bought a clock for my grandmother's room, and her name is Magdalena,' and then she became much more interested in the clock and everything since she could say her grandmother's name with pride." (Trumbull, Diaz-Meza, Hasan, & Rothstein-Fisch, 2001, p. 26)

With her 5th graders, Mrs. Altchech uses a collaborative writing strategy, which she alternates with opportunities for individual writing. Teams of students write stories together. They jointly select a topic, and each has to contribute to the writing. Students whose skills are just developing can have the satisfaction of seeing a complete piece of writing and learn from peers at the same time. She says:

"Many students aren't 'there' for writing in English, so teams are writing stories together (Godzilla stories are popular now). Students can choose to write individually and illustrate and type together. For assessment, I have them alternate so I can see individual performance." (Trumbull, Diaz-Meza, Hasan, & Rothstein-Fisch, 2001, p. 27)

Mrs. Altchech also has her students participate in "literature circles." Small groups of students select a piece of literature, and everyone reads it. Each student has responsibility for some aspect of understanding the text. These circles help to develop vocabulary, reading fluency, comprehension, oral language, and critical interpretation. The group prepares and gives a presentation to the class afterward.

Mrs. Pérez also frequently uses "choral reading" as a strategy for developing literacy skills. Students read aloud together as a whole group or as a small group. English learners can practice the rhythm and sound of English without being spotlighted. The group scaffolds everyone's performance. (They also practice the oral parallel, answering questions in chorus.)

All of the Bridging Cultures teachers have noticed that if they select, or have students select, literature that focuses on family, their students are likely to be more engaged than usual. As suggested earlier, when students bring "family" into classroom discussions, they tend to be livelier. Mrs. Pérez found that, on a schoolwide writing assessment (where it is important to get an extended sample of student writing), using "family" as a focal point led to higher performance. The prompt, "Write about an experience that you had with your family," elicited much more writing (and higher quality writing) from 3rd graders than the prompt, "Write about what it's like to be a good friend." Since Mrs. Pérez began this practice, other teachers in the project have replicated it with similar results.

Other manifestations of the value of family appear when students write personal books, not only in the topics they choose, but even on the "Author's Page," where they must describe themselves. Illustrations of the author invariably place him or her in the midst of a whole family group.

Because the bottom line of formal schooling is individual, not group, assessment, Bridging Cultures teachers make clear to students when they are allowed to help and when they aren't. For example, Ms. Daley encourages her 2nd graders to help each other complete practice tests, but she is firm in her rule that they not look at each other's papers when taking the actual tests. In the following description, she talks about preparing her students for a standardized test:

> "When it came time to prepare for the test, I had the materials I needed and the format—all I needed was a style or a process I would use. I thought a lot of the classes I had taken on cooperative learning worked so well with Bridging Cultures—it would be easy to have groups for test preparation! We would put the question on the board or overhead and work on it as a group. Or just work out of one booklet—but always in a group. I still do this; I prefer to work

my class in a whole group. Little by little we move away from the whole group as we get ready for the actual test. I make sure to explain to the students what changes are going to occur regarding group and individual work."

Historical Power Relations Between Majority and Minority Groups

Ancestral cultural roots, emphasized in the Bridging Cultures approach, are only one part of minority children's culture that educators need to understand. Another important factor minority children must cope with in their development is the history and nature of power relationships between minority and majority cultures (Ogbu, 1993, 1994; Suárez-Orozco, 1995). Anthropologist John Ogbu (1993, 1994) proposed a framework for understanding these relationships. He suggests that minority groups fall into two classifications: *involuntary* minority groups (those who become incorporated into a nation through conquest, slavery, or colonization) and *voluntary* minority groups (those who become incorporated into a nation through voluntary immigration). Refugees are considered voluntary minorities because, unlike Native Americans or African slaves, the United States in no way forced their incorporation into this country.

Involuntary minorities tend to oppose the cultural values of the majority, keeping the conquerors, enslavers, and colonizers from wiping out their indigenous cultures (Ogbu, 1993, 1994). They may resist assimilation and not trust that the education system will benefit them, at least in comparison with the majority (Conchas, 2001). They often feel they cannot adopt the ways of the majority without giving up parts of their own culture, and may develop oppositional subcultures and identities in order to resist what they perceive as pressures to adopt majority culture behaviors.

Conchas (2001) and Lee (2001) agree that voluntary minorities are both more ready to give up aspects of their home culture in order to fit in and more likely to compare their experiences in the United States favorably to those in their native countries. According to Conchas, "[a]lthough voluntary minorities may face subordination and exploitation, they perceive and react to schooling positively because they regard their current situation in the United States more favorably than their situation in their country of origin" (p. 477). For them, schooling is a new way that leads to opportunity.

Because involuntary minorities see schools as majority institutions, academic achievement challenges their group loyalties and ethnic identities. Immigrant students tend to be more optimistic about succeeding in U.S. society and enjoy greater family support than students from involuntary minority groups, such as Native Americans and African Americans (Portes, 1999).

The bottom line is that the cultural histories of minority groups create two kinds of value diversity relevant to education. The first is the diversity of values that comes from their ancestral cultures. The second is the diversity of values that comes from the ways in which groups have become part of our nation; the values that are a function of the history of relations between minority groups and the wider society (Ogbu, 1993, 1994). Understanding how these historical relations continue to affect the experiences of current-day students can be helpful to teachers and educational systems.

Avoiding Oversimplification: Intersection of Minority Status with Other Factors

Ogbu's framework should not be used to make assumptions about the potential of individual students. Some students from involuntary minority groups do quite well in school, and some from voluntary minority groups fare poorly in school (Gándara, 1995; Gibson, 1997; Mehan, Hubbard, & Villanueva, 1994). Issues of race, class, length of time in the United States, and schooling practices all influence how particular students experience schooling.

To understand how members of a particular cultural group adjust to United States society, one also needs to look across a few generations. People from the same original culture may have experiences more like those of voluntary or involuntary minorities, depending on how long they have been in the United States Among Hmong immigrants, for example, students in generation 1.5 (those born abroad but schooled in the United States from an early age) sometimes develop the oppositional frame of mind associated with involuntary minorities in contrast to those who emigrated at middle or high school age (Lee, 2001).[6] As Portes (1999) suggests, "Cultural differences may emerge reactively after intercultural contact or as each new generation borrows selectively from the mold of cultural origin" (p. 491).

---

[6] The observations about immigrant students may be quite different, depending on class. Obviously, not all immigrants are poor and uneducated. For example, within the population of Mexican immigrants nearly one in seven is a professional (Suárez-Orozco, 1995). With regard to the effects of class differences, middle-class Mexican American youth may participate in schooling in a manner more like that of their voluntary minority peers (Foley, 1991). However, other research, based on several thousand students, has shown that ethnocultural group membership still had an effect on achievement after researchers controlled for class and other factors (Portes, 1999).

The earliest Mexican Americans would be considered an involuntary minority. They became Mexican *Americans* as a result of the conquest of what is now the U.S. Southwest (previously part of Mexico). Note that Bridging Cultures is an intervention for children of voluntary immigrant families who have come to the United States from Mexico (and Central America) with a collectivistic cultural background. This generation comes to the United States with the psychology of the voluntary immigrant and has not yet been assimilated into the pre-existing Hispanic culture that stems from involuntary assimilation of the Southwest into the United States. Unfortunately, Latino school achievement may decline with each successive generation after immigration (Conchas, 2001), as students become more acculturated to the psychology of their historical roots as involuntary minorities.

Implications for Educational Practice: The Big Picture

As we see from the Bridging Cultures examples, culture is relevant not only to curriculum content, but also to home-school relations, classroom management, and instructional and assessment practices. Of course, it is also relevant to the establishment of content and performance standards, resource allocation, and structural elements, such as opportunities for parent involvement and participation in decision making. Currently, decisions about all of these elements of schooling are usually made from a single cultural perspective, that of the mainstream European American culture. This situation is unfortunate, if not absurd, in a multicultural society that claims to have the goal of educational excellence for all students.

Families should not simply be viewed as ignorant of the culture of the school (that is, of the "expected" ways to socialize their children for academic success), but recognized as operating on the basis of their own set of values. Understanding this truth can move educators to a less judgmental position and prompt a search for ways to foster bicultural development (Lee, 2001; Mehan, Villanueva, Hubbard, & Lintz, 1996).

Schools need to learn about students' cultures and historical relations with the dominant culture, and also become conscious of the unspoken values that motivate the ways schooling is provided and that represent a "culture of schooling." It is clear there *is* a culture of schooling; schools across the country exhibit a remarkable uniformity of values and practices (Hollins, 1996). This uniformity belies the multiplicity of student cultures and variations in family approaches to learning, teaching, and child rearing. It is as though only one culture, the so-called mainstream culture, counts. In fact, the norms of schools are nearly always those of the larger society. The situation can be changed; working together, school and community can forge a shared culture (Lipka, Mohatt, & The Ciulistet Group, 1998).

Our assumption is that students do indeed need to learn what Delpit (1995) has called the "power codes" of the society—the ways of interacting and communicating that are the norm in the mainstream culture. When students' ways of knowing, interacting, and communicating are known and valued by the school, schools can create a bridge between the cultures (Au & Jordan, 1981; Banks, 1988; Suina & Smolkin, 1994). At the same time, incorporating elements of students' culture in the classroom should not be just a vehicle for "bridging or explaining the dominant culture" (Ladson-Billings, 1994, p. 18). These elements should be regarded as valuable in their own right, an opportunity for enrichment of the school environment, and a sign of respect for children's cultural identity (Ladson-Billings, 1994).

Applications of the Bridging Cultures Framework to Other Cultural Groups

The Bridging Cultures approach has clearly made school a more comfortable place for Latino immigrant children and their parents. It has made the task of teaching easier and more rewarding, because teachers use the culture of the home as a foundation, rather than an obstacle they must remove. But the question remains as to how widely systems can apply it and what modifications of the approach may be necessary.

Applications to Other "Voluntary Minority" Groups

Is it possible to extend the Bridging Cultures approach to other voluntary minorities? Our response is "yes." Successful applications of the Bridging Cultures model have recently begun in the Korean American community, which has collectivistic roots in Korean culture (Jun, 2000; Kim & Choi, 1994).

Applications to "Involuntary Minority" Groups

Can the Bridging Cultures approach be applied to involuntary minorities? In all probability, for involuntary minorities, reform measures must join cultural bridges to collectivism with community control of the schools. The success of the tribal colleges for Native Americans demonstrates this principle (Boyer, 1997). The tribal colleges combine Native culture with Native control. The success of Native students in tribal colleges contrasts sharply with the high failure rates of Native students enrolled in schools controlled by non–Native American institutions. Promising outcomes are apparent in K–12 systems where Native educators have the opportunity to design schooling for Native students (McCarty, 2002; Swisher & Deyhle, 1992).

Native Americans show many collectivistic values in school settings. For instance, students from Native American communities often respond well to instruction that integrates the social with the academic. A major complaint of Native American educational leaders about the content standards national and state professional groups propose is that they fail to incorporate an ethical and social dimension. How, they ask, can you teach science without exploring the impact of scientific applications on human beings (and all life) for generations to come (Trumbull, Nelson-Barber, & Mitchell, 2002)? The well-being of the human community is at the heart of their concerns.

Researchers have characterized African American culture as a mix of individualism and collectivism (Boykin & Toms, 1985; Markus & Lin, 1999). African Americans have been in the United States for many generations. In some arenas, such as sports, they take an individualistic approach to their mode of action (Greenfield, Davis, Suzuki, & Boutakidis, 2002). Yet the struggle to survive as a group seems to have caused them to take a collectivistic stance as an ethnic group, even within the sports context (Greenfield et al., 2002). Perhaps the collectivism of African roots (Nsamenang & Lamb, 1994) has, in certain ways, survived assimilation in the African American collectivity because of the violent mode in which African slaves were incorporated into U.S. society and the ongoing racism derived from this history.

Observations in the school context indicate that, in some important respects, African Americans bring a collectivistic worldview to school with them. For example, in one study when asked about their "helping" each other with class assignments, African American high school students responded, "We're not cheating. We're helping each other out!" (Hemmings, 1996, cited in Cizek, 1999, p. 43). In this case, "cheating and sharing information were viewed not as inappropriate but as a responsibility" (Cizek, 1999, p. 88). Similarly, another study showed that African American 8th graders were more likely than white students to prefer to work in groups and to "seek out classmates and teachers for discussion, clarification, elaboration, and aid" (Nelson-LeGall & Resnick, 1998, p. 53).

Research indicates that the orientation to people rather than objects is a trait of African Americans as well (King, 1994). Research on the language development of African American children supports this contention. For example, African American children in a study on language development used social and emotional terms at an earlier age than European American children, suggesting two distinct cultural emphases in the child-rearing environments (Blake, 1994).

Possible Educational Interventions

The most constructive approach may be to accommodate selected socialization practices and values from children's home and community cultures (Au & Jordan, 1981; Gutiérrez et al., 1999; Reyes, 1992; Tharp & Gallimore, 1988). Such a cultural compatibility model stresses the simultaneous promotion of children's home-community cultures and adjustment to the mainstream culture. Classroom practices that incorporate both minority culture and mainstream values can benefit all children, majority as well as minority, in terms of learning, social behavior, attitudes, and classroom climate (Kagan, 1986).

Teacher workshops can focus on supporting the values of interdependence among members of all ethnic groups. This social and public validation of collectivistic values would allow minority or immigrant students to feel they are part of their school community. Another method might be to establish day-care centers for preschool children in elementary schools so that elementary children can help as caregivers. Such activities could develop a sense of social responsibility in the young caregivers (Whiting & Whiting, 1994). Interventions like these would also test the idea that all children, not just immigrant or minority children, benefit from a better balance between social responsibility and independence in school.

An important question remains as to the psychological price paid when pressure from an individualistic environment leads people from collectivistic cultures to surrender their way of living and child rearing. This question has only recently received attention, because educational research and practice have generally been from the perspective of the dominant society.

Communicating Among Parents, Teachers, and Students

Continuing the efforts to create a feedback loop that involves parents, students, and teachers constitutes an important strategy. Many parents, as well as teachers, may not know that children's success in school partly depends on their ability to master modes of activity and interaction that are very different from, and may even conflict with, those the parents emphasize at home. Parents with a collectivistic orientation may perceive the school's emphasis on developing each child's potential as encouraging undesirable selfishness. When the collectivistic or interdependence-oriented immigrant parent keeps a child home from school to help take care of a sick baby, he or she sees the child as both learning and enacting a responsible prosocial role. In contrast, the school, with its individualistic perspective, sees the parent as interfering with the child's independent educational development.

Parents and teachers must continue to work together to find strategies that incorporate and encourage individually oriented school achievement and development, while maintaining valued forms of interdependence, such as family unity, mutual aid, and sharing. For parents and teachers, knowing about each other's expectations facilitates communication and enables parents from collectivistic cultures to participate more actively in the schools.

Cultural Knowledge as a Component of Accountability

Accountability, or responsibility for demonstrating how students are faring vis-à-vis state and local standards, is an essential expectation of current educational policy. Research suggests schools cannot continue to do what they have done in the past: They need new knowledge and skills related to instructional practice, including new ideas about how to reach students not previously expected to perform at high levels (Elmore & Fuhrman, 2001). "Teachers' judgments are powerfully influenced by preconceptions about the individual traits of students and about the characteristics of families and communities. And they are typically uninformed by systematic knowledge of what students might be capable of learning under different conditions of teaching" (Elmore & Fuhrman, 2001, p. 69). It is clear that to be accountable, schools are going to have to begin incorporating cultural knowledge into their teacher professional development repertoires and into their whole way of approaching school reform. As Williams (2000) notes, "[T]he cumulative evidence supports the need for introducing the study of the role of culture in learning into programs of research, teacher preparation, professional development, teaching and learning interactions, and subsequently policy and comprehensive reform criteria" (p. 11).

Toward a Multicultural Model of Development

The implications for developmental and educational theory generally revolve around one major theme: the need to recognize that patterns and norms of development and education previously thought to be universal are often specific to European American culture, and this is the culture of the schools. The authors hope further understanding of the historical roots that influence minority children's development will help educators move away from a model of minority children's development that views differences as deficiencies, and beyond a coping model of minority children's development that sees differences simply as adaptations to unfavorable conditions in the dominant society (Mclloyd, 1990; Ogbu, 1994, 1995). While it is essential to replace the deficiency model, reform measures must augment the coping model with a diversity model that goes beyond identifying differences in learning, skills, and knowledge, important as these are. It is essential to recognize the diversity of invisible underlying systems of values and to acknowledge that learning differences are often rooted in historic cultural values. Instead of being assimilated out of existence, an alternative value system can make an important contribution to a diverse society.

Unfortunately, the current educational reform movement has moved to a "one-size-fits-all" model of teaching and testing; the argument and facts just presented indicate this approach is doomed to failure. Children of voluntary minority groups cannot succeed if what is most valued in school—individual achievement—is considered selfish egotism at home. Equally important, the "one-size-fits-all" model loses sight of how alternative inputs can enrich the dominant culture. For example, the U.S. ideal of the self-fulfilled individual can, at the extreme, lead to widespread isolation, alienation, and violence. Hence, an emphasis on family responsibility and solidarity, so intrinsic to collectivistic cultures, can impart a moderating influence on our society.

Acknowledgments

WestEd, the regional educational laboratory based in San Francisco, provided support to the Bridging Cultures Project research through an Office of Educational Research and Improvement grant during the years 1996–2000. Special thanks go to Dr. Sharon Nelson-Barber, director of the Culture and Language in Education Program at WestEd, for her personal support of the project. Dr. Rebeca Diaz-Meza and Ms. Aida Hasan also provided research assistance at WestEd. Of course, we give boundless credit to our participating teacher-researchers mentioned above. Thanks are also due to the University of California at Los Angeles, Urban Education Studies Center, and the University of California Linguistic Minority Research Institute for their grant support.

For the research that led most directly to the Bridging Cultures Project we would like to recognize our first teacher collaborators, Marie Altchech (also involved in Bridging Cultures) and Ana Serrano, for their invaluable roles as consultants and site facilitators. We also recognize the wonderful work of our research assistants Patricia Morales, Hedwig Woelfl, Claudia Torres, Rachel Ostroy, Mirella Benitez, and Kenichi Sakai. Finally, we express our most sincere appreciation to Stoner Avenue Elementary School and Corinne A. Seeds University Elementary School for their cooperation.

References

Au, C., & Jordan, C. (1981). Teaching reading to Hawaiian children: Finding a culturally appropriate solution. In H. Trueba, G. P. Guthrie, & K. H. Su (Eds.), *Culture in the bilingual classroom: Studies in classroom ethnography* (pp. 139–152). Rowley, MA: Newbury House.

Banks, J. A. (1988). *Multiethnic education: Theory and practice.* Boston: Allyn and Bacon.

Barakat, H. (1993). *The Arab world: Society, culture, and state.* London: University of California Press.

Berry, J. W. (1967). Independence and conformity in subsistence-level societies. *Journal of Personality and Social Psychology, 7*(4), 415–418.

Berry, J. W. (1987, August). *Ecological analyses for acculturation research.* Paper presented at the International Association for Cross-Cultural Psychology, Newcastle, Australia.

Blake, I. K. (1993). Learning language in context: The social-emotional orientation of African American mother-child communication. *International Journal of Behavioral Development, 16*(3), 443–464.

Blake, I. K. (1994). Language development and socialization in young African-American children. In P. M. Greenfield & R. R. Cocking (Eds.), *Cross-cultural roots of minority child development* (pp. 167–195). Hillsdale, NJ: Lawrence Erlbaum Associates.

Boyer, P. (1997). *Native American colleges: Progress and prospects.* An Ernest L. Boyer Project of the Carnegie Foundation for the Advancement of Teaching. Princeton, NJ: Carnegie Foundation for the Advancement of Teaching. (ERIC Document Reproduction Service No. ED 409 037)

Boykin, A. W., & Toms, F. D. (1985). Black child socialization: A conceptual framework. In H. P. McAdoo and J. L. McAdoo (Eds.), *Black children: Social, educational, and parental environments* (pp. 33–52). Newbury Park, CA: Sage Publications.

Bruner, J. S. (1990). *Acts of meaning.* Cambridge, MA: Harvard University.

Cazden, C. B. (1988). *Classroom discourse: The language of teaching and learning.* Portsmouth, NH: Heinemann.

Cizek, G. J. (1999). *Cheating on tests: How to do it, detect it, and prevent it.* Mahwah, NJ: Lawrence Erlbaum Associates.

Conchas, G. Q. (2001). Structuring failure and success: Understanding the variability in Latino school engagement. *Harvard Educational Review,* Special Issue: Immigrant Education, *71*(3), 475–504.

Correa-Chávez, M. (1999). *Bridging Cultures between home and school: Assessment of an intervention program*. Unpublished honors thesis, University of California, Los Angeles.

Delgado-Gaitan, C. (1993). Parenting in two generations of Mexican American families. *International Journal of Behavioral Development, 16*(3), 409–427.

Delgado-Gaitan, C. (1994). Socializing young children in Mexican American families: An intergenerational perspective. In P. M. Greenfield & R. R. Cocking (Eds.), *Cross-cultural roots of minority child development* (pp. 55–86). Hillsdale, NJ: Lawrence Erlbaum Associates.

Delpit, L. (1995). *Other people's children: Cultural conflict in the classroom*. New York: New Press.

Draper, P., & Cashdan, E. (1988). Technological change and child behavior among the !Kung. *Ethnology, 27*, 339–365.

Elmore, R. F., & Fuhrman, S. H. (2001). Holding schools accountable: Is it working? *Phi Delta Kappan, 83*(1), 67–72.

Foley, D. E. (1991). Reconsidering anthropological explanations of ethnic school failure. *Anthropology & Education Quarterly, 22*(1), 60–86.

Gándara, P. (1995). *Over the ivy walls: The educational mobility of low-income Chicanos*. Albany, NY: State University of New York Press.

Gibson, M. (1997). Conclusion: Complicating the immigrant/involuntary minority typology. *Anthropology & Education Quarterly, 28*, 431–454.

Graue, M. E., Kroeger, J., & Prager, D. (2001). A Bakhtinian analysis of particular home-school relations. *American Educational Research Journal, 38*(3), 467–498.

Greenfield, P. M. (1984). A theory of the teacher in the learning activities of everyday life. In B. Rogoff & J. Lave (Eds.), *Everyday cognition: Its development in social context* (pp. 117–138). Cambridge, MA: Harvard University.

Greenfield, P. M. (1994). Independence and interdependence as developmental script: Implications for theory, research, and practice. In P. M. Greenfield & R. R. Cocking (Eds.), *Cross-cultural roots of minority child development* (pp. 1–37). Hillsdale, NJ: Lawrence Erlbaum Associates.

Greenfield, P. M., Brazelton, T. B., & Childs, C. (1989). From birth to maturity in Zinacantan: Ontogenesis in cultural context. In V. Bricker & G. Gossen (Eds.), *Ethnographic encounters in southern Mesoamerica: Celebratory essays in honor of Evon Z. Vogt* (pp. 177–216). Albany, NY: Institute of MesoAmerican Studies, State University of New York.

Greenfield, P. M., & Cocking, R. R. (Eds.) (1994). *Cross-cultural roots of minority child development*. Hillsdale, NJ: Lawrence Erlbaum Associates.

Greenfield, P. M., Davis, H., Suzuki, L., & Boutakidis, I. (2002). Understanding intercultural relations on multiethnic high school sports teams. In M. Gatz, M. A. Messner, & S. Ball-Rokeach (Eds.), *Paradoxes of youth in sports* (pp. 141–157). Albany, NY: SUNY Press.

Greenfield, P. M., Raeff, C., & Quiroz, B. (1996). Cultural values in learning and education. In B. Williams (Ed.), *Closing the achievement gap: A vision for changing beliefs and practices* (pp. 37–55). Alexandria, VA: Association for Supervision and Curriculum Development.

Greenfield, P. M., Quiroz, B., & Raeff, C. (2000). Cross-cultural conflict and harmony in the social construction of the child. In S. Harkness, C. Raeff, & C. M. Super (Eds.), *Variability in the social construction of the child: New Directions in Child and Adolescent Development, 87*(Spring), 93–108.

Greenfield, P. M., & Suzuki, L. K. (1998). Culture and human development: Implications for parenting, education, pediatrics, and mental health. In W. Damon, I. E. Sigel, & K. A. Renninger (Eds.), *Handbook of child psychology, Vol. 4: Child psychology in practice* (pp. 1059–1109). New York: John Wiley and Sons.

Gutiérrez, K. (1993). Biliteracy and the language minority child. In B. Spodek & R. N. Saracho (Eds.), *Yearbook of early childhood education, Vol. 4: Language and literacy in early childhood education* (pp. 82–101). New York: Teachers College Press.

Gutiérrez, K., Baquedano-López, P., & Tejeda, C. (1999). Rethinking diversity: Hybridity and hybrid language practices in the third space. *Mind, Culture, and Activity, 64*, 286–303.

Hemmings, A. (1996). Conflicting images? Being black and a model high school student. *Anthropology & Education Quarterly, 27*(1), 27–50.

Hofstede, G. (1983). National cultures revisited. *Behavior Science Revisited, 18*, 285–305.

Hollins, E. (1996). *Culture in school learning.* Mahwah, NJ: Lawrence Erlbaum Associates.

Isaac, A. R. (1999). *How teachers' cultural ideologies influence children's relations inside the classroom: The effects of a cultural awareness teacher training program in two classrooms.* Unpublished honors thesis, University of California, Los Angeles.

Jun, C. Y. (2000). Bridging Cultures *through school counselor education.* Unpublished master's thesis, California State University, Northridge.

Kagan, S. (1986). Cooperative learning and sociocultural factors in schooling. In *Beyond language: Social and cultural factors in schooling language minority students* (pp. 231–298). Los Angeles: Evaluation, Dissemination, and Assessment Center.

Kagitcibasi, C. (1989). Approaches to studying the family and socialization. *Nebraska Symposium on Motivation, 37*, 135–200.

Kim, U. (1991, June/July). Proceedings of a workshop on continuities and discontinuities in the cognitive socialization of minority children. Department of Health and Human Services, Public Health Service, Alcohol, Drug Abuse and Mental Health Administration, Washington, DC.

Kim, U., & Choi, S. H. (1994). Individualism, collectivism, and child development: A Korean perspective. In P. M. Greenfield & R. R. Cocking (Eds.), *Cross-cultural roots of minority child development.* Hillsdale, NJ: Lawrence Erlbaum Associates.

King, J. E. (1994). The purpose of schooling for African American children: Including cultural knowledge. In E. R. Hollins, J. E. King, & W. C. Hayman (Eds.), *Teaching diverse populations: Formulating a knowledge base* (pp. 25–56). Albany, NY: State University of New York Press.

Ladson-Billings, G. (1994). *The dreamkeepers: Successful teachers of African American children.* San Francisco: Jossey-Bass.

Lebra, T. S. (1994). Mother and child in a Japanese socialization: A Japan-U.S. comparison. In P. M. Greenfield & R. R. Cocking (Eds.), *Cross-cultural roots of minority child development* (pp. 259–274). Hillsdale, NJ: Lawrence Erlbaum Associates.

Lee, S. J. (2001). More than "model minorities" or "delinquents": A look at Hmong American high school students. *Harvard Educational Review*, Special Issue: Immigrant Education, *71*(3), 505–528.

Lipka, J., Mohatt, G. V., & The Ciulistet Group (Eds.). (1998). *Transforming the culture of schools: Yup'ik Eskimo examples*. Mahwah, NJ: Lawrence Erlbaum Associates.

Markus, H. R., & Kitayama, S. (1991). Culture and the self: Implications for cognition, emotion, and motivation. *Psychological Review, 98*(2), 242–253.

Markus, H. R., & Lin, L. R. (1999). Conflictways: Cultural diversity in the meanings and practices of conflict. In D. A. Prentice & D. T. Miller (Eds.), *Cultural divides: Understanding and overcoming group conflict* (pp. 302–333). New York: Russell Sage.

McCarty, T. (2002). *A place called Navajo*. Mahwah, NJ: Lawrence Erlbaum Associates.

Mclloyd, V. C. (1990). The impact of economic hardship on black families and children: Psychological distress, parenting, and socioemotional development. *Child Development, 61*(2), 311–346.

Mehan, H., Hubbard, L., & Villanueva, I. (1994). Forming academic identities: Accommodation without assimilation among involuntary minorities. *Anthropology & Education Quarterly, 25*, 91–117.

Mehan, H., Villanueva, I., Hubbard, L., & Lintz, A. (1996). *Constructing school success: The consequences of untracking low-achieving students*. Cambridge, England: Cambridge University Press.

Merrill-Mirsky, C. (1991, June/July). *Eeny meeny pepsadeeny: Ethnicity and gender in children's musical play*. Presented at a workshop on continuities and discontinuities in the cognitive socialization of minority children. Department of Health and Human Services, Public Health Service, Alcohol, Drug Abuse and Mental Health Administration, Washington, DC.

Miramontes, O. B., & Commins, N. L. (1991). Redefining literacy and literacy contexts: Discovering a community of learners. In E. H. Hiebert (Ed.), *Literacy for a diverse society: Perspectives, practices, and policies* (pp. 75–89). New York: Teachers College Press.

Nelson-LeGall, S., & Resnick, L. (1998). Help seeking, achievement motivation, and the social practice of intelligence in school. In S. A. Karabenick (Ed.), *Strategic help seeking: Implications for learning and teaching* (pp. 39–60). Mahwah, NJ: Lawrence Erlbaum Associates.

Nsamenang, A. B., & Lamb, M. E. (1994). Socialization of Nso children in the Bamenda Grassfields of Northwest Cameroon. In P. M. Greenfield & R. R. Cocking (Eds.), *Cross-cultural roots of minority child development* (pp. 133–146). Hillsdale, NJ: Lawrence Erlbaum Associates.

Ogbu, J. U. (1993). Differences in cultural frame of reference. *International Journal of Behavioral Development, 16*(3), 483–506.

Ogbu, J. U. (1994). From cultural differences to differences in cultural frame of reference. In P. M. Greenfield & R. R. Cocking (Eds.), *Cross-cultural roots of minority child development* (pp. 365–391). Hillsdale, NJ: Lawrence Erlbaum Associates.

Ogbu, J. U. (1995). Origins of human competence: A cultural-ecological perspective. In N. R. Goldberger & J. B. Veroff (Eds.), *The culture and psychology reader* (pp. 245–275). New York: New York University Press.

Okagaki, L., & Sternberg, R. J. (1993). Parental beliefs and children's school performance. *Child Development, 64*, 36–56.

Philips, S. U. (1972). Participant structures and communicative competence: Warm Springs children in community and classroom. In C. B. Cazden,

V. P. John, & D. Hymes (Eds.), *Functions of language in the classroom* (pp. 370–394). New York: Teachers College Press.

Piaget, J. (1932/1965). *The moral judgment of the child.* New York: Free Press.

Portes, P. R. (1999). Social and psychological factors in the academic achievement of children of immigrants: A cultural history puzzle. *American Educational Research Journal, 36*(3), 489–507.

Quiroz, B., Greenfield, P. M., & Altchech, M. (1999, April). Bridging cultures with a parent-teacher conference. *Educational Leadership, 56*(7), 64–67.

Raeff, C., Greenfield, P.M., & Quiroz, B. (2000, Spring) Conceptualizing interpersonal relationships in the cultural contexts of individualism and collectivism. In S. Harkness, C. Raeff, & C.M. Super (Eds.), *Variability in the social construction of the child: New directions for child and adolescent development, 87,* 59–74.

Reyes, M. de la Luz. (1992). Challenging venerable assumptions: Literacy instruction for linguistically different students. *Harvard Educational Review, 62*(4), 427–446.

Rogoff, B. (1990). *Apprenticeship in thinking.* New York: Oxford University Press.

Rothstein-Fisch, C., Greenfield, P. M., & Trumbull, E. (1999). Bridging cultures for immigrant Latino students. *Educational Leadership, 56*(7), 64–67.

Rothstein-Fisch, C., Trumbull, E., Isaac, A., Daley, C., & Pérez, A. I. (2003, July). When "helping someone else" is the right answer: Bridging cultures in assessment. *Journal of Latinos and Education.*

Rothstein-Fisch, C., Trumbull, E., Quiroz, B., & Greenfield, P. M. (1997, June). *Bridging Cultures in the classroom.* Poster presentation at the annual meeting of the Jean Piaget Society, Santa Monica, CA.

Scribner, S. (1985). Vygotsky's uses of history. In J. V. Wertsch (Ed.), *Culture, communication, and cognition: Vygotskian perspectives* (pp. 119–145). New York: Cambridge University.

Small, M. (1998). *Our babies, ourselves: How biology and culture shape the way we parent.* New York: Anchor Books.

Smitherman, G. (1981). "What go round come round": *King* in perspective. *Harvard Educational Review, 51*(1), 41–62.

Stigler, J. W., & Perry, M. (1988). Mathematics learning in Japanese, Chinese, and American classrooms. In B. Saxe & M. Gearhart (Eds.), *Children's mathematics: New directions for child development, No. 41* (pp. 27–54). San Francisco, CA: Jossey-Bass.

Strauss, C. (2000). The culture concept and the individualism-collectivism debate: Dominant and alternative attributions for class in the United States. In L. P. Nucci, G. B. Saxe, & E. Turiel (Eds.), *Culture, thought, and development* (pp. 85–114). Mahwah, NJ: Lawrence Erlbaum Associates.

Suárez-Orozco, M. (1995). Epilogue. In M. Suárez-Orozco (Ed.), *Crossings: Mexican immigration in interdisciplinary perspectives* (pp. 413–419) Cambridge, MA: Harvard University, David Rockefeller Center for Latin American Studies. Distributed by Harvard University Press.

Sudarkasa, N. (1988). Interpreting the African heritage in Afro-American family organization. In H. P. Mcadoo (Ed.), *Black families* (2nd ed.) (pp. 27–43). Newbury Park, CA: Sage.

Suina, J. H. (1991, June/July). Discussion. In Proceedings of a workshop on continuities and discontinuities in the cognitive socialization of minority children. Department of Health and Human Services, Public Health Service, Alcohol, Drug Abuse and Mental Health Administration, Washington, DC.

Suina, J. H., & Smolkin, L. B. (1994). From natal culture to school culture to dominant society culture: Supporting transitions for Pueblo Indian students. In P. M. Greenfield & R. R. Cocking (Eds.), *Cross-cultural roots of minority child development* (pp. 115–130). Hillsdale, NJ: Lawrence Erlbaum Associates.

Swisher, K., & Deyhle, D. (1992). Adapting instruction to culture. In J. Reyhner (Ed.), *Teaching American Indian students* (pp. 81–95). Norman, OK: University of Oklahoma Press.

Tharp, R. G., & Gallimore, R. (1988). *Rousing minds to life: Teaching, learning, and schooling in social context.* Cambridge, England: Cambridge University.

Triandis, H. C. (1989). Cross cultural studies of individualism and collectivism. *Nebraska Symposium on Motivation, 37,* 41–133.

Trumbull, E., Diaz-Meza, R., & Hasan, A. (2000, April 24–28). *Using cultural knowledge to inform literacy practices: Teacher innovations from the Bridging Cultures Project.* Paper presented at the annual meeting of the American Educational Research Association, New Orleans, LA.

Trumbull, E., Diaz-Meza, R., Hasan, A., & Rothstein-Fisch, C. (2001). *The Bridging Cultures Project five-year report, 1996–2000* [Online]. Available: http://www.wested.org/bridging/BC_5yr_report.pdf

Trumbull, E., Nelson-Barber, S., & Mitchell, J. (2002). Enhancing mathematics instruction for Indigenous American students. In J. Hankes (Ed.), *Changing the faces of mathematics: Perspectives on indigenous people of North America* (pp. 1–18). Reston, VA: National Council of Teachers of Mathematics.

Trumbull, E., Rothstein-Fisch, C., & Greenfield, P. M. (2000). *Bridging Cultures in our schools: New approaches that work.* [Knowledge brief]. San Francisco: WestEd.

Trumbull, E., Rothstein-Fisch, C., Greenfield, P. M., & Quiroz, B. (2001). *Bridging Cultures between home and school: A guide for teachers.* Mahwah, NJ: Lawrence Erlbaum Associates.

Vygotsky, L. S. (1978). *Mind in society.* Cambridge, MA: Harvard University Press.

Whiting, J. W. M., Whiting, B. B. (1994). Altruistic and egoistic behavior in six cultures. In E. H. Chasdi (Ed.), *Culture and human development* (pp. 267–281). New York: Cambridge University Press.

Williams, B. (2000, August). *Strengths of diverse urban learners.* Paper presented at the American Psychological Association 2000 Convention, Washington, DC.

5

Pedagogy, Knowledge, and Teacher Preparation

Kenneth M. Zeichner

Numerous approaches to curriculum and instruction are available to help close the achievement gap between poor children of color and their middle-class peers. However, no approach to curriculum and instruction can close this achievement gap without corresponding changes in teacher education. This chapter reviews the research literature on what teachers need to be like, to know, and to be able to do to successfully teach all students to high academic standards. It also discusses the changes that must take place in teacher education to support new directions for teaching, learning, and curriculum development in urban schools.

Teaching All Students to High Academic Standards: The Research Literature

In recent years, research has drawn a clear picture of the kind of teaching, curriculum, and classroom environment that enables all students to achieve high standards. A significant proportion of this research focuses on poor students of color, whom our public schools have consistently underserved. The key elements this literature addresses are high expectations for all students, cultural responsiveness in instruction, teacher knowledge, and teaching strategies.

High Expectations for All Students

The first element common to effective teachers in urban schools is their belief that all students can be successful learners and their communication of this belief to students (Delpit, 1988; Gay, 2000). These teachers have a commitment to helping all students achieve success and truly believe they can make a difference in their students' achievement (Ladson-Billings, 1994). Winfield (1986) distinguishes between teachers who assume responsibility for their students' learning and those who shift responsibility for student failure to factors such as school bureaucracies, parents, and communities.

Despite evidence to the contrary, many students in teacher education institutions continue to believe that some students cannot learn and so hold low expectations for them (Goodlad, 1990; Pang & Sablan, 1998; Sleeter, 2001). For example, Goodlad writes:

> *The idea of moral imperatives for teachers was virtually foreign in concept and strange in language for most of the future teachers we interviewed. Many were less than convinced that all students can learn; they voiced the view that they should be kind and considerate to all, but they accepted as fact the theory that some simply cannot learn.* (p. 264)

Low expectations for student behavior and academic achievement often focus on poor students of color. Research clearly shows that teacher education students tend to view diversity of student backgrounds as a problem, rather than as a resource that enriches teaching and learning. Moreover, many of these future teachers have negative attitudes about racial, ethnic, and language groups other than their own (Zeichner & Hoeft, 1996). Such attitudes manifest as low expectations, which are then expressed in watered down and fragmented curriculum for poor students of color (Moll, 1988; Nieto, 2000; Oakes, 1985). Teachers with high expectations for all students, on the other hand, effectively translate their beliefs into more academically demanding curriculum.

Moll (1988), in describing elements that contribute to Latino students' school success, is clear about the curricular shift that needs to accompany high expectations:

> *In contrast to the assumption that working class children cannot handle an academically rigorous curriculum, or in the case of limited-English proficient students, that their lack of English fluency justifies an emphasis on low level skills, the guiding assumption in the classrooms analyzed seemed to be the opposite: that students are as smart as allowed by the curriculum. The teachers assumed that the children were competent and capable and that it was the teacher's responsibility to provide the students with a challenging, innovative, and intellectually rigorous curriculum.* (p. 467)

Standards as an Equalizer?

One attempt to overcome the differential expectations teachers sometimes hold for students is the development of curriculum standards and assessments designed to ensure that all students have access to the same knowledge and skills in the various disciplines (Fuhrman, 2001). In addition, recent reforms have sought to align the curriculum of teacher education programs with preK–12 curriculum standards and assessments (Dilworth & Brown, 2001). To date, however, neither of these reforms has led to any extensive narrowing of the achievement gap. Although many states now require reporting of data on the performance of various subgroups, very few states hold schools accountable for having all groups of students meet the same performance standards (Goertz, 2001). Thus, states are able to meet their performance goals without narrowing achievement differences.

The reality of classroom practice at the local level is often at odds with the rhetoric about the equalizing effects of curriculum standards (Spillane, 2001). Furthermore, the alignment of teacher education programs to preK–12 standards has not led to a narrowing of the achievement gap, due to the inequitable distribution of fully qualified teachers who complete teacher education programs aligned with the standards. Currently, students who are poor and of color are frequently taught by teachers who are less than fully qualified (Dilworth & Brown, 2001). In addition, although some standards for teacher licensing address aspects of what teachers need to know and be able to do to teach all students (Walton & Carlson, 1997), some researchers believe the standards that are most influential on teacher education programs throughout the United States (such as Interstate New Teacher Assessment) have failed to include elements of effective pedagogy as applied to a culturally diverse classroom (Murrell, 2001, Zeichner, 2003).

Cultural Responsiveness in Instruction

Culturally responsive instruction contains two critical elements: first, the incorporation of aspects of students' languages, cultures, and daily experiences into the academic and social context of schooling; and second, the explicit teaching of the school's codes and customs (for example, the culture of the classroom) so that students will be able to participate fully in the social dynamic of the classroom.

Bridging home and school cultures. It is not enough simply to make the curriculum more rigorous. The literature is clear about the need for a scaffolding or bridge between the cultures of the school and the home in order to teach all students to high academic standards.

Building scaffolding or a bridge consists of constructing a set of supports to enable students to relate school to experiences at home and vice versa (Mehan & Trujillo, 1989). The literature sometimes refers to such supports as "cultural synchronization" (Jordan Irvine, 1989). The point is to make curriculum and instruction responsive to what is important to students in their home cultures.

Ways of providing this kind of support include the use of teaching strategies such as sheltered bilingual education (Echevarria & Graves, 1998) and assisted teaching (Tharp & Gallimore, 1988), as well as the reorganization of lesson formats, discourse patterns, behavior standards, curriculum materials, and assessment practices to make teachers more sensitive to linguistic and cultural variations (Garcia, 1993; Gay, 2000; Jordan Irvine & Armento, 2001; Olsen & Mullen, 1990; Strickland & Ascher, 1992).

Effective teachers understand the cultures of students in their classrooms and adapt curriculum and instruction accordingly. Cultural responsiveness supports academic learning and helps students identify with and maintain pride in their home cultures (Cummins, 1986, 1989; Foster, 1997; Gay, 2000; Nieto & Rolon, 1997). In culturally responsive classrooms, students can apply to new learning the language and task completion skills already in their repertoires (Cole & Griffin, 1987). An example would be using a knowledge of Spanish to learn to read English texts (Au & Kawakami, 1994).

Other examples of restructuring classroom practices around the cultural resources students bring to school are using peer learning centers and turn-taking in reading groups (Tharp & Gallimore, 1988); incorporating community-related themes into classroom writing projects (Moll & Diaz, 1987); and employing interaction patterns such as choral and responsive reading commonly found in African American churches in classrooms with many African American students (Foster, 1997; Hollins, 1982).

Explicit teaching of school culture. The second critical element in congruent instruction is the explicit teaching of the school's codes and customs (such as the culture of the classroom), so that students will be able to participate fully in the mainstream or "culture of power" (Delpit, 1988; Villegas, 1991; Vilegas & Lucas, 2002). Knapp and Turnbull (1991) succinctly capture this principle of cultural congruence in their synthesis of factors associated with school success for poor children. They argue that poor children will be better able to meet academic challenges if schools abide by the following principles:

> Teachers know and respect the students' cultural/linguistic backgrounds and communicate this respect in a personal way to the students. The academic program allows and encourages students to draw and build on experiences they have, at the same time it exposes them to unfamiliar experiences and ways of thinking. The assumptions, expectations, and ways of doing things in school—in short, its culture, are made explicit to the students by teachers as they explain and model these dimensions of academic learning. (p. 334)

Maintaining students' ethnocultural identities while simultaneously familiarizing them with the codes of power requires teachers to combine culturally congruent and consciously incongruent teaching and curriculum strategies (Singer, 1988). Because several cultures are present in many classrooms, total cultural congruence in instruction is not possible. Teachers can, however, incorporate culture and language-sensitive practices into their classroom instruction so that all students feel respect for their cultural roots (Gay, 2000; Nieto, 2002). One component of culture involves students' daily experiences in their homes and communities, such as the types of knowledge, activities, and social interactions that occur outside the school. Understanding the daily experiences of students can help teachers manage the complexity of multiple cultures represented in their classrooms.

Teacher knowledge of and respect for cultural traditions. In order for teachers to implement a culturally responsive approach to teaching, they must have knowledge of and respect for the various cultural traditions and languages of students in their classrooms. Anything less ensures that many ethnic and language minority students will continue to fall short of meeting high academic standards. Teachers need general sociocultural knowledge about child and adolescent development; about second language acquisition (Carrasquillo & Rodriguez, 1996); and about the ways socioeconomic circumstances, language, and culture shape school performance (Cazden & Mehan, 1990; Comer, 1988). Finally, according to some (Banks, 1991; Hollins, 1990), teachers need a clear sense of their own ethnic and cultural identities in order to understand and appreciate those of their students (Carter & Goodwin, 1994; McAllister & Jordan Irvine, 2000). They also must be aware of how their own cultural biases may influence their judgments about student performance and obstruct their students' ability to learn.

The literature discusses at length the importance of giving teachers information about the values, practices, and learning styles of particular cultural groups (Coballes-Vega, 1992). However, the danger in this strat-egy is that general knowledge about cultural group characteristics may strengthen any stereotypes teachers already hold (McDiarmid & Price, 1990). One way to circumvent this is to teach teachers how to learn about, and then incorporate into instruction, information about students, their families, and their communities (Cazden & Mehan, 1990; Trueba, 1989). Strategies for acquiring such information include making home visits, conferring with community members, talking with parents, consulting with minority teachers, and observing children in and out of school (Villegas & Lucas, 2002).

Teachers essentially become researchers of their students and their students' communities (Heath, 1983; Moll, 1992), then adjust their classroom practices to make the local cultural community the baseline for curriculum and instruction. Garcia (1993) identifies the following three ways in which successful teachers of culturally and linguistically diverse students do this:

1. By using cultural referents in both verbal and nonverbal forms to communicate instructional and institutional demands,
2. By organizing instruction to build on rules of discourse from the home and community cultures, and
3. By showing equal respect to the values and norms of the home and community cultures and to those of the school culture.

Teaching Strategies for Making Meaning

Methods of instruction that appear to work most successfully with poor ethnic and language minority students tend to focus on making meaning out of content. This is the exact opposite of the decontextualized skills that schools most often teach these students (Moll, 1988). Research (Knapp & Shields, 1990) challenges the notion that teacher-directed instruction of a skills-based and sequentially ordered curriculum develops students' analytic and conceptual skills and their ability to express themselves in writing. Research attributes the failure of this approach in urban schools to teachers not providing students with a larger meaning or purpose for learning.

Cummins (1986, 1989) contrasts two general orientations to teaching—the transmission model and the reciprocal interaction model. Cummins (1986) argues that the transmission model contributes to the disempowerment of poor students of color:

The teacher's task is to impart knowledge or skills that he or she possesses to students who do not yet have these skills. . . . The teacher initiates and controls the interaction, constantly orienting it toward the achievement of instructional objectives. The curriculum . . . frequently focuses on the internal structure of the language or subject matter. Consequently, it focuses predominately on surface features of language or literacy . . . and emphasizes correct recall of content taught by means of highly structured drills and workbook exercises. (p. 28)

According to Cummins (1986), in the reciprocal interaction model, an orientation that supports the empowerment of ethnic and language minority students and their academic success, genuine dialogue takes place between teachers and students. Rather than maintaining absolute control of student learning, teachers guide and facilitate instruction. "A central tenet of the reciprocal interaction model is that talking and writing are a means to learning" (p. 28). This orientation encourages collaborative learning and interaction among students and between students and teachers. Students tend to see academic tasks as relevant to their lives (Garcia, 1991). Also, according to Cummins (1986), "This model emphasizes the development of higher level cognitive skills rather than just factual recall, and meaningful language use by students rather than the correction of surface forms" (p. 28). Often in this approach, teachers organize instruction in basic skills and academic content around themes students and teachers select together (Garcia, 1991).

The reciprocal interaction model builds ethnic and language minority students' academic success through a variety of teaching methods and curricular programs. Teachers need this variety to respond appropriately to student needs (Nieto, 2000; Villegas & Lucas, 2002).

Although researchers try to identify classroom practices that successfully promote learning among ethnic and language minority students (Natriello, McDill, & Pallas, 1990; Slavin & Madden, 1989), their work instead raises important questions about the efficacy of some allegedly successful practices. For example, Reyes (1992) argues that currently popular forms of "process instruction" are not always successful with language minority students unless teachers make culturally and linguistically supportive adaptations:

Teachers must rise above the euphoria over whole language and writing process and recognize that these programs are not perfect or equally successful for all. They are successful only to the extent that teachers understand the theories, assume the role of mediators, not merely facilitators, and create culturally and linguistically sensitive learning environments for all learners. (p. 440)

The literature also agrees on the need for teachers to have a deep understanding of the subjects they teach so they can present material in

multiple ways to address the diversity of prior experiences and understandings present in their classrooms (McDiarmid, 1994).

Other strategies teachers can employ to teach all students to high academic standards include modifying or developing curriculum materials
to represent the perspectives and practices of different cultural groups
(Sleeter & Grant, 1999); assessing students in ways that are sensitive to
cultural and linguistic variations (Goodwin, 1997); and creating collaborative classroom environments through such practices as cooperative
grouping, peer tutoring, and mixed-ability grouping (Garcia, 1991; Hixson,
1991; Quality Education for Minorities Project, 1990; Waxman & Padron,
2002). There is almost universal condemnation of ability grouping in elementary schools and tracking in secondary schools, and a strong feeling
that teachers need to be aware of how schools use these practices to structure inequality (Hodge, 1990).

A final strategy for teachers that has substantial instructional benefits is to involve parents and other community members in authentic ways
in the school program (Ada, 1986; Grant, 1991; Murrell, 2001). Parents
and other community members can play a significant role in determining
what constitutes an appropriate education for their children and youth
(Delgado-Gaitan, 1991; Murrell, 2001; Valdes, 1996). According to Comer
(1988), when adults cross racial, class, and cultural lines and share information and power within a school, students are more likely to be able to
cross these lines and perform well in both languages and cultures. Harrison (1993) argues that these interactions must be culturally appropriate in
order for trust to develop between the school and the community. Harrison also contends that genuine parent and community empowerment is a
more significant influence on school success than are particular instructional approaches.

Figure 5.1 summarizes this discussion of what teachers need to be
like, to know, and to be able to do to teach all students to high academic
standards.

The Inadequacy of Classroom-Based Solutions for Narrowing the Achievement Gap

Having high expectations for students, cultural congruence in instruction,
culturally inclusive curriculum, knowledgeable teachers, and appropriate
instructional strategies all contribute to narrowing the achievement gap in
urban schools. However, they are still not enough to overcome the effects
of racism, language discrimination, social stratification, unequal resource
distribution, and a history of discrimination against poor people of color

FIGURE 5.1

A Pedagogy for Narrowing the Achievement Gap in Urban Schools

- Teachers have a clear sense of their own ethnic and cultural identities.
- Teachers communicate high expectations for the success of all of their students.
- Teachers are personally committed to achieving equity for all students and believe that they are capable of making a difference in their students' learning.
- Teachers have developed a personal bond with their students and cease seeing their students as "the other."
- Students are provided with an academically challenging curriculum that includes attention to the development of higher-level cognitive skills.
- Instruction focuses on student creation of meaning about content in an interactive and collaborative learning environment.
- Students often see learning tasks as meaningful.
- The curriculum includes the contributions and perspectives of the different ethnic and cultural groups that make up the society.
- Teachers provide scaffolding that links the academically challenging and inclusive curriculum to the cultural resources that students bring to school.
- Teachers explicitly teach students the culture of the school and classroom and seek to maintain students' sense of ethnic and cultural pride and identity.
- Parents and community members are encouraged to become involved in students' education and are given a significant voice in making important school decisions related to programs (i.e., resources and staffing).

(Carter & Goodwin, 1994; Villegas, 1988). As Weiner (1989) points out, while teacher education programs can turn out teachers who can instruct students in their classrooms with respect, creativity, and skill, they are no substitute for larger political and social movements that can effectively alter systemic deficiencies in school systems and in society. Granted, there are examples of schools where poor students of color achieve at high levels (Bensman & Meier, 2000; National Coalition of Advocates for Students, 1991; Taylor & Pearson, 2002). However, most urban teachers work in conditions where they cannot engage in the complex and demanding teaching that makes high achievement possible (Weiner, 1993). Changes in the ways in which teachers interact with students in classrooms must be accompanied by or preceded by changes in schools' systemic and structural conditions. Otherwise, the highly interactive and demanding teaching this chapter advocates will become an urban reality only in a few exceptional schools. The kinds of changes schools need include equalizing spending between rich and poor schools (Rotberg, Harvey, & Warner, 1993), restructuring teachers' professional development (Lieberman & Miller, 2001;

Smylie, 1996), and eliminating bureaucratic regulations that interfere with teachers' main academic mission (Weiner, 1999).

The Task of Teacher Education

Proposals to narrow the achievement gap in urban schools often overlook teacher education. Proposals for urban school reform often imply that if it were possible to identify the teaching and curriculum practices that lead to high achievement for all students, then we could "train" teachers to use these practices. This model of teacher development dominates teacher education in urban schools. However, it is incompatible with the ambitious vision of teaching and schooling necessary for narrowing the achievement gap (Little, 1993).

Research on teacher learning makes it clear that putting strategies such as cooperative learning and multicultural curriculum materials into the hands of culturally encapsulated and largely white, monolingual teachers and prospective teachers without changing the way in which these teachers view poor students of color will accomplish little. Teacher education initiatives need to transform some of the assumptions and attitudes teachers bring to teacher education. Nieto (2000) points out that the most important way to become a multicultural teacher is to become a multicultural person. Teachers, like their students, interpret and give meaning to instruction through the concepts, categories, and worldviews they bring to learning (Wubbels, 1992).

Developing teaching skills is only part of the job. Teacher education institutions also need to affect the types of people who go into urban schools to teach. Research identifies three dimensions to the task of preparing teachers for culturally diverse classrooms (Zeichner, 1996).

First, teacher education programs are limited in their ability to overcome the negative attitudes and low expectations that many prospective and current teachers hold for students of color and their families (Wideen, Mayer-Smith, & Moon, 1998). Therefore, teacher education programs need mechanisms that admit into teaching only people committed to teaching all students to high academic standards. Currently, grade point averages, test scores, and the glowing testimony of young college students who want to be teachers because they "love kids" dominates admission practices in teacher education programs. But alternatives exist. One is to use alternative route programs, which tend to attract more diverse and mature prospective teacher cohorts than university-based programs. Another is to employ selection procedures such as Haberman's interviews, which screen people especially for their potential to teach in urban schools (Haberman & Post, 1998).

A second dimension to educating teachers for diverse classrooms involves developing teachers' cultural sensitivity and intercultural teaching competence. Research shows that practices such as giving prospective teachers service learning and community field experiences and using non-certified community members as teacher educators (under particular conditions) contributes to teachers' ability to engage in culturally congruent instruction (Boyle-Baise & Sleeter, 2000; Burant & Kirby, 2002; Seidel & Friend, 2002; Zeichner, 1996). However, just as classroom solutions are inadequate without changes in the institutional context of teachers' work, socializing teachers within teacher education programs is inadequate without changes in the institutional environment in which teacher education programs operate.

The institutional context of teacher education programs is the third dimension of preparing teachers for cultural diversity. Many colleges and universities lack institutional commitment to diversity (Grant, 1993). This, in turn, insulates faculty (Howey & Zimpher, 1990). Together, these findings raise serious questions about the capacity of teacher education institutions to support and sustain programs that prepare teachers for urban schools. Fortunately, research does identify several promising strategies for strengthening the capacity of teacher education programs. One strategy gaining particular favor is the establishment of consortia that provide faculty expertise in multicultural education and staff development for teacher educators (Melnick & Zeichner, 1997; Price & Valli, 1998).

Final Thoughts

The research literature contains a growing consensus about what teachers need to be like, to know, and to be able to do to teach all students to high academic standards. This vision rests on teachers believing that all students can learn, and teachers taking responsibility for this task regardless of students' economic circumstances or skin color. To narrow the achievement gap in urban schools, classrooms must be highly interactive and collaborative. Teachers must let students know they care about them and hold high expectations for them. Instruction in these classrooms builds upon and respects the cultural resources and traditions students bring to school. They integrate a variety of cultural perspectives, often around thematic units. At the same time, they induct students into the culture of the school.

Constance Clayton, former superintendent of the Philadelphia Public Schools, maintains we do not need more research to tell us what we need to do to narrow the achievement gap in urban schools. What the situation requires, rather than a new pedagogy, is the emergence of a new politics.

Clayton (1989), reiterating the position of the late Ronald Edmonds, contends we already know how to teach all children successfully. The real issue is whether our society is serious about creating schools in which this pedagogical agenda can flourish. Similarly, we need to create the kinds of teacher education programs and professional development opportunities that can build this ambitious vision of schooling.

Ultimately, because of the impossibility of creating equal schools in an unequal society, narrowing the achievement gap between poor students of color in urban schools and their middle-class peers depends on establishing the social preconditions necessary for school reform. This means dealing with massive inequities in society as a whole. Culturally responsive curriculum and instruction are only one small part of a society that provides all children access to decent and rewarding lives.

References

Ada, A. F. (1986). Creative education for bilingual teachers. *Harvard Educational Review, 56*(4), 386–393.

Au, K., & Kawakami, A. (1994). Cultural congruence in instruction. In E. Hollins, J. King, & W. Hayman (Eds.), *Teaching diverse populations* (pp. 5–23). Albany, NY: SUNY.

Banks, J. (1991). Teaching multicultural literacy to teachers. *Teaching Education, 4*(1), 135–144.

Bensman, D., & Meier, D. (2000). *Central Park East and its graduates.* New York: Teachers College Press.

Boyle-Baise, M., & Sleeter, C. E. (2000). Community-based service learning for multicultural teacher education. *Educational Foundations, 14*, 33–50.

Burant, T. J., & Kirby, D. (2002). Beyond classroom-based early field experiences: Understanding an educative practicum in an urban school and community. *Teaching and Teacher Education, 18*, 561–575.

Carrasquillo, A. L., & Rodriguez, V. (1996). *Language minority students in the mainstream classroom.* Philadelphia: Multilingual Matters.

Carter, R. T., & Goodwin, A. L. (1994). Racial identity and education. In L. Darling-Hammond (Ed.), *Review of research in education, 20* (pp. 291–336). Washington, DC: American Educational Research Association.

Cazden, C., & Mehan, H. (1990). Principles from sociology and anthropology: Context, code, classroom, and culture. In M. Reynolds (Ed.), *Knowledge base for the beginning teacher* (pp. 47–57). Washington, DC: American Association of Colleges for Teacher Education.

Clayton, C. (1989). We can educate all our children. *The Nation, 31*, 132–135.

Coballes-Vega, C. (1992). *Considerations in the teaching of culturally diverse children.* ERIC Clearinghouse on Teacher Education. Washington, DC: American Association of Colleges for Teacher Education.

Cole, M., & Griffin, P. (1987). *Contextual factors in education.* Madison, WI: Wisconsin Center for Education Research.

Comer, J. (1988). Educating poor minority children. *Scientific American, 25*(5), 42–48.

Cummins, J. (1986). Empowering minority students: A framework for interventions. *Harvard Educational Review, 56*(1), 18–36.

Cummins, J. (1989). *Empowering minority students.* Sacramento, CA: California Association for Bilingual Education.

Delgado-Gaitan, C. (1991). Involving parents in the schools: A process of empowerment. *American Journal of Education, 100*(1), 20–46.

Delpit, L. (1988). The silenced dialogue: Power and pedagogy in educating other people's children. *Harvard Educational Review, 58*(3), 280–298.

Dilworth, M., & Brown, C. (2001). Consider the difference: Teaching and learning in culturally rich schools. In V. Richardson (Ed.), *Handbook of research on teaching* (pp. 643–667). Washington, DC: American Educational Research Association.

Echevarria, J., & Graves, A. (1998). *Sheltered content instruction: Teaching English language learners with diverse abilities.* Boston: Allyn & Bacon.

Foster, M. (1997). *Black teachers on teaching.* New York: New Press.

Fuhrman, S. (Ed.). (2001). *From the capitol to the classroom: Standards-based reform in the United States.* Chicago: University of Chicago Press.

Garcia, E. (1991). *Education of linguistically and culturally diverse students: Effective instructional practices.* Santa Cruz, CA: National Center for Research on Cultural Diversity & Second Language Learning.

Garcia, E. (1993). Language, culture, and education. In L. Darling-Hammond (Ed.), *Review of research in education, 19* (pp. 51–100). Washington, DC: American Educational Research Association.

Gay, G. (2000). *Culturally responsive teaching.* New York: Teachers College Press.

Goertz, M. (2001). Standards-based accountability: Horse trade or horse whip. In S. Fuhrman (Ed.), *From the capitol to the classroom: Standards-based reform in the United States* (pp. 39–59). Chicago: University of Chicago Press.

Goodlad, J. (1990). *Teachers for our nation's schools.* San Francisco: Jossey-Bass.

Goodwin, A. L. (Ed.). (1997). *Assessment for equity and inclusion.* New York: Routledge.

Grant, C. (1991). *Educational research and teacher training for successfully teaching limited English proficient students.* Paper presented at the Second National Research Symposium, Washington, DC.

Grant, C. (1993). The multicultural preparation of U.S. teachers: Some hard truths. In G. Verma (Ed.), *Inequality and teacher education* (pp. 41–57). London: Falmer.

Haberman, M., & Post, L. (1998). Teachers for multicultural schools: The power of selection. *Theory into Practice, 37*(2), 96–104.

Harrison, B. (1993). Building our house from the rubbish tree: Minority directed education. In E. Jacobs & C. Jordan (Eds.), *Minority education: Anthropological perspectives* (pp. 147–164). Norwood, NJ: Albex.

Heath, S. B. (1983). *Ways with words: Language, life, and work in communities and classrooms.* New York: Cambridge University.

Hixson, J. (1991). *Multicultural issues in teacher education: Meeting the challenge of student diversity.* Paper presented at the annual meeting of the American Educational Research Association, Chicago.

Hodge, C. (1990). Educators for a truly democratic system of schooling. In J. Goodlad & P. Keating (Eds.), *Access to knowledge: An agenda for our nation's schools* (pp. 259–272). New York: College Entrance Examination Board.

Hollins, E. (1982). The Marva Collins story revisited: Implications for regular classroom instruction. *Journal of Teacher Education, 33*(1), 37–40.

Hollins, E. (1990). Debunking the myth of a monolithic white American culture; or moving toward cultural inclusion. *American Behavioral Scientist, 34*(2), 201–209.

Howey, K., & Zimpher, N. (1990). Professors and deans of education. In W. R. Houston (Ed.), *Handbook of research on teacher education* (pp. 349–370). New York: Macmillan.

Jordan Irvine, J. (1989). *Cultural responsiveness in teacher education: Strategies to prepare majority teachers for successful instruction of minority students.* Paper presented at the annual meeting of Project 30, Monterey, CA.

Jordan Irvine, J., & Armento, B. J. (2001). *Culturally responsive teaching.* Boston: McGraw Hill.

Knapp, M. S., & Shields, P. M. (1990). Reconceiving academic instruction for children of poverty. *Phi Delta Kappan, 71*, 752–758.

Knapp, M., & Turnbull, B. (1991). Alternatives to conventional wisdom. In M. Knapp & P. Shields (Eds.), *Better schools for the children in poverty: Alterations to conventional wisdom* (pp. 329–353). Berkeley, CA: McCutchan.

Ladson-Billings, G. (1994). *The dreamkeepers: Successful teachers of African American children.* San Francisco: Jossey Bass.

Lieberman, A., & Miller, L. (2001). *Teachers caught in the action: Professional development that matters.* New York: Teachers College Press.

Little, J. W. (1993). Teachers' professional development in a climate of educational reform. *Educational Evaluation and Policy Analysis, 15*(2), 129–151.

McAllister, G., & Jordan Irvine, J. (2000). Cross cultural competency and multicultural teacher education. *Review of Educational Research, 70*(1), 3–24.

McDiarmid, G. W. (1994). The arts and sciences as preparation for teaching. In K. Howey & N. Zimpher (Eds.), *Informing faculty development for teacher educators* (pp. 99–137). Norwood, NJ: Ablex.

McDiarmid, G. W., & Price, J. (1990). *Prospective teachers' views of diverse learners: A study of the participants in the ABCD project.* East Lansing, MI: National Center for Research on Teacher Learning.

Mehan, H., & Trujillo, T. (1989). *Teacher education issues* (Research and Policy Series No. 4). Santa Barbara, CA: University of California, Linguistic Minority Research Project.

Melnick, S., & Zeichner, K. (1997). Enhancing the capacity of teacher education institutions to address diversity issues. In J. King, E. Hollins, & W. Hayman (Eds.), *Preparing teachers for cultural diversity* (pp. 23–39). New York: Teachers College Press.

Moll, L. (1988). Some key issues in teaching Latino students. *Language Arts, 65*(5), 465–472.

Moll, L. (1992). Literacy research in community and classrooms: A sociocultural approach. In R. Beach, J. L. Green, M. L. Kamil, & T. Shanalas (Eds.), *Multidisciplinary perspectives on literacy research* (pp. 211–244). Urbana, IL: National Council of Teachers of English.

Moll, L., & Diaz, R. (1987). Teaching writing as communication: The use of ethnographic findings in classroom practice. In D. Bloome (Ed.), *Literacy and schooling* (pp. 55–65). Norwood, NJ: Ablex.

Murrell, P. (2001). *The community teacher: A new framework for effective urban teaching.* New York: Teachers College Press.

National Coalition of Advocates for Students. (1991). *The good common school: Making the vision work for all students.* Boston: Author.

Natriello, G., McDill, E., & Pallas, A. (1990). *Schooling disadvantaged children: Racing against catastrophe.* New York: Teachers College Press.

Nieto, S. (2000). *Affirming diversity: The sociopolitical context of multicultural education.* New York: Longman.

Nieto, S. (2002). *Language, culture, and teaching.* Mahwah, NJ: L. Erlbaum.

Nieto, S., & Rolon, C. (1997). Preparation and professional development of teachers: A perspective from two Latinas. In J. Jordan Irvine (Ed.), *Critical knowledge for diverse teachers and learners* (pp. 89–124). Washington, DC: American Association of Colleges for Teacher Education.

Oakes, J. (1985). *Keeping track: How schools structure inequality.* New Haven, CT: Yale University.

Olsen, L., & Mullen, N. (1990). *Embracing diversity: Teachers' voices from California's classrooms.* San Francisco: California Tomorrow Project.

Pang, V., & Sablan, V. (1998). Teacher efficacy: How do teachers feel about their ability to teach African-American children? In M. Dilworth (Ed.), *Being responsive to cultural differences: How teachers learn* (pp. 39–60). Thousand Oaks, CA: Corwin.

Price, J., & Valli, L. (1998). Institutional support for diversity in preservice teacher education. *Theory into Practice, 37*(2), 114–120.

Quality Education for Minorities Project. (1990). *Education that works: An action plan for the education of minorities.* Cambridge, MA: Author.

Reyes, M. (1992). Challenging venerable assumptions: Literacy instruction for linguistically different students. *Harvard Educational Review, 62*(4), 427–446.

Rotberg, I., Harvey, J. J., & Warner, K. (1993). *Federal policy options for improving the education of low income students.* Washington, DC: Rand Corporation.

Seidel, B., & Friend, G. (2002). Leaving authority at the door: Equal-status community-based experiences and the preparation of teachers for diverse classrooms. *Teaching and Teacher Education, 18,* 421–433.

Singer, E. (1988). *What is cultural congruence and why are they saying such terrible things about it?* (Occasional Paper No. 120). East Lansing, MI: Michigan State University, Institute for Research on Teaching.

Slavin, R., & Madden, N. (1989). What works for students at risk. *Educational Leadership, 46*(5), 4–13.

Sleeter, C. (2001). Epistemological diversity in research on preservice teacher preparation for historically underserved children. In W. Secada (Ed.), *Review of research in education, 25,* (pp. 209–250). Washington, DC: American Educational Research Association.

Sleeter, C., & Grant, C. (1999). *Making choices for multicultural education* (3rd ed.). Upper Saddle River, NJ: Merrill.

Smylie, M. (1996). From bureaucratic control to building human capital: The importance of teacher learning in educational reform. *Educational Researcher, 25*(9), 9–11.

Spillane, J. (2001). Challenging instruction for all students. In S. Fuhrman (Ed.), *From the capitol to the classroom: Standards-based reform in the United States* (pp. 217–241). Chicago: University of Chicago Press.

Strickland, D., & Ascher, C. (1992). Low income African-American children and public schooling. In P. Jackson (Ed.), *Handbook of research on curriculum* (pp. 609–625). Washington, DC: American Educational Research Association.

Taylor, B., & Pearson, P. D. (2002). *Teaching reading, effective schools, accomplished teachers.* Mahwah, NJ: Lawrence Erlbaum.

Tharp, R., & Gallimore, R. (1988). *Rousing minds to life: Teaching learning and schooling in social context.* New York: Cambridge University.

Trueba, H. (1989). *Raising silent voices: Educating the linguistic minorities for the 21st century.* New York: Newbury.

Valdes, G. (1996). *Con respecto: Bridging the distances between culturally diverse families and schools.* New York: Teachers College Press.

Villegas, A. M. (1988). School failures and cultural mismatch: Another view. *The Urban Review, 20*(4), 253–265.

Villegas, A. M. (1991). *Culturally responsive pedagogy for the 1990's and beyond.* Princeton, NJ: Educational Testing Service.

Villegas, A. M., & Lucas, T. (2002). *Educating culturally responsive teachers: A coherent approach.* Albany, NY: SUNY Press.

Walton, P., & Carlson, R. (1997). Responding to social change: California's new standards for teacher credentialing. In J. King, E. Hollins, & W. Hayman (Eds.), *Preparing teachers for cultural diversity* (pp. 222–240). New York: Teachers College Press.

Waxman, H., & Padron, Y. (2002). Research-based teaching practices that improve the experiences of English language learners. In L. Minaya-Rowe (Ed.), *Teacher training and effective pedagogy in the context of student diversity* (pp. 3–38). Greenwich, CT: Information Age Publishing.

Weiner, L. (1989). Asking the right questions: An analytic framework for reform of urban teacher education. *The Urban Review, 21*(3), 151–161.

Weiner, L. (1993). *Preparing teachers for urban schools.* New York: Teachers College Press.

Weiner, L. (1999). *Urban teaching: The essentials.* New York: Teachers College Press.

Wideen, M., Mayer-Smith, J., & Moon, B. (1998). A critical analysis of the research on learning to teach: Making the case for an ecological perspective on inquiry. *Review of Educational Research, 68*(2), 130–178.

Winfield, L. (1986). Teacher beliefs toward at-risk students in inner urban schools. *The Urban Review, 18*(4), 253–267.

Wubbels, T. (1992). Taking account of student teachers' preconceptions. *Teaching and Teacher Education, 8*(2), 137–150.

Zeichner, K. (1996). *Educating teachers for cultural diversity.* In K. Zeichner, S. Melnick, & M. Gomez (Eds.), *Currents of reform in preservice teacher education* (pp. 133–175). New York: Teachers College Press.

Zeichner, K. (2003). The adequacies and inadequacies of three current approaches to the reform of teacher education in the U.S. *Teachers College Record, 105*(3), 490–519.

Zeichner, K., & Hoeft, K. (1996). Teacher socialization for cultural diversity. In J. Sikula (Ed.), *Handbook of research on teacher education* (2nd ed.) (pp. 176–198). New York: Macmillan.

6

Turnaround Teachers and Schools

Bonnie Benard

*How do we help each teacher envision a future for his or her stu-
dents that is not pathological? How do we counter society's in-
difference toward poor children of color? This is a monumental
task, a teacher's task. Teachers must believe their students can
experience a future that is full of hope, promise, and potential,
or they should, quite simply, not teach our children.*

—William Ayers and Patricia Ford (1996, p. 326)

In the five years since the first edition of this volume, our society has
witnessed only beginning progress in closing the achievement gap. The
strategies called for five years ago in the first edition of this book
remain even more critical today: providing school-linked services and
resources for urban communities and families; making urban schools and
classrooms culturally compatible with students' home backgrounds and
conditions; having teachers who communicate high expectations, caring,
and cultural sensitivity; giving urban students opportunities to learn; creating school environments that foster students' resilience; and fostering
high levels of teacher engagement (Williams, 1996).

In fact, given that five of the above six strategies are directly related to
the quality of teaching, it should come as no surprise that quality teaching was identified in a recent analysis of the National Assessment of Educational Progress (Wenglinsky, 2000) as the most powerful influence on
academic achievement. "After all," states yet another study, "the only path
to greater academic achievement that is open to all students is the one
they and teachers travel daily together" (Wilson & Corbett, 2001, p. 119).

While quality teaching might mean many things, when students, the
ultimate consumers of quality teaching, are asked what this means to
them, they are unequivocal in their answer: a caring teacher who accepts

"no excuses" and who refuses to let them fail (Wasley, Hampel, & Clark, 1997; Wilson & Corbett, 2001).

These students are also saying what long-term research into human resilience has found. Lifespan developmental studies of how young people successfully overcome risks and challenges—such as troubled families, poverty, and disadvantages—to become "competent, confidant, and caring" (Werner & Smith, 1992) individuals, as well as successful students, clearly document the power of caring teachers and schools that convey high expectations and provide opportunities for their active participation in the learning process (Higgins, 1994; Masten & Coatsworth, 1998; Rutter, Maughan, Mortimore, Ouston, & Smith, 1979; Werner & Smith, 1989, 1992, 2001).

Resilience studies provide critical information to closing the achievement gap, because they give educators clear evidence that all children and youth have the capacity to be educated, and that teachers and schools do have the power to educate them successfully. According to Lisa Delpit (1996), "When teachers are committed to teaching all students, and when they understand that through their teaching change CAN occur, then the chance for transformation is great" (p. 208).

Resilience research identifies the specific practices and beliefs of "turnaround" teachers and schools. Moreover, these studies are corroborated by research into the characteristics of teachers and schools that successfully motivate and engage youth, including those now labeled "high performing, high poverty schools" (Baldwin, 2001; Comer, Haynes, Joyner, & Ben-Avie, 1996; Diero, 1996; James, Jurich, & Estes, 2001; Ladson-Billings, 1994; Meier, 1995; Resnick et al., 1997; Rutter et al., 1979; Sergiovanni, 1996, 2000). Perhaps most importantly, anyone who has had a personal experience of transformative teachers and schools would probably find that experience validated by both resilience research and the successful school studies.

This chapter will examine the transformative power of teachers and schools and describe the practices of these turnaround people and places, providing some case studies as well as self-assessment tools for moving transformation forward in teaching and school dynamics.

The Power of a Teacher

Can you identify a special teacher or mentor in your life? What impact did that person have on your life? What was it about that person that influenced you?

A common finding in resilience research is the power of a teacher—often without realizing it—to tip the scale from risk to resilience. Werner and Smith (1989) found that, "Among the most frequently encountered positive role models in the lives of the children . . . outside of the family circle, was a favorite teacher. For the resilient youngster, a special teacher was not just an instructor for academic skills but also a confidant and positive model for personal identification" (p. 162). The following story provides an example of this long-term influence through short-term involvement.

Becky was a senior taking a class on study methods. Her teacher, Bruce Wilkinson, described Becky's story in the following manner:

"When grading my first set of papers, I came to one that was one page long, looked as if it had been wadded into a ball and then smoothed out and had ketchup smeared on the bottom right corner. Immediately I put an F at the top of the paper.

"The next time the class met, I made an effort to find out more about this student. Becky sat in the back of the room. Her hair was a mess, her clothes looked like her paper, and she was not in good shape. When I collected papers, I looked for Becky's. Trying to maintain an optimistic outlook, I thought to myself, 'Maybe Becky is supposed to be my pet project this semester.'

"At the top of Becky's paper I wrote, 'Dear Becky: I believe that this paper does not truly reflect your true talents and abilities. I can't wait to see what you can really do.' I didn't place a grade on the paper. What good would another F do?

"Her next paper improved to a D–. This time I wrote another note. 'Dear Becky: Thanks for cracking the door just a bit. I didn't think I was wrong about you. How about the privilege of seeing what you can really do when you apply yourself? I'm on your team.' Each paper that came in that semester improved over the last one.

"Finally, Becky received an A+. On that paper I wrote, 'Dear Becky: Your improvement is nothing less than astonishing. I always knew you had it in you. It has been a pleasure to watch you grow in my class.' "

Several years later, Wilkinson received a letter. He didn't recognize the name on the return address. The letter went something like this: "Dear Dr. Wilkinson: I just had to write you a letter after all these years. You don't recognize my name because I am now married. I don't know how to thank you. You are the first person in my entire life to help me believe there was anything good about me. Your class changed my life. I am happily married and the mother of two sons." (Cash, 1997)

Practices of Turnaround Teachers

Students desire authentic relationships in which they are trusted, given responsibility, spoken to honestly and warmly, and treated with dignity and respect. They feel adults inside schools are too busy, don't understand, or just don't care about them. (Poplin & Weeres, 1992)

In story after story, turnaround teachers like Bruce Wilkinson are described as providing, in their own personal styles and ways, three supports and opportunities (also called *protective factors*) critical to healthy development and school success: caring relationships, high expectations, and opportunities for participation/contribution (Benard, 1991, 1996). Closing the achievement gap depends on teachers providing these protective factors, no matter what subject, grade, or students they teach.

Caring Relationships

"What is the difference between scribble and a letter of the alphabet to a child? The only reason the letter is meaningful and worth learning and remembering is because a meaningful other wants him or her to learn and remember it" (Comer, cited in Steele, 1992).

Turnaround teachers are, first and foremost, caring. They convey *loving support*—the message of being there for a youth, of trust, of unconditional love. Resilient survivors talk about such teachers' "quiet availability," "fundamental positive regard," and "simple sustained kindness" (Higgins, 1994, pp. 324–25). This can be—and often is—a brief one-to-one connection: words of encouragement written on a paper as Wilkinson's were in the above vignette, a touch on the shoulder, a smile, a greeting. *Respect*, the giving of acknowledgement, seeing students for who they are, as equals "in value and importance," figures high in turnaround relationships and schools, according to renowned urban educator Deborah Meier (1995, p. 120). Clearly, Becky felt this respect from her teacher.

Wilkinson also conveys a sense of *compassion*—nonjudgmental love that looks beneath a student's negative behavior and sees the pain and suffering. Turnaround teachers do not take their students' behavior personally. They understand that no matter how negative behavior is, that student is doing the best thing possible given present circumstances. Sandy McBrayer, founder of an alternative school for homeless youth and 1994 National Teacher of the Year, declares, "People ask me what my 'methods' are. I don't have a method. But I believe one of the things that makes me an adequate or proficient teacher is that I never judge and I tell my kids I love them every day" (Bacon, 1995, p. 44).

Finally, being *interested in, actively listening to,* and *getting to know the gifts* of students conveys the message, "You are important in this world; you matter." Wilkinson takes the time, "makes an effort" to find out more about Becky's life, even makes her his "pet project" for the semester. Knowing the stories of their students' lives is an absolute must if teachers are to have the empathy necessary to establish caring relationships.

Turnaround teachers not only establish caring relationships between themselves and students, they consciously promote these between students, between themselves and family/community members, and between students and family/community members. Inviting family and community members into the classroom to mentor and work with students, either one on one or in small groups, is a win-win way to increase caring in the classroom exponentially and to promote caring family-school-community partnerships. Some strategies for increasing these caring relationships are listed below (Figure 6.1) and can be used as a self-assessment checklist.

FIGURE 6.1

Caring and Support

Place a check mark by the items already being implemented. Place a plus sign by items you would like to improve or strengthen.

____Creates and sustains a caring climate	____Is nonjudgmental
____Aims to meet developmental needs for belonging and respect	____Looks beneath "problem" behavior
	____Reaches beyond the resistance
____Is available/responsive	____Uses humor/smiles
____Offers extra individualized help	____Is flexible
____Has long-term commitment	____Shows patience
____Creates one-to-one time	____Uses community-building process
____Actively listens/gives voice	____Creates small, personalized groups
____Shows common courtesy	____Creates opportunities for peer-helping
____Respects others	
____Uses appropriate self-disclosure	____Uses cross-age mentors (older students, family/community members)
____Pays personalized attention	
____Shows interest	
____Checks in	
____Gets to know hopes and dreams	Creates connections to resources
____Gets to know life context	____*Education*
____Gets to know interests	____*Employment*
____Shows respect	____*Recreation*
____Fundamental positive regard	____*Health, counseling, and social services*

High Expectations

Regardless of the specific elements of a "no-excuses" strategy, wherever the term is used, it conveys the integral role that educators who do not give up on any students can play in the educational lives of children and youth who have traditionally not performed well. (Wilson & Corbett, 2001, p. 121)

At the core of caring relationships are high expectations that reflect the teacher's deep belief in the student's innate resilience and capacity to learn. Werner (1996) states, "One of the wonderful things we see now in adulthood is that these children really remember one or two teachers who made the difference . . . who looked beyond outward experience, their behavior, their unkempt—oftentimes—appearance and saw the promise" (p. 24). She could have been describing Bruce Wilkinson. A consistent description of turnaround teachers is their *seeing the possibility:* "They held visions of us that we could not imagine for ourselves" (Delpit, 1996, p. 199).

As Wilkinson demonstrates, these teachers not only see the possibility, they *recognize existing strengths, mirror them back,* and help students see where they are strong. They assist youth, especially those who have been labeled or oppressed, in understanding their personal power to *reframe* their life narratives from damaged victim or school failure to resilient survivor and successful learner. Turnaround teachers help youth see the power they have to think differently about their lives and construct alternative meanings for them. They help them

- To not take *personally* the adversity in their lives ("You aren't the cause—nor can you control—your father's drinking or your friend's racist remarks"),
- To not see adversity as *permanent* ("This too shall pass"), and
- To not see setbacks as *pervasive* ("You can rise above this"; "This is only one part of your life experience"). (Adapted from Seligman, 1995)

Inherent in high expectations is the "no-excuses" message. In Wilson and Corbett's (2001) study of Philadelphia schools, "Teachers' refusal to accept any excuses for failure separated the classrooms in which students succeeded from those in which they did not. . . . The teacher, according to students, acted out of a determination to promote success. . . . [Teachers] 'stayed on students' until they got it" (pp. 120–121).

As Warren Bennis (1994) related in his classic examination of leadership, "In a study of school teachers, it turned out that when they held high expectations for their students, that alone was sufficient to cause an increase of 25 points in the students' I.Q. scores." Of course, high expectations must be accompanied by the supports necessary to achieve them. High standards without concomitant supports would not only be ludicrous but cruel and frustrating, robbing students of their intrinsic motivation for learning.

High-expectation messages from turnaround teachers are *student-centered*. These teachers understand that successful learning means engaging the *whole* child, not just the cognitive but the social, emotional, physical, and spiritual parts. They also understand that student *motivation* is driven by needs for love and belonging, respect, autonomy/power, mastery, challenge, fun, and meaning, and that successful learning experiences are designed to meet as many of these needs as possible (for example, cooperative learning or arts-based games and projects can actually meet all of these).

Being student-centered also means connecting learning to students' lives, using the student's own culture, strengths (or intelligences), interests, goals, and dreams as the beginning point for learning. Wilkinson showed how *starting with students' strengths*, instead of their problems and deficiencies, can enlist students' intrinsic motivation, keeping them in a hopeful frame of mind to learn and work on any concerns. Multiple intelligence research studies provide support for this approach (Gardner, 2000).

Some strategies for conveying high expectations to students—and many apply to working with family and community members as well—are listed in Figure 6.2 and can be used as a self-assessment checklist.

Opportunities for Student Participation and Contribution

When one has no stake in the way things are, when one's needs or opinions are provided no forum, when one sees oneself as the object of unilateral actions, it takes no particular wisdom to suggest that one would rather be elsewhere. (Sarason, 1990, p. 83)

Creating opportunities for active student participation and contribution is a natural outgrowth of working from this strengths-based perspective. If teachers care for their students and believe in them, they must give them a "voice," the chance to be heard. This means they must listen deeply. As one successful teacher of culturally diverse students puts it, "You have to know the kids; they may be from all kinds of backgrounds and cultures, but if you really *listen* to them, they'll tell you how to teach them." Moreover, you will be supporting their autonomy and initiative, two personal strengths associated with healthy development and lifelong learning (Deci, 1995; Werner & Smith, 1989).

FIGURE 6.2

High Expectations

Place a check mark by the items already being implemented. Place a plus sign by items you would like to improve or strengthen.

____ Sustains a high-expectation climate

____ "No-excuses/Never-give-up" philosophy

____ Aims to meet developmental needs for mastery and challenge

____ Believes in innate capacity of all to learn

____ Focuses on whole child (social, emotional, cognitive, physical, spiritual)

____ Understands the needs motivating student behavior and learning

____ Sees culture as an asset

____ Challenges and supports ("You can do it; I'll be there to help.")

____ Connects learning to students' interests, strengths, experiences, dreams, goals

____ Encourages creativity and imagination

____ Conveys optimism and hope

____ Affirms/encourages the best in others

____ Attributes the best possible motive to behavior

____ Articulates clear expectations/boundaries/structure

____ Disciplines strictly and fairly

____ Provides clear explanations

____ Holds students accountable

____ Models boundary-setting/adaptive distancing

____ Uses rituals and traditions

____ Recognizes strengths and interests

____ Mirrors strengths and interests

____ Uses strengths and interests to address concerns/problems

____ Uses a variety of instructional strategies to tap multiple intelligences

____ Employs authentic assessment

____ Groups students heterogeneously

____ Continuously challenges racism, sexism, ageism, classism, homophobia

____ Helps to reframe self-image from at-risk to at-promise

____ Helps to reframe problems to opportunities

____ Conveys message to students that they are resilient

____ Sees students as *constructors* of their own knowledge and meaning

____ Teaches critical analysis

____ Encourages self-awareness of moods and thinking

____ Relates to family and community members with high expectations

____ Calls home to report students' good behavior and achievements

____ Helps family members see students' strengths, interests, goals

Turnaround teachers give students lots of opportunities to *make choices*, including creating the governing rules of the classroom. They involve students in curriculum planning, hold regular class meetings, give them choices in their learning experiences, and use participatory evaluation strategies such as portfolios and other forms of authentic assessment. They engage students in active problem solving by asking questions that encourage self-reflection, critical thinking, consciousness, and dialogue (especially around salient social and personal issues).

Even with respect to classroom discipline, Kohn's (1993, 1996) main advice is, "Bring the kids in on it! . . . Instead of reaching for coercion, engage children and youth in a conversation about the underlying causes of what is happening and work together to negotiate a solution. . . . It is in classrooms and families where participation is valued above adult control that students have the chance to learn *self-control*" (1993, pp. 14, 18).

Rutter and colleagues (1979) did seminal research on effective urban schools in poor communities—that is, schools in which the rates of delinquency and dropping out actually *declined* the longer students were in them. Rutter found them to be schools in which students "were given a lot of responsibility. They participated very actively in all sorts of things that went on in the school; they were treated as responsible people and they reacted accordingly" (Pines, 1984, p. 65).

These schools provide lots of opportunities for *experiential learning* in which students do hands-on work and engage with materials, people, projects, and experiences. One student explains why she likes her science class: "We have lots of fun. All we do is projects where we try and understand how variables affect each other. Everyone understands what we are doing 'cause we do lots of hands-on stuff. We also sing and dance in there. The teacher comes up with songs for things that help everyone remember stuff" (Wilson & Corbett, 2001, p. 99).

Evaluations of adventure/outdoor experiential learning (ropes/challenge courses, wilderness adventures) have found, once again, positive social, emotional, behavioral, and cognitive (academic) outcomes in students involved in these programs (Hattie, Marsh, Neill, & Richards, 1997). Furthermore, their grades in school actually *increased* the further away they were in time from the experience. *Arts-based learning*, having the opportunities for creative expression, including poetry, creative writing, and all other forms of the arts, is a highly successful research-proven strategy for improving school success in all students (Catterall, 1997). The creative arts also serve as a critical tool for teachers to learn about students' lives.

Another powerful approach for promoting school and life success lies in giving students the opportunity to work with and help others through research-proven strategies such as cooperative learning, reciprocal peer tutoring, peer-helping, project-based learning, and service-learning. Service-learning evaluations, both national and at the state level, have consistently found this strategy to promote holistic positive outcomes in students, including their core subject grade point averages and standardized test scores (Melchior, 1996, 1998; RPP International, 1998). When students have teachers who encourage them to work with and help others, and to give their gifts back to the community, youth develop the attitudes and competencies characteristic of healthy development and successful learning, such as social competence, problem solving, and a sense of self and future.

Some strategies for increasing student participation and contribution—many of which apply to working with family and community members as well—are listed below (Figure 6.3) and can be used as a self-assessment checklist.

The following story told by a continuation high school teacher captures the turnaround process that can happen when teachers provide the three critical protective factors for students—when they care enough to find out

FIGURE 6.3

Participation / Contribution

Place a check mark by the items already being implemented. Place a plus sign by items you would like to improve or strengthen.

_____Builds a democratic, inclusive community

_____Practices equity and inclusion

_____Aims to meet developmental needs for power/autonomy and meaning

_____Provides opportunities for planning

_____Provides opportunities for decision making

_____Provides opportunities for problem solving

_____Empowers students to create classroom rules

_____Holds regular and as-needed class meetings

Infuses communication skills into all learning experiences

_____*Reading*

_____*Writing*

_____*Relationship*

_____*Cross-cultural*

Creates opportunities for creative expression

_____*Art*

_____*Music*

_____*Writing/poetry*

_____*Storytelling/drama*

Provides opportunities for students to use/contribute their

_____*Strengths and interests*

_____*Goals and dreams*

_____*Gives meaningful responsibilities*

Includes and engages marginalized groups

_____*Girls/women*

_____*Students of color*

_____*Students with special needs*

_____Infuses service/active learning

_____Uses adventure/outdoor, experience-based learning

_____Offers community service

_____Offers peer-helping

_____Offers cross-age helping

_____Offers peer support groups

_____Uses cooperative learning

_____Provides ongoing opportunities for personal reflection

_____Provides ongoing opportunities for dialogue/discussion

_____Uses small interest-based groups

_____Uses group process/cooperative learning

_____Uses restorative justice circles in place of punitive discipline

_____Engages students—especially those on the margin—in a school climate improvement task force

_____Invites the participation and contribution of family and community members in meaningful classroom activities—not just cookie-baking!

---

a student's story, start with the student's strengths, and give the student an opportunity to give back a "gift" to the community:

One student who'd been in a bad car accident was really depressed. He didn't want to be here. . . . He would come into the class and put his head down on the desk. . . . The only thing that captured any of his interest was reptiles. We got him involved in a service-learning project at a local botanical garden. He became a docent and a virtual expert on reptiles. One Saturday a USDA forester and I were scheduled to give a talk at the botanical gardens. I had to leave early, so I asked this student if he'd come and fill in after I left. He agreed to come and speak about reptiles. His presentation especially impressed a woman in the audience, a director at a local museum. She asked the student if he'd come to take care of reptiles at the museum. Now this student is the director of the children's discovery section at the museum. (RPP International, 1998, p. 55)

These three protective factors are so powerful because they are how students—and everyone else—meet the basic human needs for love and belonging; for respect, power, accomplishment, and learning; and ultimately for meaning. No matter what subject matter teachers teach, they can do it in the same caring and empowering way as the turnaround teachers—and at no extra cost.

It is what teachers *model* that makes the final difference. Social learning theorists say that most of learning comes from the models around the learner. If teachers are caring and respectful, if they never give up on their students, if they help them discover and use their strengths, if they give them ongoing responsibilities as active decision makers—the students will learn empathy, respect, the wise use of power, self-control, responsibility, persistence, and hope. Moreover, when teachers model this invitational behavior, they create a *classroom climate* in which caring, respect, and responsibility are the behavioral norms.

The Power of Schools

"A school can create a coherent environment," a climate more potent than any single influence—teachers, class, family, neighborhood—"so potent that for at least six hours a day it can override almost everything else in the lives of children" (Edmonds, 1986).

Young people continually describe schools and classrooms that have been turnaround experiences as being like "a family," "a home," "a community"—even "a sanctuary." One young woman writes, "School was my church, my religion. It was constant, the only thing that I could count on every day. . . . I would not be here if it was not for school" (Children's Express, 1993). What turnaround schools do is illustrated by the following story of one school:

Emiliano Zapata Street Academy

Oakland, California, has a high school where there are no fights, no security guards, no metal detectors, no guns, and the police department visits to ticket meter violators rather than to arrest students. California and several other states that earned an F in "Student Climate" on Education Week's *latest state-by-state report card* (Quality Counts '98, *Special Issue, Jan. 8, 1998) would do well to examine this school's innovations.*

It is not a private school. It has low-income students and little technology, but it earned California's Distinguished School Award in 1990, and many students say it is the best school they have ever attended. A teacher who has been there for 25 years says she wouldn't teach anywhere else.

Asked to explain the difference in atmosphere at the Oakland Emiliano Zapata Street Academy, one student says this: "There was a fight a day at my old school. Here we are a family. Students will stop each other from fighting, because we don't want anyone to mess up the good thing we have here."

When teachers are pressed to explain how fights are avoided, several core ideals stand out. First, the Street Academy is an institution of tight relationships. Every staff member, for example, is the "consulting teacher" for 15 or 20 students. The teacher meets with those students twice a day and reviews a sheet on which other teachers have recorded information on that day's academic performance and behavior. The consulting teacher responds immediately to any problems—calling a parent, conferring with another student if there are conflicts. Problems are not allowed to fester and grow. Even verbal altercations are taken seriously, and students are not sent back to class until they have worked out a solution.

When I asked one student his response to all this scrutiny, he has a ready answer: "I like it. I don't have to watch my back all the time, and I'm going to graduate."

A second factor in play at the Street Academy is that, while many schools espouse multiculturalism, this school practices it in earnest. The staff's ethnic composition mirrors that of the students—mostly African American and Latino—and many staff members live in the community. Cultural content is not a tack-on item, but at the deep essence of the school. Racism is explicitly discussed; staff members embrace and respect each other across racial lines; and there is a stern response to cross-racial disrespect among students.

A third factor is that the Street Academy is small and its campus closed. Those who think that the 3,000-student American high school is the only possibility should look at the private schools where the wealthy send their children. They are small places where teachers are required to watch closely over the academic and personal development of their charges. Public high schools in other industrialized countries are also much smaller—averaging around 400 students in some European countries, for example.

Because the Street Academy is small and treats its students as whole human beings, youngsters tell the teachers what is actually happening in their lives. The English teacher might take a kid to McDonald's when his family is short on cash. The social studies teacher will find another youngster a shelter or a bus ticket. Every year, thousands of American candidates for teaching credentials are taught Maslow's hierarchy of needs as part of their educational psychology courses. And each year, those thousands of new teachers go to work in high schools that don't even acknowledge, let alone resolve, the most basic of those needs: food, shelter, safety, and a sense of belonging. Urban high schools cannot solve the array of problems confronting poor people in America, but no school can earn the respect of its students if it makes those problems and their victims invisible.

Finally, the Street Academy is self-renewing, creating teachers who get better every year instead of burning out. The principal has led the school for 21 years with a magical mix of democracy and toughness. Teachers have enormous latitude in creating new teaching methods and procedures, but the school's leader is demanding of everyone, including herself, when it comes to meeting student needs.

Many schools have a poor climate, because American adolescents have huge, unmet needs in the typical high school. Some parents have said that the Street Academy is like a "private school for poor kids." And that is what poor kids need—schools with the same atmosphere of discipline, hopeful expectation, and camaraderie that wealthy parents provide for their children.

—Kitty Kelly Epstein, "An Urban High School with No Violence,"
Education Week, March 4, 1998.

Practices of Turnaround Schools

Can you remember going to a school that felt like "family" or had a sense of community? What did this look like? What was going on?

The practices of turnaround schools like the Emiliano Zapata Street Academy provide the three protective factors: caring relationships, high expectations, and opportunities for participation and contribution. These exist through schoolwide structures, supports, and opportunities, not only for students, but for teachers, families, and the community. They create an "atmosphere of camaraderie, discipline, and hopeful expectation." These characteristics map closely to studies of schools that are successfully closing the achievement gap (James et al., 2001; MacBeath, Boyd, Rand, & Bell, 1995). The following strategies describe schools that have a vision and mission based on caring relationships, high expectations, and opportunities for participation. The list can be used as a school self-assessment tool.

- **Quality of relationships between teachers and students** is the primary focus of turnaround schools, according to Wilson and Corbett's study of Philadelphia schools (2001). Leaders of successful schools understand everything this chapter has discussed to this point. None of the other reforms that follow will be transformative unless the teacher-student relationship is caring, has high expectations, and is reciprocal. "Small classrooms [or any other reform] were not necessarily better if the teachers in them still accepted failure. It was the quality of the relationships in the classrooms that determined the educational value of the setting" (Wilson & Corbett, 2001, p. 122). This clearly seems to be the case in the Street Academy example, as it is "an institution of tight relationships," according to the writer.
- **Supporting teachers is sine qua non,** given they are the critical factor in turnaround schools. As one wise school administrator has remarked, "If you don't feed the teachers, they'll eat the students!" In other words, it's hard to give what you don't get. This means teachers need resources, time, professional development opportunities, and materials, as well as the three protective factors themselves. In order to develop a "self-renewing" school like Emiliano Zapata Street Academy, they need caring relationships with their colleagues, mentors, and school leaders, high expectations on the part of school leaders, and opportunities and time for collegial decision making and planning themselves. Most of the strategies on the checklists for teacher-student relationships apply also to the administrator-teacher relationship. Staff retreats, shared rituals, and team teaching also support turnaround teachers (Diero, 1996), as do teacher support and reflection groups (Palmer, 1998). Some schools even have "resiliency coordinators," volunteer therapists who mentor teachers in the three protective factors.
- **Consistency** across the school in discipline, pedagogy, and content creates clear, high expectations for all students. They know where they stand academically and behaviorally—and they all know they stand together. This is clear from the way all the students and teachers deal

128

with conflict at Emiliano Zapata Street Academy. This consistency creates an orderly, safe school—the number one prerequisite for learning to take place, according to brain science (Diamond & Hopson, 1998).

- **A shared mission based on meeting the needs of the whole student**—the physical, social, emotional, cognitive, and spiritual dimensions—describes turnaround schools (Baldwin, 2001; Diero, 1996). Attending to the students' needs for food, safety, belonging, respect, power, challenge, and meaning was the bottom line for the principal of the Emiliano Zapata Street Academy. She understood that real learning could not take place without this holistic focus.

- **Small learning communities** are an absolute must for lowering the achievement gap. Study after study has borne out the positive academic and other developmental outcomes of this strategy (Finn, Gerber, Achilles, & Boyd-Zaharias, 2001; Wasley et al., 2000). Smaller classes and smaller schools are two of the most powerful structural facilitators of relationships between teachers and students, teachers and parents, and students and students.

- **School-based mentoring** during and after school is now the most prevalent form of mentoring (Herrera, Sipe, & McClanahan, 2000). Rigorous documentation shows that mentoring produces positive health as well as positive social and academic outcomes in students (Tierney, Grossman, & Resch, 1995). Moreover, it is a primary approach in breaking down the walls between a school and the community. Hundreds of schools have created mentoring programs, linking community volunteers to students in after-school programs. In Street Academy's case, the teachers each served as mentors for small groups of their students. Other forms of mentoring include cross-age peer-helping/tutoring in which older students help younger ones. Research has documented that the tutor receives the most academic, social, and emotional benefits (Bearman, Bruckner, Brown, Theobald, & Philliber, 1999).

- **Career exploration,** and for older students, **high school transition programs,** are a high priority for keeping learning meaningful and connected to students' lives. Effective examples of the latter in closing the achievement gap are tech prep, AVID, I-Have-A-Dream, Sponsor-A-Scholar, and Upward Bound (James et al., 2001). Having a sense of purpose, goals, and a future is a primary characteristic of resilient survivors and learners (Benard, 1991, 1996), and is both a motivator and an outcome of academic success. Many of the programs and schools identified as closing the achievement gap have a school-to-career focus.

- **Early intervention services** in the form of counseling, support groups, and student assistance programs provide learning supports that are often critical to helping students stay in school and achieve academically. These services are inherently collaborative, with the school interfacing with student services professionals, social services providers, community-based organizations, law enforcement officials, and business and community leaders.

- **Diversity** of all sorts is seen as a strength and an attribute to celebrate. With this value, successful schools serving students of color, like Emiliano Zapata Street Academy, have a diverse teaching staff that reflects their student body, and staff that are able to form positive relationships with students' families and communities. These schools see family members as cultural resources, inviting them into the classroom to serve as resources in educating their children. Comer's work in this arena is a classic example of the positive academic and social outcomes for students and their families in using this approach (Comer et al., 1996).

- **After-school programs** are becoming a critical link in promoting school-community partnerships, as well as a vital support to students in promoting academic success and providing a safe haven in the after-school hours (U.S. Departments of Education, Justice, and Health and Human Services, 1998). A recent survey by the National Association of Elementary School Principals (2001) found that these programs have more than doubled during the 1990s. Beacon schools in New York City, San Francisco, and several other cities are a wonderful model of after-school programs based on providing the three protective factors. They consistently find positive youth development outcomes, including that of the academic dimension (Walker & Arbreton, 2002; Warren, Brown, & Freudenberg, 1999).

- **Ongoing assessment of students for quality improvement** is the bottom line for educational reform to close the achievement gap. This means schools need a structure for hearing the student perspective, especially in terms of how well the school is providing the three protective factors. Assessment can include regular breakfast meetings with the principal, as some schools have established. Several other schools (Laboratory Network Project, 2001) use student focus groups as an ongoing way to monitor the school climate or aid in schoolwide decision making. Fullan, considered an educational change guru, states, "Educational change, above all, is a people-related phenomenon for each and every individual. Students, even little ones, are people, too. Unless they have some meaningful (to them) role in the enterprise, most educational change, indeed most education, will fail. I ask the reader not to think of students as running the school, but to entertain the following question: What would happen if we treated the student as someone whose opinion mattered in the introduction and implementation of reform in schools?" (1991, p. 170).

- **Family-school-community partnerships** are valued and recognized as essential in closing the achievement gap. Turnaround schools know they can't bring about the change alone and welcome the contribution of families, community-based organizations, and community volunteers. They also recognize that families and community members—especially in resource-challenged communities—need supports and opportunities themselves in order to be contributing partners. Therefore, turnaround schools work together with community-based organizations to provide not only *after-school and mentoring programs* for students, but *family math, writing, and mediation programs,* as well as *family resource centers, full-service schools, early childhood programs, school-community gardens,* and even *community schools* that serve students, their families, and their communities (Dryfoos, 1998; Schor, 1997). Just as supporting teachers is critical to student achievement, so is supporting families and community members who, in turn, serve youth.
- **Students are out in the community doing service-learning.** Just as mentoring gets community adults into the lives of students, community service-learning gets students into the lives of adults. A schoolwide oral history project of the community can not only help engage students in their schooling, but build a real sense of community among all the partners. It is hard to imagine a strategy more research based, more grounded in the three protective factors, and more motivating to students, for the underlying message of community service-learning is, "You are a valued member of our community; we need you to help us make our community a better place for everyone." Nothing is more transformative for a struggling or challenged student than to be seen as a community resource—instead of a school problem.

It All Starts with Our Beliefs

We contend that something else is missing in recipes for urban reform: an underlying belief that all children can succeed and that it is the schools' responsibility to ensure that this happens. . . . Some educators say "all children can succeed—if they make an effort"; others say "all children can succeed—if only the parents would help"; and still others, fewer in number, assert "all children can succeed—and it's my job to make sure they do. . . ." This [last] philosophy must infuse all efforts to improve urban education. (Wilson & Corbett, 2001, pp. 117–118)

The bottom line and starting point for creating turnaround classrooms and schools that provide caring relationships, high expectations, and opportunities for participation is the deep belief on the part of teachers and school staff that every child and youth has innate resilience, the capacity for healthy development and successful learning (see Figure 6.4). What this implies, then, is that, "Professional development [must be] focused on adults' underlying beliefs about a school's role in supporting student learning rather than discrete 'best practices'. . . . Even if a teacher tried to adhere to current thinking about best instructional practices, students in these schools would still fall through the cracks unless teachers believe it is his or her responsibility to construct a supportive net to catch them" (Wilson & Corbett, 2001, pp. 120–121).

So how do we change beliefs? A few simple strategies follow:

- **Provide for teachers what students need.** As discussed earlier, and as seen in Figure 6.4, caring relationships, high expectations, and opportunities for participation promote teacher self-efficacy, "a belief

FIGURE 6.4

Teacher Resilience in Action

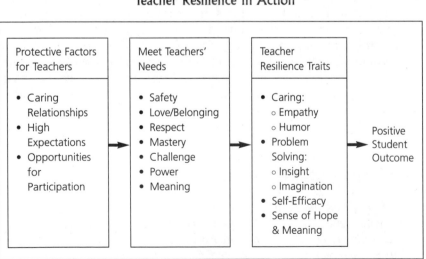

that students can learn if taught and a belief in one's own ability to successfully teach them" (Sergiovanni, 2000, p. 131).

- **Reflect personally and dialogue as a staff on beliefs about innate resilience.** This means every adult in the school must personally grapple with questions like: "What does it mean in my classroom and school if ALL kids have the capacity for healthy development and successful learning?" "What tapped my resilience?" "What occurred in my life that brought out my strength and capacity?" "How am I connecting this knowledge to what I do in the classroom?"

- **Form a resiliency study group.** Read the research on resiliency, including the studies of successful city schools. Share stories—both personal and literary—of successfully overcoming the odds. "It is important to read about struggles that lead to empowerment and to successful advocacy, for resilient voices are critical to hear within the at-risk wasteland" (Polakow, 1993, p. 269). It is through hearing others' stories and telling one's own that it becomes clear all stories, including those of students and their families, are really the *human* story. As Remen (1996) reminds us, "Stories that touch us in this place of common humanness awaken us and weave us together as a family once again" (p. xxvii). We develop the empathy that undergirds the belief in ourselves and others.

- **Try an initial experiment using the resiliency approach.** A teacher who finds this approach appealing can choose the most challenging student. Look for and identify all the student's strengths and mirror them back to her. Teach her she has innate resilience and the power to create her own reality. Create opportunities to have her participate and contribute her strengths. Be patient. A focus on small victories (which often grow into major transformations) helps dispel doubts about the approach.

- **Relax, have fun, and trust the process!** Working from one's own innate resilience and well-being engages the innate resilience and well-being of one's students, creating a positive self-fulfilling prophecy. Teaching becomes much more effortless, enjoyable, and self-renewing. Moreover, resiliency research, as well as research on nurturing teachers and successful schools, gives all the proof needed for teachers to lighten up, let go of their tight control, be patient, and trust the process.

When teachers care, believe in, and invite back "city kids," and when schools support teachers, students, and families and work in partnership with them, the achievement gap narrows and even closes. Both the "good" and "bad" news of closing the achievement gap is contained in Edmonds'

133

nearly 20-year-old prophetic statement: "We can, whenever and wherever we choose, successfully teach all children whose schooling is of interest to us. We already know more than we need to do that. . . . Whether or not we will ever effectively teach the children of the poor is probably far more a matter of politics than of social science" (Edmonds, 1986).

The bad news, according to even our most current reports (James et al., 2001), is that the national and state political will to provide a long-term commitment to policies supporting the needs of teachers and students on a large scale appears as much of a challenge today as it ever was. The good news is that social science validates a fairly simple recipe that each teacher has the power to accomplish, teacher by teacher, classroom by classroom, and school by school. And if educational change experts like Fullan are right, this is, indeed, the only way educational change to close the achievement gap can happen.

References

Ayers, W., & Ford, P. (Eds.). (1996). *city kids, city teachers: Reports from the front row.* New York: New Press.

Bacon, J. (1995). The place for life and learning: National teacher of the year, Sandra McBrayer. *Journal of Emotional and Behavioral Problems, 3*(4), 42–45.

Baldwin, J. (2001). Tales of the urban high school. *Carnegie Reporter,* 23–29.

Bearman, P., Bruckner, H., Brown, B., Theobald, W., & Philliber, S. (1999). *Peer potential: Making the most of how teens influence each other.* Washington, DC: National Campaign to Prevent Teen Pregnancy.

Benard, B. (1991). *Fostering resiliency in kids: Protective factors in the family, school, and community.* Portland, OR: Northwest Regional Educational Laboratory.

Benard, B. (1996). Fostering resilience in urban schools. In B. Williams (Ed.), *Closing the achievement gap: A vision for changing beliefs and practices* (pp. 96–119). Alexandria, VA: Association for Supervision and Curriculum Development.

Bennis, W. (1994). *On becoming a leader* (2nd ed.). New York: Perseus.

Cash, J. (1997, November/December). What good leaders do. *Thrust for Educational Leadership,* 22–25.

Catterall, J. (1997). Involvement in the arts and success in secondary school. *Americans for the Arts Monographs, 1*(9).

Children's Express (1993). *Voices from the future: Children tell us about violence in America.* New York: Crown.

Comer, J., Haynes, N., Joyner, E., & Ben-Avie, M. (Eds.). (1996). *Rallying the whole village: The Comer process for reforming education.* New York: Teachers College Press.

Deci, E. (1995). *Why we do the things we do: Understanding self-motivation.* New York: Penguin.

Delpit, L. (1996). The politics of teaching literate discourse. In W. Ayers and P. Ford (Eds.), *City kids, city teachers: Reports from the front row* (pp. 194–208). New York: New Press.

Diamond, M., & Hopson, J. (1998). *Magic trees of the mind: How to nurture your child's intelligence, creativity, and healthy emotions from birth through adolescence.* New York: Dutton.

Diero, J. (1996). *Teaching with heart: Making healthy connections with students.* Thousand Oaks, CA: Corwin Press.

Dryfoos, J. (1998). *Safe passage: Making it through adolescence in a risky society.* New York: Oxford University Press.

Edmonds, R. (1986). Characteristics of effective schools. In E. Neisser (Ed.), *The school achievement of minority children: New perspectives* (pp. 93–104). Hillsdale, NJ: Lawrence Erlbaum.

Epstein, K. (1998, March 4). An urban high school with no violence. *Education Week,* 45.

Finn, J., Gerber, S., Achilles, C., & Boyd-Zaharias, J. (2001). The enduring effects of small classes. *Teachers College Record, 103*(2), 145–183.

Fullan, M. (with Stiegelbauer, S.). (1991). *The new meaning of educational change.* New York: Teachers College Press.

Gardner, H. (2000). *Intelligence reframed: Multiple intelligences for the 21st century.* New York: Basic Books.

Hattie, J., Marsh, H., Neill, J., & Richards, G. (1997). Adventure education and Outward Bound: Out-of-class experiences that make a lasting difference. *Review of Educational Research, 67,* 43–87.

Herrera, C., Sipe, C., & McClanahan, W. (2000). *Mentoring school-age children: Relationship development in community based and school-based programs.* Philadelphia: Public/Private Ventures.

Higgins, G. (1994). *Resilient adults: Overcoming a cruel past.* San Francisco: Jossey-Bass.

James, D., Jurich, S., & Estes, S. (2001). *Raising minority academic achievement: A compendium of education programs and practices.* Washington, D.C.: American Youth Policy Forum.

Kohn, A. (1993, September). Choices for children: Why and how to let students decide. *Phi Delta Kappan, 75*(1), 8–20.

Kohn, A. (1996). *Beyond discipline: From compliance to community.* Alexandria, VA: Association for Supervision and Curriculum Development.

Laboratory Network Project. (2001). *Listening to students: Self-study toolkit.* Washington, DC: Office of Education and Research Improvement.

Ladson-Billings, G. (1994). *The dreamkeepers: Successful teachers of African American children.* San Francisco: Jossey-Bass.

MacBeath, J., Boyd, B., Rand, J., & Bell, S. (1995). *Schools speak for themselves: Toward a framework for self-evaluation.* London: The National Union of Teachers.

Masten, A., & Coatsworth, D. (1998). The development of competence in favorable and unfavorable environments: Lessons from research on successful children. *American Psychologist, 53*(2), 205–220.

Meier, D. (1995). *The power of their ideas.* Boston: Beacon Press.

Melchior, A. (1996). *National evaluation of Learn and Serve America school and community-based programs: Interim report: Appendices.* Washington, DC: Corporation for National Service.

Melchior, A. (1998). *National evaluation of Learn and Serve America school and community-based programs: Final report.* Washington, DC: Corporation for National Service.

National Association of Elementary School Principals (NAESP). (2001). *Survey of after-school programs.* Washington, DC: NAESP.

Palmer, P. (1998). *The courage to teach: Exploring the inner landscape of a teacher's life.* San Francisco: Jossey-Bass.

Pines, M. (1984, March). Resilient children: An interview with Michael Rutter. *Psychology Today,* 57–65.

Polakow, V. (1993). *Lives on the edge: Single mothers and their children in the other America.* Chicago: University of Chicago Press.

Poplin, M., & Weeres, J. (1992). *Voices from the inside: A report on schooling from inside the classroom.* Claremont, CA: Claremont Graduate School, Institute for Education in Transformation.

Remen, R. (1996). *Kitchen table wisdom: Stories that heal.* New York: Riverhead Books.

Resnick, M., Bearman, P., Blum, R., Bauman, K., Harris, K., Jones, J., Tabor, J., Beuring, T., Sieving, R., Shew, M., Ireland, M., Bearinger, L., & Udry, J. (1997). Protecting adolescents from harm: Findings from the National Longitudinal Study on Adolescent Health. *Journal of the American Medical Association, 278,* 823–832.

RPP International. (1998). *An evaluation of K–12 service-learning in California.* Sacramento, CA: California Department of Education.

Rutter, M., Maughan, B., Mortimore, P., Ouston, J., & Smith, A. (1979). *Fifteen thousand hours.* Cambridge, MA: Harvard University Press.

Sarason, S. (1990). *The predictable failure of educational reform.* San Francisco: Jossey-Bass.

Schor, L. (1997). *Common purpose: Strengthening families and neighborhoods to rebuild America.* New York: Doubleday.

Seligman, M. (1995). *The optimistic child.* Boston: Houghton Mifflin.

Sergiovanni, T. (1996). *Leadership for the schoolhouse.* San Francisco: Jossey-Bass.

Sergiovanni, T. (2000). *The lifeworld of leadership: Creating culture, community, and personal meaning in our schools.* San Francisco: Jossey-Bass.

Steele, C. (1992). Race and the schooling of Black Americans. *Atlantic Monthly, 29*(4), 67–78.

Tierney, J., Grossman, J., & Resch, N. (1995). *Making a difference: An impact study of big brothers/big sisters.* Philadelphia: Public/Private Ventures.

U.S. Departments of Education, Justice, and Health and Human Services. (1998). *Safe and smart: Making the after-school hours work for kids.* Washington, DC: Author.

Walker, K. & Arbreton, A. (2002). *Working together to build Beacon Centers in San Francisco: Evaluation findings from 1998–2000.* Philadelphia: Public/Private Ventures.

Warren, C., Brown, P., & Freudenberg, N. (1999). *Evaluation of the New York City Beacons: Summary of Phase 1 findings.* New York: Academy for Educational Development.

Wasley, P., Fine, M., Gladden, M., Holland, N., King, S., Mosak, E., & Powell, L. (2000). *Small schools, great strides: A study of new small schools in Chicago.* New York: Bank Street College of Education.

Wasley, P., Hampel, R., & Clark, R. (1997). *Kids and school reform.* San Francisco: Jossey-Bass.

Wenglinsky, H. (2000). *How teaching matters.* Princeton, NJ: Educational Testing Service.

Werner, E. (1996). How kids become resilient: Observations and cautions. *Resiliency in Action, 1*(1), 18–28.

Werner, E., & Smith, R. (1989). *Vulnerable but invincible: A longitudinal study of resilient children and youth.* New York: Adams, Bannister, & Cox.

Werner, E., & Smith, R. (1992). *Overcoming the odds: High-risk children from birth to adulthood.* New York: Cornell University Press.

Werner, E., & Smith, R. (2001). *Journey to the midlife: Risk, resilience, and recovery.* New York: Cornell University Press.

Williams, B. (Ed.). (1996). *Closing the achievement gap: A vision for changing beliefs and practices.* Alexandria, VA: Association for Supervision and Curriculum Development.

Wilson, B., & Corbett, H. (2001). *Listening to urban kids: School reform and the teachers they want.* New York: State University of New York Press.

7

Implementing Opportunity-to-Learn Assessment Strategies and Standards

Floraline I. Stevens

Opportunity to learn (OTL) is a concept recognized as an important macrolearning variable. This determination came about through such international research as the Second International Mathematics Study and Third International Mathematics and Science Study sponsored by the International Association for the Evaluation of Educational Achievement and studies by the Organization for Economic Cooperation Development (OECD). In these studies, content coverage was the major variable that differentiated high- and low-achieving schools. This finding led OECD (1991) to advocate standardizing content coverage or the "content has been taught" theory from country to country and from teacher to teacher when investigating students' academic achievement. In the United States, the National Assessment of Educational Progress used this same definition of OTL content coverage.

In the United States, much of the educational research has attributed differences among ethnic groups' academic achievement to race and socioeconomic status. In contrast, other countries cite content coverage as the major contributor of differentiated achievement. The question the United States needs to address is whether the lack of OTL or race and social class are the principal contributors to low academic achievement of students in urban schools. In international studies, race was not a contributor because the countries studied were overwhelmingly white.

OTL was meant to guarantee high standards of instruction. That is, what teachers needed to do in their classrooms was to ensure that the curriculum was covered through high-quality instruction. Prior to the development of a conceptual framework, OTL research was limited to investigation of one variable at a time, principally content coverage.

Educational equity issues surfaced as part of the school reform efforts in the 1990s. Researchers wanted to determine what practices and conditions public schools needed in order to ensure they could offer a quality education to all students, particularly poor and minority students. A more comprehensive and operational definition of OTL developed in response to these equity issues (Stevens, 1993b). A conceptual framework with four connected variables emerged that researchers found had a powerful influence on improving teachers' instructional practices and student learning (Stevens, 1993a).

The variables covered by the OTL conceptual framework include content coverage, content exposure, content emphasis, and quality of instructional delivery (Brophy & Good, 1986; Leinhart, 1983; McDonnell, Burstein, Catterall, Ormseth, & Moody, 1990; Stevenson & Stigler, 1992; Winfield, 1987). Descriptions of the variables are as follows:

- **Content coverage.** Teacher arranges for all students to have access to the core curriculum and to critical subject matter topics. Teacher ensures that there is curriculum content and test content overlap.
- **Content exposure.** Teacher organizes class time to include time-on-task for students. Teacher provides enough time for students to learn the content of the curriculum and to cover adequately a specific topic or subject.
- **Content emphasis.** Teacher selects topics to teach from the core curriculum and a dominant level of instruction. Teacher determines which skills to teach and emphasize to all students.
- **Quality of instructional delivery.** Teacher presents lessons that are coherent so students are able to understand and use the information learned. Teacher connects activities logically and sequentially with a beginning, middle, and end.

Transformation of Knowledge: From Declarative to Procedural

From 1993 to 1995, much time went into presenting educators with the expanded definition of OTL. In 1995, the Laboratory for Student Success, the Mid-Atlantic Regional Educational Laboratory at Temple University, funded an applied research project that investigated how to transform the concept of OTL into a set of assessment strategies and then train teachers to use and apply it in classrooms.

Some of those concerned with education reform have assumed that because research knowledge was available, schools would use and implement it in real-life situations. With respect to OTL research, dissemination of information had occurred through the development, production, and presentation of several papers on OTL, as well as speeches, seminar participation, and informal discussions. The result was a heightening of the awareness level of OTL for educators in the United States. However, what was missing was information about whether classroom teachers in U.S. public schools were considering OTL seriously. Therefore, the major thrust of further research has been to move or transform research knowledge on OTL to procedural knowledge. In other words, the goal was to transform theory into practice and assess its impact. Hence, classroom teachers received information about the four OTL variables and their accompanying OTL assessment strategies and practices in a series of workshop sessions with appropriate follow-up activities. What was still necessary to know was to what extent teachers were implementing OTL procedural knowledge in their classrooms.

Several researchers (Goertz, 1994; Porter, 1993; Schmidt, 1983; Stevens, 1993b) suggested strategies and practices to assess OTL in classrooms. These included having teachers keep journals or teacher logs, observing classroom instruction, conducting surveys of teachers and students, and doing periodic ongoing assessment of subject content. In addition, Bailey (1996) conducted a review of research to learn whether educators were continuing to advocate the suggested OTL assessment strategies and practices and if they had suggested additional options. The review found that the OTL strategies were still relevant and that no additional strategies and practices had surfaced.

Based on the findings from a national survey of urban classroom teachers (Stevens, Wiltz, & Bailey, 1998), a review of OTL research (Bailey, 1996), and information from the research on professional development (Fullan, 1990; Griffin, 1986; Loucks-Horsley et al., 1987; McLaughlin, 1991), the Laboratory for Student Success developed the format for an OTL Assessment Strategies Workshop and produced a workshop handbook. The workshop format followed the research that advocated professional development should be

- Schoolwide and context specific,
- Supportive of school principals,
- Long-term with adequate support and follow-up, and
- Encouraging of collegiality.

The workshop handbook included the following sections for each OTL assessment strategy: research on the strategy, an applicable definition, workshop activities, and a follow-up homework assignment. The appendix had a compilation of research articles that provided enhanced information on

OTL assessment strategies and their relationship to teaching and learning in the classroom.

Figure 7.1 describes the six OTL assessment strategies selected for the workshop that became the topical content of the materials included in the handbook. Figure 7.2 identifies the OTL framework variables that are relevant to each of the OTL assessment strategies.

During the workshop, the leader reviewed the OTL variables, introduced the OTL assessment strategy, and requested that participants read the introductory statement about the OTL assessment strategy. The leader selected a participant to read aloud the research on the strategy, then introduced the activity to enable participants to practice the strategy within the workshop. During the activity, participants worked in subgroups divided according to grade level, subject taught, or special assignment (counselor, coordinator, administrator) to allow them to practice the activity in smaller units. When appropriate, the subgroup leaders reported the results of their group assignment. The participants received a similar follow-up assignment to complete outside the workshop. The leader asked them to complete an evaluation form at the end of the workshop to rate the teacher-friendliness of the OTL assessment strategy and the quality of the workshop presentation. Finally, the workshop leader scheduled monthly visits to allow time for the teachers to conduct their follow-up work assignments.

Coming to Scale in Multiple Sites

Over a five-year period, the Laboratory for Student Success spent four years in seven schools and four school districts implementing and assessing the OTL project. One school district was on the West Coast, and three were in the mid-Atlantic region of the United States. Five of the schools were at the elementary level, and two were middle schools. All of the schools, whether in the pilot phase or in the implementation phase, were low-achieving schools with a high majority or 100 percent population of minority students. All of the schools had high percentages of poor students as evidenced by their participation in the free-lunch program. Six of the schools were already identified as at risk. In one school district, two schools in the project were originally identified in 1994–95 as being among five lowest achieving elementary schools; in another, state monitors were assigned to the project schools in 1998–99. It was not easy to bring an innovative research-based project to these schools, because many of the teachers felt demoralized and stigmatized. However, the interactive discussions during the sessions allowed the teachers to express their hurt and concerns. Consequently, they became more enthusiastic about the potential of the OTL activities to improve their students' academic achievement.

FIGURE 7.1

Description of the OTL Assessment Strategies

Strategy	Description
1. **Using networking and collaboration to improve instructional practices**	Teachers network to exchange information or services with other teachers. They meet to work jointly in an intellectual endeavor. Teachers work cooperatively and willingly to assist other teachers in an activity or project.
2. **Keeping journals**	Teachers keep a written record for their personal use of the assessment/effects of classroom lessons and activities; student behaviors, knowledge, and skills; and content covered, time allotted, and skills and concepts emphasized.
3. **Assessing student mastery of skills and concepts**	Teachers find out whether their teaching is successful and for which students. They learn in what respects their teaching needs improvement through assessment information. Teachers gain assessment information from norm-referenced testing, criterion-referenced testing, performance-based assessment, and portfolios.
4. **Conducting observations for constructive feedback**	Based on a mutually agreed-upon observation process, teachers will observe a colleague to provide feedback to improve teaching practices. Has a coherent lesson been presented? If not, the colleague can observe an example of good teaching practices to learn an effective teaching strategy.
5. **Conducting surveys about teacher practices**	A group of teachers is surveyed to measure the percent of time or frequency with which a teacher guides and coaches the development of students using various teaching approaches or strategies, e.g., lectures, cooperative learning, and hands-on activities. Teachers are surveyed to determine the extent that a topic assessed on a test was taught to students.
6. **Conducting surveys about school resources needed for effective teaching**	A group of teachers is surveyed to determine the amount of materials and equipment available for use in classrooms. Teachers are surveyed to determine the frequency with which students use those materials and equipment.

(continued)

FIGURE 7.2

Identification of the OTL Framework Variables
for Each OTL Assessment Strategy

OTL Assessment Strategy	OTL Framework Variable

1. **Using networking and collaboration to improve instructional practices**	1. *Content Coverage.* Teachers meet to decide on the core curriculum for the grade level or subject.
	2. *Content Exposure.* Teachers meet to share and learn effective strategies to organize their classes for time-on-task.
	3. *Content Emphasis.* Teachers meet to select critical topics, skills, and concepts from the curriculum to teach.
	4. *Quality of Instructional Delivery.*
	  a. Teachers meet to share information about and learn effective teaching practices and strategies.
	  b. Teachers meet to discuss journal-recorded information on the outcomes and effectiveness of the teaching practices and strategies used in their classrooms.
	  c. Teachers meet to discuss interval or unit assessment-testing information related to the outcomes and effectiveness of their teaching practices and strategies used in their classrooms.

2. **Keeping journals**	1. *Content Coverage.* Teachers record information on the content covered in the core curriculum. 2. *Content Emphasis.* Teachers select topics to record in their journals. 3. *Quality of Instructional Delivery.* Teachers record information on the effectiveness and outcomes of their teaching practices and strategies used in their classrooms.
3. **Assessing student mastery of skills and concepts**	1. *Content Coverage.* Teachers and administrators identify the required core curriculum. 2. *Content Emphasis.* Teachers and administrators determine which topics, skills, and concepts are essential for each grade level or subject and how many must be taught to mastery within a year. 3. *Quality of Instructional Delivery.* At grade level or departmental meetings, teachers determine which skills and concepts need improved teaching practices or strategies based on information from interval or unit assessment information.

(continued)

FIGURE 7.2 (cont.)

Identification of the OTL Framework Variables
for Each OTL Assessment Strategy

OTL Assessment Strategy	OTL Framework Variable
4. Conducting observations for constructive feedback	1. *Quality of Instructional Delivery.* Teachers present lessons on core curriculum topics for observation by a teacher colleague or administrator for constructive feedback, or teachers provide videos of lessons for constructive feedback.
5. Conducting surveys about teacher practices	1. *Content Coverage.* Teachers determine what is the core curriculum to teach. 2. *Content Exposure.* Teachers determine the amount of time to devote to teaching various topics, skills, and concepts. 3. *Content Emphasis.* Teachers determine which topics, skills, or concepts in the curriculum to teach.
6. Conducting surveys about school resources needed for effective teaching	1. *Quality of Instructional Delivery.* Teachers determine the instructional materials needed and available in their classrooms.

They gave evidence of their support for the OTL project by their cooperation in doing their "homework" assignments.

The development of OTL materials and the format for the workshops
occurred during 18 months of the project. Workshop piloting and field-
testing followed in the remaining years. Figure 7.3 shows the schedule for
implementation of the OTL project's development.

1996–97 School Year

Two elementary schools in a poor section of a large West Coast city
were pilots for both the format of the workshops and the use of the workshop materials. Both schools had low socioeconomic status, with very
high percentages of students on the free-lunch program. Project administrators made minor revisions based on the following criteria:

- The workshop leader's critical analysis of the implementation of the
  workshop format

FIGURE 7.3

Schedule for Implementation of the OTL Project

School Year	Activity	School
1995–96	Conduct national survey and develop handbook material	--
1996–97	Pilot the workshop format and handbook materials	Two elementary schools in large West Coast city
1997–98	Hold OTL workshops for six months	Two elementary schools in large East Coast city
1998–99	Hold OTL workshops for six months	Two middle schools in mid-Atlantic state
1999–2000	Hold OTL workshops for six months	One elementary school in mid-Atlantic state

- The workshop participants' positive evaluations
- The participants' use of the materials

An important preliminary finding was that the school where the principal attended all workshop sessions and was an active participant had better teacher participation in and enthusiasm for the workshop and higher students' test scores at the end of the school year. This finding emphasized that school principals needed to make a commitment to attend the workshops before they were conducted in the schools.

1997–98 School Year

The first year of the project's implementation was on the East Coast in a large city. The two elementary schools were both situated adjacent to or surrounded by public project housing. The two schools were identified as part of the group of the five lowest achieving elementary schools in the school district. Although both principals had agreed to attend the workshops with their teachers, only one held to the commitment. The other principal attended intermittently and did not stay throughout the sessions attended.

One finding was that beginning the workshop sessions with the "Networking and Collaboration" OTL assessment strategy was critical to the implementation of the other strategies. Another finding verified the preliminary finding that the principal's continuous attendance at the workshop sessions had a positive impact on teachers' attitudes and their commitment and ability to implement the strategies outside of the workshop sessions. Although teachers found all of the OTL assessment strategies to be teacher-friendly, finding the time to implement the "Networking and Collaboration" strategy was a major obstacle. Unless the principal made an effort to reconfigure the schedule or to uphold the scheduled times for teachers to meet, full implementation of this strategy was thwarted.

During this year, project administrators developed an implementation assessment checklist following the model of the degree of implementation checklist developed for a school intervention project (Wang, 1992). They used the checklist to interview the teachers at the end of the school year to determine if they were using any of the strategies after the workshop ended. It could also be used at designated intervals to determine progress toward full implementation of the OTL assessment strategies.

1998–99 School Year

In an effort to become more comprehensive in its scope of operation, the project moved to the middle school level. Selected schools were in another state in the mid-Atlantic region. As in the previous school district, authorities had identified the two middle schools as among those that should be taken over by the state. This meant that the state would assign monitors during the next school year. Again, there was a difference in the attendance of the two principals: One principal attended more of the sessions, but neither attended all of the sessions. Teachers rated the assessment strategies as teacher-friendly and committed themselves to doing the follow-up assignments. The interactive discussions in the workshop sessions allowed the teachers to voice their concerns about the issues in the schools. These discussions sometimes segued into how to use the OTL assessment strategies to address some of their school-related issues. These included low academic achievement of the students and discipline problems.

1999–2000 School Year

The last year of the project was spent in the same state as the middle schools. This time the principal and teachers of an elementary school requested the project. This request was in contrast to the situation in previous years, where predetermined school districts received service because they were extremely low-achieving and appeared in need of the project. In those schools, the project had contacted the principals but had not queried the teachers about what they wanted.

In the last elementary school, as in the other schools, the handbook provided for each teacher, the interactive discussions, and the follow-up homework assignments again appeared to constitute an effective format for the workshops.

Principal Buy-In for Site Participation

It is important that principals understand the potential impact of the OTL Assessment Strategies Workshops before being asked for their commitment to have the workshops in their schools. School principals should attend a one- or two-day intensive orientation workshop covering all of the strategies. This way, if the duties and responsibilities at the principals' schools do not allow them to attend workshop sessions continuously, they will nevertheless be knowledgeable already about the content of the workshops and the conditions needed to create a successful workshop experience for teachers and support staff. Therefore, the principals will be on an equal level with their school faculties about the workshop's content and processes. In addition, after the principals attend the orientation workshops, they can explain to their staff what the workshops are about and get their commitment to have the workshops in their schools. This process facilitates the implementation of the workshop for professional development staff.

A Tale of Two Elementary Schools

The workshop leader went to two elementary schools in January of the second year of the OTL project and made monthly visits until May. Teachers were initially wary of the leader because the principal of each school had accepted the idea of having the OTL workshops but had not discussed them with the teachers. When the workshop leader arrived for the first workshop sessions at the two schools, the teachers were polite but not wholly receptive to attending OTL Assessment Strategies Workshops. However, as the sessions continued, the teachers' attitudes became more positive. Their positive evaluations of the sessions mirrored their behavior in the sessions. Each month, the leader gave a workshop on one of the OTL assessment strategies.

The first workshop topic was "Using Networking and Collaboration to Improve Instructional Practices." The leader asked participants to read the definitions of networking and collaborating found in their workbooks. Next, the leader appointed teacher-participants to read aloud the research about networking and collaborating. Then the leader asked the teachers to form groups according to their grade level. Their first activity required that they meet in their groups and list the achievement problems in their school. Next, they read a case study found in the workbook about a school district with student achievement problems and reviewed the OTL variables (i.e., content coverage, content exposure, content emphasis, and quality of instructional delivery). Using the case study information and the OTL variables information, the teachers were to determine strategies to address the reading and mathematics achievement problems presented in the case study. Representatives from each grade level were to share the information about the strategies generated within their respective groups. Participants observed that the workshop activities were catalysts for having teachers meet and discuss instructional problems. As the workshop leader moved from group to group, the discussions focused on problem solving. One teacher commented that it was a new experience for her and her teacher-colleagues to meet solely to discuss issues of instruction.

The workshop leader then assigned a follow-up activity to move teachers from the workshop activity to their own school's educational problems. The assignment was for the teachers to meet within their grade levels and list the achievement problems in their school. They then chose from among the problems one in particular that their team would work to address. To prepare them for their grade-level meetings, the entire workshop group reviewed Schmoker's model for an efficient meeting, and the leader asked them to use this model when convening grade level meetings (Schmoker, 1996). Each grade level was to select one team member to report its work at the next professional development session.

The leader observed that by assigning "homework" to the teachers in each of the grade levels and allowing at least three weeks for them to meet prior to the next workshop, the possibility of implementation of "Networking and Collaboration" and other assessment strategies outside of the workshop environment greatly increased. Also, the knowledge that they would be reporting back to their teacher peers increased their drive to complete the assignment. At the next meeting, before going to a new topic, the group leaders reported their identified problems. There was discussion about the overlap of problems identified at each school and a decision to share the list with each school principal for further planning.

The two-and-one-half-hour workshop sessions were lively, with an interactive format that included multiple activities such as reading, discussing, planning, and reporting. Teachers were not passive participants. The leader provided them with information and asked them to meet and plan based on the information and their experiences. The workshop leader did not define any preset behaviors or outcomes. Therefore, many of the participants' responses were innovative once they met, developed actions, and designed their own OTL assessment strategies in the context of the topic presented. For example, at one of the schools, the 3rd grade chair reported that her group had met to solve the problem of a very heavy workload. Prior to attending the workshop on "Networking and Collaboration," the 3rd grade teachers were working singularly. At the grade level meeting following the workshop, they solved their workload problem by agreeing to divide up the work. At their meetings, they agreed on what they needed to teach during a certain period of time. Then each teacher assumed responsibility for preparing lessons and materials for one subject area. Teacher #1 was responsible for reading, Teacher #2 for mathematics, and Teacher #3 for English/language arts. Also, they agreed to meet regularly to discuss and assess where they were going with their classes and the progress or problems they needed to address. Teachers on several occasions wanted the workshop leader to remind their principals that they needed additional time for meeting and planning together.

At the end of the five months of professional development, the workshop leader asked the teachers to think about all of the OTL assessment strategies presented in the workshop sessions and to grade each as "not teacher-friendly," "teacher-friendly," and "very teacher-friendly." Again, the teachers said that all of the OTL assessment strategies were teacher-friendly. In particular, "Networking and Collaboration" was rated as very teacher-friendly. They assessed it as a form of professional development because they were able to share information about successful teaching practices used in the classrooms and obtain good ideas about how to improve their teaching. However, the teachers noted a common concern about this strategy—it required a commitment of time for meeting. On visits to the schools following the workshop year, the teachers urged the workshop leader to remind the principals to keep their commitment of providing time for the teachers to meet regularly so they could network and collaborate about instructional issues and practices in their schools.

In 1996–97, the year prior to the OTL Assessment Strategies Workshops, the two low-achieving schools had improved. The amount of positive change was not as large, however, as in 1997–98, when the project actually conducted the workshops. In fact, in one school, the increase in percentile scores in 1997–98 was almost double the amount of change in 1996–97.

For the 1996–97 school year, the two schools improved in reading. The reading percentile score for School #1 increased 11 points, from 20 to 31. The increase for School #2 was 10 points, from 32 to 42. For the 1997–98 school year, the two schools improved in reading at a greater rate, with their scores nearly reaching the median, that is, the 50th percentile. In School #1, the scores increased 14 points to 44 points between Fall 1997 and Spring 1998. In School #2, the percentile score was 47 in Spring 1998, up 19 points from its Fall 1997 score. A summary of these scores appears in Figure 7.4.

FIGURE 7.4

Percentile Reading Scores for Two Schools, 1996–98

School	Fall 1996	Spring 1997	Difference	Fall 1997	Spring 1998	Difference
#1	20	31	+11	30	44	+14
#2	32	42	+10	28	47	+19

Levels of demonstrated leadership played an important role in the schools' success. Achievement scores were higher at the school where the principal and assistant principal were consistent attendees at the workshop sessions. This was in contrast to the school where the assistant principal did not attend any workshop sessions and the principal's attendance was brief and intermittent.

OTL Standards and Assessment: Accountability in the Classroom

According to Lewis (1995), OTL standards have to do with the conditions and resources necessary to give students an equal chance to meet performance standards. The OTL variables describe teaching conditions needed to meet school districts' academic achievement requirements based on districtwide assessments. Schools can use these assessment scores to determine graduation from high school, grade promotion or retention at the same grade level, and other decisions as they emerge.

Educators hear very little about OTL standards (for example, of teacher-based teaching performance) and more about content and performance standards (for example, of student-based performance). Yet student outcomes are contingent upon the quality of teaching in the classroom. In large urban school districts, large numbers of teachers have no preservice training. How will the system hold these teachers accountable for providing good teaching conditions and producing good teaching in their classrooms if they do not have an intellectual or working knowledge of either?

The OTL Assessment Strategies Workshops were important because they introduced teachers to the OTL variables and to OTL assessment strategies that can assist them in becoming better teachers. These workshops dealt with the processes for learning. However, to be really effective and accountable, teachers need to have in-depth knowledge of the content of the subjects they are teaching. Content coverage, content exposure, and content emphasis have no meaning if teachers do not know or understand, or have only rudimentary knowledge of, the subject being taught. This is particularly true at the secondary level and is less evident at the elementary level.

When we read about performance standards, "performance" refers to students and not their teachers. However, if the teacher's performance is not satisfactory, it is very difficult to achieve satisfactory student performance. Neither knows what encompasses a high level of performance. They have not seen examples of outstanding student work nor had practice producing it.

Teacher performance standards are closely related to OTL standards. However, Lewis (1995) believes that currently there is no professional curriculum for teachers to learn and use to meet teacher performance standards. According to Lewis, the professional curriculum would "require time for teachers to study student work and the work of other teachers, and to collaborate with other teachers to improve their knowledge of the material, of students' thinking, and of how to teach in ways that would be likely to improve student performance" (p. 146). In response, the OTL Assessment Strategies Workshop does present a professional curriculum for teachers. Teachers who learned about the OTL variables and the OTL assessment strategies attempted to improve students' opportunities to learn in their classrooms by doing the assignments, implementing the OTL assessment strategies, and working toward improving the conditions for students to learn and enhance their academic achievement. That is being accountable.

References

Bailey, M. (1996). *Assessing opportunity to learn in urban schools: A report on the review of research documents to identify current OTL practices.* Philadelphia: Temple University Center for Research in Human Development and Education.

Brophy, J., & Good, T. (1986). Teacher behavior and student achievement. In M. C. Wittrock (Ed.), *Handbook of research on teaching* (pp. 328–375). New York: McMillan.

Fullan, M. (1990). Staff development, innovation, and institutional development. In B. Joyce (Ed.), *Changing school culture through staff development* (pp. 3–25). Newark, DE: International Reading Association.

Goertz, M. (1994). *Opportunity to learn: Instructional practices in eighth-grade mathematics: Data from the 1990 NAEP Trial State Assessment, CPRE* [Research Report No. 32]. New Brunswick, NJ: Rutgers, the State University of New Jersey.

Griffin, G. (1986). Clinical teacher education. In J. Hoffman & S. Edwards (Eds.), *Reality and reform in clinical teacher education* (pp. 1–24). New York: Random House.

Leinhart, G. (1983). Overlap: Testing whether it is taught. In G. F. Madaus (Ed.), *The courts, validity, and minimum competency* (pp. 152–170). Boston: Kluweer-Nijhoff.

Lewis, A. (1995). An overview of the standards movement. *Phi Delta Kappan, 76*(10), 744–750.

Loucks-Horsley, S., Harding, C., Arbuckle, M., Murray, L., Dubea, C., & Williams, M. (1987). *Continuing to learn: A guidebook for teacher development*. Andover, ME: Regional Laboratory for Educational Improvement of the Northeast and Islands/National Staff Development.

McDonnell, L., Burstein, L., Catterall, J., Ormseth, T., & Moody, D. (1990). *Discovering improved course-work indicators*. Santa Monica, CA: Rand.

McLaughlin, M. (1991). Enabling professional development: What we have learned. In A. Lieberman & L. Miller (Eds.), *Staff development for education in the '90s* (pp. 61–82). New York: Teachers College Press.

Organization for Economic Cooperation Development. (1991). *Outcomes of education: OECD international education indicators network A: Report of phase 2*. Paris: Author.

Porter, A. (1993). *Opportunity to learn* [Brief No. 7]. Madison, WI: Center on Organization and Restructuring of Schools.

Schmidt, W. (1983). High school course taking: A study of variation. *Journal of Curriculum Studies, 15*(2), 167–182.

Schmoker, M. (1996). *Results: The key to continuous school improvement*. Alexandria, VA: Association for Supervision and Curriculum Development.

Stevens, F. (1993a). Applying the opportunity to learn conceptual framework to the investigation of the effects of teaching practices via secondary analyses of multiple-case-study summary data. *Journal of Negro Education, 62*(3), 232–248.

Stevens, F. (1993b). *Opportunity to learn: Issues of equity for poor and minority students*. Washington, DC: National Center for Education Statistics.

Stevens, F., Wiltz, L., & Bailey, M. (1998). *Teachers' evaluations of the sustainability of opportunity to learn (OTL) assessment strategies: A national survey of classroom teachers in large urban school districts*. Philadelphia: Temple University Center for Research in Human Development and Education.

Stevenson, H., & Stigler, J. (1992). *The learning gap: Why our schools are failing and what we can learn from Japanese and Chinese education*. New York: Summit Books.

Wang, M. (1992). *Adaptive education strategies: Building on diversity*. Baltimore: Paul H. Brookes Publishing.

Winfield, L. (1987). Teachers' estimates of test content covered in class and first-grade students' reading achievement. *Elementary School Journal, 87*(4), 438–445.

8

Schools That Work for Teachers and Students

Karen Seashore Louis and Debra Ingram

T wo facts about public education in the 21st century are inescapable: The student population is increasingly multicultural, and students are coming from families of lower socioeconomic status. These demographic shifts challenge schools to mount massive reforms that range from providing on-site social services, to developing curricula that spark interest among the new generations of students (Rong & Brown, 2002), to initiating organizational changes that challenge the status quo (Ravitch, 1998).

However, effects on teachers from these demographic shifts still receive limited attention. This chapter considers the prospects for improving urban schools through professional and organizational reform. Creating a teaching force that has the energy and skill to teach today's urban students requires more than matching students and teachers or improving the skills of individual educators. Rather, it necessitates creating schools where all teachers are learners together with their colleagues (Leithwood & Louis, 1998).

The systemic reform literature suggests real improvement in schools will not occur unless the professional development of teachers focuses more clearly on specific student learning outcomes and a common curriculum (Desimone, 2000). This chapter argues that skills and knowledge will not be enough unless other aspects of teachers' work also improve. In particular, the changing conditions of schools decrease traditional intrinsic rewards for teachers and increase uncertainty, a situation that in turn reduces teacher commitment to and engagement in their work. The research reported here indicates that modest changes in teachers' working conditions can make dramatic differences in their engagement.

Note: Quotes in this chapter that appear without parenthetical citation are drawn from the authors' unpublished notes on interviews with teachers.

Urban Education as a Special Context for Teaching

According to Englert (1993), "The conditions in some of our schools are so bad, and the physical and social environments in which these schools are located so frightful, that we may have to cross off some . . . as expendable" (p. 3).

Creating high-quality working environments for teachers is an issue in all schools, but is particularly problematic in large cities, where the dilemmas and failures of our educational system have been apparent for decades (Kantor & Brenzel, 1992). These include socioeconomic, political, and organizational conditions that, while not unique, converge to make urban schools both vulnerable and demanding places for teachers.

Socioeconomic Conditions

The social and economic characteristics of urban communities have significant implications for teachers' work. Urban schools may be overwhelmed by the problems their students bring to school, making it more difficult for them to engage successfully with normal dilemmas of pedagogy (Picus, 1996). The double disadvantage of poor students and poor communities puts an extra strain on teachers, who are often from different socioeconomic backgrounds than those of their students, yet who must organize a pedagogy that will engage and connect the classroom to the student's own experience (Ladson-Billings, 2000). Although some educational reformers rail against the proportion of nonteaching professionals in schools (Odden, 1997), urban schools lack the internal or external support systems to help teachers work with students whose personal lives are in disarray.

Urban schools are hard to reform because many of them are weakly linked to the professional networks through which ideas are diffused. During the mid-1980s, only a tiny fraction of urban schools were basing change efforts on the then-popular "effective schools" literature (Louis & Miles, 1990), suggesting they were not well-connected to the many change agents promoting these principles at the time. Major comprehensive school reform interventions of the 1990s, such as those funded by the Annenberg Challenge, have had disappointing results (Finn, 2000; Glennan, 1998).

The socioeconomic setting also limits human resources: Teachers who staff the Chicago Public School System are by and large those who went through that system, received their teacher training locally, and have taught in no other district (Rollow & Bryk, 1995). In addition, urban schools are less likely to attract and keep the most talented teachers (Kantor & Brenzel, 1992). Urban school systems may prefer to "hire their own," but many teachers also prefer the easier and better-paid teaching opportunities of the suburbs.

Political Conditions

In urban settings, interest group politics mix with educational politics in a more volatile way than in smaller towns (Brown, 1997; McDermott, 2000), and teachers are not insulated from this conflict. Many urban settings display fragmented values concerning education and are more likely to exhibit distance or even antagonism between the professional values of teachers and the concerns of parents and community members (Fainstein & Fainstein, 1978).

Recent restructuring efforts in major cities have almost uniformly revealed deep-seated differences between proponents of parental control over schooling and professional judgments. Urban communities are often ethnically and racially heterogeneous, so the "community" may also be deeply divided (Louis, in press). When diversity is present in a school, it can negatively affect decentralized school improvement efforts (Bryk, Camburn, & Louis, 1999). Under these conditions, many urban districts exhibit the attributes of a "policy vacuum"—an absence of clear, organized constituencies, clear understanding of policy issues and choices, consistency in policy initiatives, and coordination between overlapping or complementary policies (Corwin & Louis, 1982). Policy vacuums lead to unstable educational policies, which in turn undermine school and teacher efforts to reform (Louis & Miles, 1990).

Organizational Conditions

Urban school districts are, almost by definition, large, and individual urban schools are larger than average (although they are not, especially at the high school level, the largest in the United States). Recent efforts to look at the effects of district and school size suggest that big equals bureaucratic—and also bad for children—at least where students are of lower socioeconomic status (Lee & Smith, 1997). For teachers, there is an added problem: Larger schools in lower socioeconomic status communities tend to develop a lesser "sense of community" among teachers than do other schools (Bryk, Lee, & Holland, 1993), and a sense of community is associated with student achievement (Louis & Marks, 1998).

Creating an engaged teaching force focused on the common problems of teaching demands a great deal of the faculty, yet urban schools have more difficulty than others in recruiting and retaining the most talented teachers (Englert, 1993). Teacher shortages are now a national problem, exacerbating the recruitment dilemma for urban schools. Even committed urban teachers may leave the profession or move because they are often subjected to unprofessional working conditions, less involved in policy decisions, treated with less respect by administrators, and have fewer opportunities to engage in significant work with each other (Corcoran, Walker, & White, 1988; Coyle, 1997).

The nature of work in urban schools is, in addition, hurried, focused on the short term, and subject to the same interruptions shared by teachers in other contexts. Few teachers and administrators are easily able to be "reflective practitioners" who eagerly seek complex information to improve their work. Rather, they are often harassed and are looking for information to solve today's problems today. In this regard, they get little assistance because urban schools typically lack basic information that would encourage reflection and experimentation (Cibulka, 1992).

Teacher Engagement and Student Achievement[1]

Reformers often attribute the problems of student learning to poorly prepared teachers, but evidence suggests an equally if not more serious problem is an increasing level of teacher detachment and alienation from their work and students (Shoho & Martin, 1997), a problem institutions have ignored for some time (National Education Association, 1987). Because teachers' work and students' work are inextricably intertwined, alienation is a primary stumbling block to improving student engagement. From the student's point of view, teacher engagement is a prerequisite for student engagement. From the teacher's point of view, student engagement is, in turn, the most important predictor of a teacher's interest and effort. *In this sense, teacher engagement is a subset of the broader objective of creating effective schools that increase student learning opportunities and improve student achievement.*

Teachers' Dependence on Students: The "Iron Law of Social Class"

Teachers get psychological rewards from watching their students learn. Dedicated teachers are able to point with pride to a student who has made

---

[1] Our conceptualizations of teacher engagement and the "iron law of social class" draw on previous work by Louis and Smith (1992).

progress on a particular concept this week, or another who has picked up basic cognitive skills that were lacking at the beginning of the year. See-ing the results of their own efforts is, for teachers, as important as it is for physicians to see patients getting well, or for lawyers to see clients whose lives have been changed because of their interventions.

But learning is not equally distributed among our students, and neither is teachers' sense of efficacy in their work. Striving to ensure that all stu-dents learn does not ensure that all will learn at the same rate or with the same ease. Research suggests a strong association between the socio-economic characteristics of students and their communities, and teacher satisfaction and engagement with teaching (Derlin & Schneider, 1994; Metz, 1990). Compared with teachers of more affluent children, teachers who work with students from poorer families are more likely, for exam-ple, to believe their students bring behaviors into the classroom that make teaching difficult, and to believe they have little influence over their stu-dents' learning. In addition, teachers in schools with a higher proportion of minority children are more likely to feel their efforts are not rewarded with student engagement in learning. Yet many teachers claim, "If you gave me students who were prepared to learn, I could be a great teacher."

Here is the "Catch 22" for urban schools: Unless teachers are engaged with teaching and feel they are effective, students are less likely to make rapid progress in learning (Firestone & Rosenblum, 1988; Hoy, Hannum, & Tschannen-Moran, 1998). And, from the students' point of view, teacher engagement is a necessary prerequisite for student engagement. This is particularly true for large schools and for districts and schools with a high concentration of lower income and minority students (Kennedy, 1995; Lee & Smith, 1997). Because teachers' work is linked to students' work, alien-ated teachers pose a major stumbling block to students' engagement with their own education.

In the majority of schools, teachers' lives focus almost exclusively on their classrooms. Hence, it is not surprising teachers prefer to work with the most responsive and quickest students—predominantly those of the middle classes and the higher tracks. Such students feed teachers' profes-sional satisfactions (Metz, 1990).

The argument that teachers depend on their students for their profes-sional satisfactions is empirically accurate, but there is an alternative per-spective. The authors' work with reforming urban schools over the last decade suggests that while it is not possible for teachers to change stu-dents' social origins or community resources, *it may be possible to change the relationship between social class and teacher commitment and engage-ment under the right organizational conditions.*

What Is Teacher Engagement?

Unengaged teachers have been described as "bored teachers who just go through the textbook and aren't thinking" or as having "taught one year for 30 years"; they have been nicknamed "Mrs. Ditto or Mr. Filmstrip," and known as teachers "who barely know their student's names" (Louis & Smith, 1992, p. 119).

Teacher engagement falls into four distinct types, two of which are *affective* and focus on human relationships in the school, and two of which are *instrumental* and focus on the goals of teaching and learning (Firestone & Rosenblum, 1988; Bryk, Lee, & Holland, 1993). Each form of engagement is vital and must be present for teaching to remain effective for all students. Thus, redesigning the school so that teachers of disadvantaged students have the same opportunities for engagement as those who work in more advantaged schools is fundamental to improving education. The following are the four types of engagement:

- **Engagement with the school as a social unit.** This form of engagement reflects a sense of community and personal caring among adults within the school and promotes integration between personal life and work life. This form of engagement is a mark of teachers who "wouldn't want to work at any other school," who refer to peers and students as friends and family, who attend after-hours school events as often as they can, and who are quick to rally together if faced with a troubling event.
- **Engagement with students as unique, whole individuals rather than as "empty vessels to be filled."** Teachers demonstrate this type of engagement when they lead classes in ways that acknowledge and respond to students' thoughts and knowledge, listen to their ideas, involve themselves in students' personal as well as school lives, and in general make themselves available to students who need support or assistance. Many types of formal and informal coaching, sponsoring, mentoring, and counseling activities are additional examples of engagement with students.
- **Engagement with academic achievement.** Curriculum writing and development, sharing ideas and experiences about teaching as a craft with other teachers, making good and creative use of class time, expressing high expectations for performance, providing useful feedback to students, and actively considering student assessment are all ways teachers can engage in their students' achievement.
- **Engagement with a body of knowledge needed to carry out effective teaching.** Particularly in secondary schools, teachers need to

keep current in their content fields and incorporate new subject-related ideas into their classrooms. Expressing one's personal passion for a subject, seeking ways to connect the subject to students' lives, being involved in professional organizations, and pursuing advanced degrees in one's field can be examples of this form of engagement.

Most teachers engage with their work in multiple dimensions when they enter the profession. Over time, engagement is almost always affected by the presence and absence of various demands on teachers—demands they place on themselves as well as those made by students, principals, and parents. Demands are stressful, but they can also energize. Students who want more, as well as parents who are involved, create an environment of high expectations for teachers. Although being observed at work is not easy, teachers whose colleagues observe their classes report higher levels of satisfaction than those whose classrooms are their singular domain (Louis & Marks, 1998).

In order to sustain teachers' engagement, however, teachers (like students) also need consistent positive reinforcement that is meaningful and rewarding. According to some popular case studies, the most unpromising contexts can still generate some forms of teacher engagement, often based on friendships among the faculty (Kidder, 1989). But teachers engaged on only a few of these dimensions will not necessarily serve students well. A staff may be highly engaged with the social community of adults in their school, but neglect student achievement (Hoy et al., 1998). Or they may become so obsessed with achievement that they remain distant from less able students. Dramatic imbalances can be counterproductive to the functioning of schools.

A Profile of Urban Schools with High Engagement

Since the late 1980s, the authors have conducted research in public schools actively involved in reform, ranging from projects that chose a diverse national sample of school community environments to those that involved intensive case studies and surveys in two urban districts. To illustrate how schools serving the disadvantaged can secure for their teachers working conditions similar to those of schools serving more advantaged students, this section focuses on three schools, referred to here by pseudonyms. These schools had poorer students than others in their respective districts, yet all showed evidence of student achievement that was well above the average for their districts. In addition, when we analyzed available survey data and looked at measures of engagement, they scored as high as or higher than more affluent schools.[2] Nevertheless, they brought effort, energy, and hope to their teaching tasks in excess of what would be expected. Particularly striking was the fact that teacher engagement in the three schools was higher than in other schools where most of the students were from minority and non-English-speaking populations, but where more students came from middle-class homes. Thus, we believe that in these schools the effects of the racial composition of the school were not particularly important.

City Park Secondary School

City Park is a small, innovative secondary school located in an impoverished section of a major northeastern city. In the shadow of a public housing project, poverty, crime, drugs, and violence touch the lives of the community members on a daily basis. The school shares a large 1950s-era building with two other small schools. Although the immediate neighborhood is largely Hispanic, the school aims for a diverse enrollment and has largely succeeded: Its student body is approximately 45 percent black, 35 percent Hispanic, and 20 percent white, with a broad range of academic ability. The school is renowned for the academic success of its students, 95 percent of whom go on to postsecondary education, and virtually all of whom are able to pass the state's rigorous high school exit examinations.

The school is rooted in the progressive education tradition, and is structured around the following principles:

- Minimization of bureaucracy
- A humanistic, open environment characterized by equal respect for staff and students (students do not need passes to go to the bathroom, and students and staff are both addressed by their first names)
- No tracking
- A core curriculum planned and developed by teams of teachers
- Significant team planning time that is used primarily for curriculum development

---

[2] Specific survey measures of teacher engagement are available elsewhere. See Lewis, K.S. (1988). Effects of teacher quality of work life in secondary schools on commitment and sense of efficacy. *Effectiveness and School Improvement, 9*(1), 1–27.

- Instructional/learning strategies that emphasize "essential questions" and inquiry
- Parent involvement
- An overall sense of family

The school enrolls around 600 students in three divisions (7–8, 9–10, and 11–12) that are further divided into houses of about 80 students. There are no traditional departments, but within each division there is a Math-Science Team and a Humanities Team, each consisting of about five teachers. Teams meet weekly for two hours to develop and coordinate curriculum and share ideas about what has and has not worked. Scheduling is nontraditional, with students and teachers meeting for two-hour blocks. Because of the division structure, students stay with the same teachers for two years and are also attached throughout the high school years to a single advisor. A daily one-hour advisory period focuses on guidance for academic and personal growth and reinforces the "family" atmosphere of the school.

Taft Community School

Taft Community School is a 308-student elementary school located in an impoverished section of a midwestern city. As a "community school," it receives its students on the basis of residence. Taft was recently awarded a quality performance award from the district for meeting or exceeding student achievement improvement goals. Scoring well above average for the district is not what one would expect from a school where students are both poor (nearly 75 percent of the students qualify for free or reduced-price lunch) and more diverse (30 percent of the students are white, 30 percent black, 22 percent Asian American, 13 percent Hispanic, and 6 percent Native American) than the city's typical elementary school. An additional challenging factor at Taft is that it enrolls a large recent immigrant population. Students' first languages range from Sudanese and Arabic to Chinese and Russian.

The Taft mission calls for fostering student self-confidence, social responsibility, and sense of community. To build strong relationships with students and provide support for learning, teachers in grades 1–4 remain with the most "educationally fragile" students for two or three years. Although not a magnet school, Taft teachers have agreed to integrate arts and technology into the subject matter curriculum. For example, the school recently purchased 25 laptop computers that students may check out for use in their classrooms, and the teachers engage in collaborative instruction with artists from four well-established cultural centers in the city. Curriculum focus is also a feature agreed upon by consensus: 50 percent of each day is spent on language arts and mathematics, and the other half is composed of science, social studies, health, physical education, and world languages.

Taft also reaches out to build collaborative relationships with parents and the community. On a typical day at Taft, many parents, community members, and university students work alongside teachers in the classroom as volunteers. It is a Taft policy that all staff, not just the principal and teachers, are responsible for making the community feel welcome in the school.

Lakeside High School

Lakeside High School is a grades 9–12 comprehensive high school located in a middle-income urban neighborhood. It draws its student body of about 1,900 students from across the city. The high school contains two popular magnet programs. The third program in the school, which enrolls students who have not selected a specific high school program, is called the General Program. The majority (63 percent) of Lakeside's students are white, with 18 percent African American, 9 percent Asian, and 6 percent Native American students; 31 percent of the students are eligible for free or reduced-price lunch. There are approximately 100 certified teachers on staff. This section focuses on the 9th grade "Diversity Team," described by its teachers as a disadvantaged population in the middle of a more affluent setting. "Only one-third of Lakeside's student body is part of the General Program, [but] many General students feel inferior and disenfranchised because of the selective Open and Liberal Arts programs which encompass the rest of school."

Ninth grade Diversity Team teachers were particularly concerned about the very high dropout rate between 9th and 10th grades and reasoned that until they could address the dropout problem, there was little point in trying to meet the district's goals for improvement on state test scores (given in 10th grade). They applied for a grant to engage in interdisciplinary teaching and began to collect data on student daily attendance and engagement with school. Over a three-year period, they made major changes in curriculum and teaching and were able to show significant differences in student behavior and continued enrollment. One teacher summarized the team's sense of success as follows: "We had 64 10th grade Native Americans this year [that is, students who completed 9th grade and enrolled again at Lakeside]. I guess that was enough for me to think we needed to do it again; it's that connectedness thing and creating a sense of community."

Perhaps more importantly, teacher efforts to change the curriculum and instruction led them to a very different understanding of their students, their capabilities, and what they needed to succeed. Teachers are committed to changing pedagogies and using demonstrations to permit students who have a record of school failure to express themselves in meaningful ways that are connected to core subject matter and civic values. The authors' classroom observations suggest that Lakeside teachers and their students have succeeded in creating classrooms that demand higher order thinking and are culturally sensitive.

How Do Some Urban Schools Organize to Increase Teacher Engagement and Student Achievement?

City Park, Taft, and Lakeside are very different schools, and have achieved different levels of success in "closing the gap." But what do they have in common that helps explain how changing the conditions of teachers' work will lead to improved conditions for student work? There appear to be three major factors: school culture, school organization, and school leadership.

School Culture

All three of these schools share norms and values that make teachers' work life different from conventional schools and that have a significant positive impact on teacher engagement.

A strong sense of being in "a school with a mission." Teachers in all three schools emphasized the importance of being part of a school (or a team) that was striving for a collective definition not just of *goals* (high achievement) but also of *strategies* for reaching them. A teacher at Lakeside, which was relatively new to the process of reform, expressed the importance of mission in the following way: "Our interdisciplinary activities [are] something everybody has a stake in. . . . I know our expectations were higher [this year]. . . . We expect to end up feeling like we HAVE more when we get done with something now than we did last year. Last year, we didn't know what we WANTED to have."

In City Park, where the pedagogical approach was most clearly articulated, the need to both live the mission and draw energy from it were mentioned by many faculty: "People know that . . . if you want to work in this school . . . [the team approach] is the bottom line. . . . I think [it] makes the job of teaching a creative experience, and creativity feeds on itself."

Taft teachers also emphasized the importance of collective focus: "The number one school improvement goal is to improve the reading achievement of students. So many of our collaborations are focused on that. . . . All the conversations that artists have with teachers deal with how does this teach a child to read? How does teaching a child drumming make them a better reader? It's about focus."

An emphasis on closeness among staff members. Teachers in the three schools view each other as sources of personal and intellectual support. Mutual reliance engenders frequent discussion about the nature of interpersonal relations in the school and how they are different from other settings. In all three schools, there was talk about trust, and staff viewed interpersonal relationships as a way of helping teachers continue to make the efforts required to meet student needs.

An emphasis on respect and caring for students. "Part of teaching is lending your ego for a kid to learn. . . . If you are only teaching a subject, [you're] not teaching kids" (teacher from City Park).

Respect and caring are significant aspects of teachers' work in restructured schools. The theoretical basis for caring has been extensively developed elsewhere (Noddings, 1984; Shann, 1999), but is empirically demonstrated in these urban schools. A City Park teacher articulated the importance of concerned and compassionate teacher-student relationships and pointed out that meeting each student as an individual—no matter how difficult that student might be—is stimulating in itself:

"If you are teaching the kids, you see where each kid is and what their next step is. You have to perceive all of the differences. . . . You have to handle the resistance so that they may make steps for themselves. . . . You have to do that, and that is an engaging process."

In Lakeside, students talked openly about teachers' respect for them, which was reinforced by the way in which teachers sought continuous feedback about their changes in curriculum and pedagogy. Not all student comments were thoughtful, but teachers took them seriously, and used them to make changes in their plans. As one teacher put it, "We get feedback from the kids, and we feel that it's really important for the kids to learn how to critique things and to give us input on . . . whether they felt they learned anything from this."

Taft teachers, with their large and diverse immigrant population, embraced the informal focus on the arts as a means of caring for and valuing student differences. Three of the four arts partners with whom they regularly collaborated had a strong focus on reflecting the deep culture of minority and immigrant groups.

Caring is good for students, of course, but it is also good for the adults who work with them. *Caring makes schools into ethical and moral environments, not just arenas for "getting the job done."* Studies of beginning teachers indicate that the desire to be involved with a profession that has a moral character is a significant motivation. This motivation is not simple altruism, but reflects the teacher's need to be engaged with work that has significance.

A demand for active problem solving among teachers. Urban teachers encounter a powerful form of empowerment when they believe they are responsible for finding and solving problems—a theme that arose repeatedly in the three schools. At City Park, one teacher commented about the way in which the problem-solving focus was reflected in student-teacher relationships: "The assumption is that the kids are basically trying to do the best that they can, and that might not be so great at a given point in time, and you try to get everybody together and acknowledge that there's a problem . . . rather than trying to blame someone. You try to deal with what the problem is, what are the different factors, and what can we do to change the situation. And that's the way problems are dealt with, even academically."

Teachers in Lakeside and Taft also emphasized problem solving and the responsibility given to teachers to manage their own environment. An external visiting committee at Taft wrote the following critique: "The profile that emerges is that of a school that has collectively valued and assertively sought to acquire skills, procedures, and resources that are known to develop and expand learning opportunities for adults and children."

Although part of taking responsibility comes from demands, it is also evidence that teachers felt they were given permission to solve problems in ways they had not previously experienced. A Taft teacher commented, "The opportunity and the experiences I have had [here] have really given me a greater sense of freedom and license to do stuff in the classroom that I might not do otherwise."

It is notable that all schools expected teachers, and not just administrators or counselors, to help students preserve constructive human relations at all times and in all places. At Lakeside, for example, the Diversity Team did not give up on students who were initially unable to attend an event outside school without "acting up"; they integrated culturally appropriate civic virtues (based on Ojibwe teaching) into the curriculum of core subjects and measured their success by behavior not only in their classrooms, but also outside. As one teacher announced, "We were going to look to see if the number of suspensions went down. And so we do have that information and yes, they have."

As a consequence of a strong focus on teachers and students working together to solve problems at their source, the disciplinary problems that plague many urban schools were rare.

Peer pressure to work. Life in the three schools was more demanding than in most schools—but worth it because the high expectations teachers had of one another were coupled with stimulation and support. City Park teachers talked about being exhausted, feeling that the work of curriculum development and active teaching had no end. But no teacher suggested that the effort made him or her want to leave. Lakeside's Diversity Team members had to meet over the summer and after school in order to develop the new curriculum and pedagogical strategies they were using, as well as to confront the interdisciplinary teacher for the first time. Even the math teacher worked on ways to incorporate the civic virtues theme into his classroom, as demonstrated by the following comment: "We're doing a probability unit in some of my math classes, and I talked to them about how important the data they come up with is . . . that if they make up the data it's not going to accurately reflect the truth of the situation, and that's what we're trying to find out. . . : What is the TRUTH about the probability of this situation?"

Why is pressure to work engaging? Because it is tied to a sense of doing work that addresses the vision of the school, and because it has visible payoff in the impacts on students—kids who are often viewed as dull and uninterested in school. Peer pressure increases teacher engagement because it is usually coupled with valued professional feedback from peers. When teachers collaborate with demanding colleagues, their best work becomes more visible. Of course, their failures may also be visible, but other norms, especially teachers helping one another, cushion the potentially negative impact of more exposure.

School Organization

Although professional culture is at the heart of teacher engagement, a variety of organizational changes can reinforce or revive the staff's commitments to teaching.

Creating structures to promote teacher decision making. When teachers take part in making important decisions, they also begin to take responsibility for finding and solving problems. The principals of these schools went beyond informal, open-door discussions and problem solving. They also built new decision-making structures and clearly delegated important decisions to teachers. Although teachers valued informal opportunities to give opinions or make suggestions, formal decision making authority was an important symbol of their professional position and responsibilities.

Teachers at all three schools clearly articulated the connection between involvement in decision making and their responsibilities for making the school function effectively. By consensus, teachers at Taft redesigned their school committees to better align them with goals in the school improvement plan. The new structures were to reflect faculty areas of expertise related to school goals, how each area influenced increases in student learning, and how data could be used to monitor change. At City Park the faculty saw the entire school structure as designed for empowerment and viewed the democratic process as integral to the educational experience they structured for students. As one faculty member stated, "We are a decision-making school. We work as a whole school, we work . . . within our team and . . . within our classrooms where even kids are allowed to make some decisions about how things are to be done."

Creating structures to promote collaboration. Changing the way in which time is used is one of the most difficult tasks of school reform (Smith, 2000). But all of these schools restructured so that teachers had more time to work together. Working together not only strengthened personal bonds but also infused teachers with new enthusiasm about instruction. City Park's schedule provides teams with a weekly two-hour meeting in which they develop curriculum, teaching strategies, and student assignments. The schedule reflects the value the school places on teachers' own engagement with their academic program. As one teacher observed, "In my other school, what I was good at, I stayed good at. What I wasn't good at, I never improved. . . . I really could have been in the building all by myself. There were never times when you could get together and discuss issues with other teachers. . . . "

The reduction in isolation was apparent in all settings. Teachers at Lakeside pointed out that developing a clear statement of their goals "is providing an opportunity that otherwise would not have been there for us to have dialogue, as teachers who support students." Another Lakeside teacher stated that the collaboration permitted a level of spontaneity in teaching that she had not previously felt: "It's like an idea will come up, and Tracy will say, well, I have a book that will tie in so well with that, so we'll do that. It just seems easier for us to do this year—I don't know if it's just a function of . . . having a little more experience under our belt working with other people."

In City Park, the principal's work is based on a philosophy of the need for collaboration, tying it to both teacher engagement and student engagement, as in the following statement: "You must remove teachers from isolation and make learning exciting. To make learning exciting for students, you must make learning exciting for teachers, because when learning is exciting for both teachers and students, kids can't get lost."

The theme that time spent with colleagues provided zest and stimulation for the lonelier task of teaching in the classroom was universal. Time spent with adults in these schools was not "down time" for relaxing, but creative time used for professional growth. Active use of collegial discussion was particularly evident at Taft, where staff used an annual daylong retreat to plan both buildingwide and individual professional development, and to relate professional development to school goals. Collegiality boosts engagement, in part because it increases interpersonal knowledge and the "family" feeling. It is important, however, to tie collegiality directly to the development of professional competence.

Yet all three schools considered the official staff development days as less important than the more ad hoc or partially planned development opportunities invented by teachers. A teacher from City Park best summarized the importance of continuing experimentation and skill development to engagement with the following comment: "We're not always doing the same thing. There's always something new to be thinking about. . . . It encourages you to think about issues, to grapple with important questions."

Creating structures to improve curriculum. Giving teachers the support they need to write or adapt curriculum for the students they teach can increase engagement. The problem of curriculum in urban schools is complex, and research-based comprehensive school reforms are a legitimate part of the urban educational renewal landscape. However, some autonomy over curriculum is a feature in virtually all of the successful urban schools that the authors have studied—collectively and individually—over the last decade.

In the three schools covered here, teachers develop curriculum, units, lesson plans, and instructional designs in teams. Curriculum development and discussion of instruction are the central purposes of Lakeside's daily meetings and City Park's weekly team meetings, while at Taft the school's reorganized committees serve the same function.

As noted earlier, collaborative group experiences benefit teachers. Beyond that, curriculum writing involves teachers in thinking about and discussing fundamental issues relating to knowledge and learning. Furthermore, they can calculate what levels of knowledge and instruction are best for the specific students they teach. That process engages teachers in their students, in the academic program of the school, in the craft of teaching, and in the subject they teach.

School Leadership

Teachers agreed with a consensus that a school with an ineffective principal was unlikely to be exciting no matter how talented the staff, and also that schools can become exciting quite rapidly after the arrival of a supportive principal. This is because the origins of the positive features associated with engagement all lie within the purview of each school's administrative leadership.

At the time of this study, City Park was a relatively new school, and its teachers had transferred from other schools to work there. Choice created a sense of being in a special place and of working with a special team. At Taft, on the other hand, many teachers had worked there for a long time, and few experienced it as unique. Finally, the Diversity Team at Lakeside High was composed primarily of new teachers, because experienced teachers preferred teaching in the magnet programs.

The factor that all the schools had in common, however, was an administrative leadership pattern that promoted engagement. The effective principal helps facilitate staff to develop the culture described above, while taking responsibility for designing and maintaining the organizational features that support it. However, there are some aspects of the leadership role that cannot be fully subsumed under the categories described above.

Buffering teachers. Studies of conventional schools emphasize the role of the principal in buffering the teacher from unwanted outside interventions by parents (Rossmiller, 1992). In these schools, parents and community were invited in, but principals had to work at buffering teachers from the district office and from state policies. City Park is located in a highly politicized district, and the principals and other school advocates have lobbied extensively to maintain the school's autonomy, particularly under a growing demand for increased student testing at the secondary level. Lakeside and Taft are located in a less volatile district that endorses site-based management, but principals actively encourage teachers to pursue goals beyond state and district expectations for improvement in test scores by looking at multiple sources of data about student learning and by focusing on long-term effects rather than short-term gains.

Spending time on daily routines. Leadership in the schools did not conform to the image of the efficient executive who participates as a policy broker and leaves the daily work of the organization to others. Instead, the principals were visible, had open doors, and were available for spontaneous discussion or problem solving. They spent time with students and tried to be ever-present at school activities, even when informal rewards were given. They were in the lunchroom and around the halls, not to discipline, but to gather information that would help them continue to support teachers' work (Louis & Miles, 1990).

Delegating and empowering. Another quality the principals of these three schools shared was their promotion of conditions that acknowledged the professional capabilities and judgments of teachers. Principals who create healthy environments for teachers "make teachers invent solutions to problems—they aren't the only problem solver." The effective principal "can leave the building without things falling apart or hitting snags, and has staff empowered to respond to crises." At Taft, the following comment, made by an individual outside of the school, was typical: "There has been a significant contribution of knowledge and expertise regarding democratic organization leadership by the building principal. The level of trust and commitment among school personnel and community members is notably high, and seems to be due in large part to the principal's ability to sense and respond to organization needs and to engage and support processes and structures that are effective."

It is important to note that at all three schools the philosophical conviction was to empower the group rather than the individual teacher. Communal decisions prevailed (even when the administrators were not enthusiastic), and it was up to the individual to implement these collective resolutions, with some autonomy and flexibility.

Providing leadership about values. Teachers agreed that the principal set the tone for developing a vision and a value orientation in the school. It is important for the principal to understand and reflect the best in community ethical standards and values, and to "make clear what is valued— don't keep faculty guessing about what is important." Leadership articulating strong values was most visible in City Park, where the first principal founded the school based on a particular educational philosophy that directly incorporated teacher engagement. In the large and well-established Lakeside, the influence of leadership values was more subtle, but still acknowledged by all teachers, particularly with regard to increasing parent involvement, a focus on interdisciplinary curriculum development, and caring for students.

Implications for Teachers

Teachers cannot change the social, political, and organizational conditions that affect urban schools. But, along with the principal, they share control of their own professional culture. For example, unless teachers willingly join in discussions about values and what makes for good teaching, the most valiant efforts of an enthusiastic principal will not be rewarded. There are trade-offs that teachers must be willing to make if they want to work in settings like these.

For many good teachers, one of the joys of teaching is the freedom to experiment freely within their own classroom. In all three of these schools, however, teachers were willing to trade some of their traditional autonomy for the collective responsibility for curriculum, student and teacher behavior, and quality of instruction. For many teachers, including those in City Park, which placed the greatest emphasis on the role of the group, this trade-off is not without costs. Some teachers pointed out, for example, that they couldn't spend as much time working on their disciplinary-based teaching as in other schools. In other schools, even enthusiastic teachers noted there were some times when they wished they could just shut the door and use their old "stand and deliver" strategies for teaching. As well as the gains, it is important for teachers to be able to discuss the losses they encounter as part of the autonomy-collective responsibility trade-off.

Implied in collective responsibility is accountability—if not to external constituencies, at least to peers. Open discussions of teaching are not always comfortable because they sometimes require admitting one's own deficiencies, or pointing out the flaws in a colleague's approach. Genuine peer review and discussion are still rare in most U.S. schools. Of the three schools profiled in this monograph, only City Park had achieved this fully. In Taft and Lakeside, such discussions were still relatively rare and confined largely to smaller groups consisting of other teachers who were viewed as like-minded friends.

A key aspect of teacher leadership in all three schools was the teachers' consistent belief that they had full responsibility for the curriculum—even under current state mandates. Owning the curriculum is harder in practice than most teachers expect. Not all curriculum was teacher-constructed, but teachers needed to accept the obligation to question all aspects of both content and pedagogy, and to "fix" parts that didn't work for their students, even where district requirements and external assessment procedures created pressure to use a more traditional approach.

Defining a clear body of expertise needed to work in an urban setting is a very tough job, but it appears to be central to the work of these schools. Part of elaborating a basis for professional expertise involved taking charge of professional development. While all the schools sought help from "outside experts," they also defined professional development as learning from each other.

The average U.S. teacher already works hard—the typical workweek is more than 40 hours. But highly engaged teachers in urban schools appear to work even harder. The issue is not just hours (although teachers who accepted unusual leadership responsibilities for committees or curriculum work often did encounter exceptional demands on their time), but the demand for collective work. Teachers in these schools reorganized the schedule to accommodate additional meetings, or used time after school in ways they had not previously done. But enthusiasm may yield to frustration when meetings are unproductive (as some meetings always are), and not directly related to classroom and student work in the short run.

Conclusion

A teacher at City Park told us of a visit to her class by a Shakespearean actor: "This guy . . . transformed my class in a way I could never have done. I was overawed by how good he was with my kids. . . . He had one of my kids standing on her head!" Perhaps all of us dream of schools full of such people, but the prospect of transforming schools through charisma is unrealistic. Such people are rare, and, as this teacher said, "You would run out of them pretty quickly!" It is also a mistake to allow teachers to depend only on students as a source of external support and feedback. Doing so may put thousands of teachers in frustrating and lonely work environments, with dim prospects for high teacher engagement. City Park, Taft, and Lakeside have teachers who energetically invest in the personal and academic progress of their students. A variety of collegial, administrative, and structural supports help them remain engaged. And these examples can become models as schools begin to think about how to change in ways that encourage a productive mix of teacher engagement.

Teachers' engagement with the school as a social unit or community intensified most profoundly when there was a sense of vision or purpose about education and the specific students they served. While it is important not to underestimate individual purpose and motivation, the cases suggest that a supportive culture within the school can compensate significantly for the lower expectations from community and parents in those areas where socioeconomic status is low.

Engagement with student achievement is also sustained by opportunities for teachers to collaborate, both on schoolwide decisions and on curriculum and instruction. Collaborative activities often converge only on the margins of school life, such as paperwork or holiday performances. At the three schools, teachers participated as a whole and in smaller groups in decisions regarding the fundamental issues of the school, including the abilities and needs of the students, the nature of teacher-student relationships, the content of the curriculum, the methods of instruction, and the setting or abolishing of policies. Collaboration also contributes to teachers' engagement with achievement because it provides opportunities for teachers to support and give feedback they may not always get from their students. Finally, opportunities to develop curriculum and instructional plans specifically for the students they serve allows teachers to assess an appropriate level of challenge for their students, increasing the likelihood of student engagement in their work.

Structures that allow teachers to interact with students informally and in small groups nourish engagement with students as whole individuals. Beyond providing structures and pedagogies to enhance teachers' understanding of students, a cultural norm among engaged teachers acknowledges the links between students' emotional well-being and their readiness to learn. Teachers understand that engagement with subject matter, while important to academic achievement, cannot be the only priorities of the school. Teachers stayed current with developments in their field through participation in local and national associations, yet it was clear they often subordinated engagement with their individual subject to a more interdisciplinary curriculum when doing so could address fundamental concepts students would need.

The relationship between teacher engagement and organizational leadership, culture, and structure is not simple. But the organizational reforms accomplished by these schools demonstrate how schools serving disadvantaged students can sustain levels of teacher engagement comparable to schools in higher socioeconomic circumstances.

The success of these three schools is not easy to reproduce. Districts and states increasingly pressured these schools to perform on standardized tests, but the schools also generated high demands for teacher performance and engagement. Furthermore, the schools the authors studied successfully freed teachers from depending *only* on students' daily classroom success as a source of professional satisfaction by providing a richer array of feedback and rewards from adults. At the same time, as a result of feedback and increased professional interaction, teachers in these schools also felt a higher sense of efficacy in their professional competence that encouraged them to make greater investments in their success with students. Teachers in these schools gave themselves freely to the task of instruction and student achievement but also had resources to turn to if classroom success was not immediate or as profound as they hoped. This is, perhaps, the balance to which any restructured school must aspire in order to break the "iron law of social class."

References

Brown, F. (1997). Privatization and urban education—More political and less educational. *Education and Urban Society, 29*(2), 204–216.

Bryk, A. S., Camburn, E. M., & Louis, K. S. (1999). Professional community in Chicago elementary schools: Facilitating factors and organizational consequences. *Educational Administration Quarterly, 35*(5), 751–781.

Bryk, A. S., Lee, V. E., & Holland, P. B. (1993). *Catholic schools and the common good.* Cambridge, MA: Harvard University Press.

Cibulka, J. (1992). Urban education as a field of study: Problems of knowledge and power. In J. Cibulka, R. Reed, & K. Wong (Eds.), *Politics of urban education in the United States* (pp. 15–38). Washington, DC: Falmer Press.

Corcoran, T., Walker, L. J., & White, J. L. (1988). *Working in urban schools.* Washington, DC: Institute for Educational Leadership.

Corwin, R., & Louis, K. S. (1982). Organizational barriers to knowledge use. *Administrative Science Quarterly, 27*(4), 623–640.

Coyle, M. (1997). Teacher leadership versus school management: Flatten the hierarchy. *Clearing House, 70*(5), 236–239.

Derlin, R., & Schneider, G. (1994). Understanding job satisfaction: Teachers and principals, urban and suburban. *Urban Education, 29*(1), 63–88.

Desimone, L. (2000, July). The role of teachers in urban school reform. *ERIC Clearinghouse on Urban Education Digest, 5.*

Englert, R. (1993). Understanding the urban context and conditions of practice of school administration. In P. Forsyth & M. Tallerico (Eds.), *City schools: Leading the way.* Newbury Park, CA: Corwin.

Fainstein, N., & Fainstein, S. (1978). The future of community control. *Political Science Review, 70*(3), 905–923.

Finn, C. (2000). *Can philanthropy fix our schools? Appraising Walter Annenberg's $500 million gift to public education.* Washington, DC: Thomas B. Fordham Foundation.

Firestone, W., & Rosenblum, S. (1988). The alienation and commitment of teachers and students in urban high schools: A conceptual framework. *Educational Evaluation and Policy Analysis, 10*(2), 285–300.

Glennan, T. (1998). *New American schools after six years.* Santa Monica, CA: RAND Corporation.

Hoy, W., Hannum, J., & Tschannen-Moran, M. (1998). Organizational climate and student achievement: A parsimonious and longitudinal view. *Journal of School Leadership, 8*(4), 336–359.

Kantor, H., & Brenzel, B. (1992). Urban education and the "truly disadvantaged": The historical roots of the contemporary crisis, 1945–1990. *Teachers College Record, 94*(2), 214–278.

Kennedy, E. (1995). Contextual effects on academic norms among elementary school students. *Educational Research Quarterly, 18*(4), 5–13.

Kidder, T. (1989). *Among school children*. Boston: Houghton Mifflin.

Ladson-Billings, G. (2000). Fighting for our lives—Preparing teachers to teach African American students. *Journal of Teacher Education, 51*(3), 206–214.

Lee, V., & Smith, J. (1997). High school size: Which works best and for whom? *Educational Evaluation and Policy Analysis, 19*(3), 205–227.

Leithwood, K., & Louis, K. S. (Eds.). (1998). *Organizational learning in schools*. Lisse, The Netherlands: Swets and Zeitlinger.

Louis, K. S. (in press). Creating democratic schools: International perspectives. In L. Moos (Ed.), *International congress of school effectiveness and school improvement*. Copenhagen, Denmark: Universitetsforlaget.

Louis, K. S., & Marks, H. (1998). Does professional community affect the classroom? Teacher work and student work in restructuring schools. *American Journal of Education, 106*(4), 532–575.

Louis, K. S., & Miles, M. B. (1990). *Improving the urban high school: What works and why*. New York: Teachers College Press.

Louis, K. S., & Smith, B. (1992). Cultivating teacher engagement: Breaking the iron law of social class. In F. Newmann (Ed.), *Student engagement and achievement in American secondary schools* (pp. 119–152). New York: Teachers College Press.

McDermott, K. A. (2000). Barriers to large-scale success of models for urban school reform. *Educational Evaluation and Policy Analysis, 22*(1), 83–89.

Metz, M. (1990). How social class differences shape the context of teachers' work. In M. McLaughlin, J. Talbert, & N. Bascia (Eds.), *The contexts of teaching in secondary schools* (pp. 40–110). New York: Teachers College Press.

National Education Association (NEA). (1987). *Status of the American public school teacher*. Washington, DC: Author.

Noddings, N. (1984). *Caring, a feminine approach to ethics and moral education*. Berkeley, CA: University of California Press.

Odden, A. (1997). Raising performance levels without increasing funding. *Journal of School Business Affairs, 63*(6), 4–12.

Picus, L. O. (1996). Current issues in public urban education. *Housing Policy Debate, 7*(4), 715–729.

Ravitch, D. (1998). *A new era in urban education* (Policy Brief #35). Washington, DC: Brookings Institution.

Rollow, S. G., & Bryk, A. S. (1995). Building professional community in a school left behind by reform. In K. S. Louis & S. Kruse (Eds.), *Professionalism and community: Perspectives on reforming urban schools* (pp. 105–132). Newbury Park, CA: Corwin Press.

Rong, X. L., & Brown, F. (2002). Immigration and urban education in the new millennium: The diversity and the challenges. *Education and Urban Society, 34*(2), 123–133.

Rossmiller, R. (1992). The secondary school principal and teachers quality of work life. *Educational Management and Administration, 20*(3), 132–146.

Shann, M. H. (1999). Academics and a culture of caring: The relationship between school achievement and prosocial and antisocial behaviors in four urban middle schools. *School Effectiveness and School Improvement, 10*(4), 390–413.

Shoho, A., & Martin, N. (1997). Alienation among alternatively certified and traditionally certified teachers. *ERS Spectrum, 17*(3), 27–33.

Smith, B. (2000). Quantity matters: Annual instructional time in an urban school system. *Educational Administration Quarterly, 36*(5), 652–682.

9

Reframing the Reform Agenda

Belinda Williams

> *Those engaged in educational reform are those engaged in societal development: those engaged in societal development are those engaged in the evolution of virtue. It is time to return to large-scale reform with even more ambitious goals than we had in the 1960s, armed with the sophisticated knowledge that we can turn complexity's own hidden power to our advantage.*

> —Michael Fullan (1999, p. 84)

Building the mind and character of every child." President George W. Bush posed this challenge to the educational community and society to close the achievement gap. It is a call to tackle the complexity Fullan describes. Education reforms of the past several decades, limited to improving achievement with fragmented strategies, proposals, and programs, have not required the rigor of identifying and addressing the complex variables that affect socioeconomic, racial, and ethnic group differences in academic achievement (Annenberg Institute for School Reform, 2002; Lee, 2002). The proposals in the No Child Left Behind Act could be strengthened with the recommendations offered by a rigorous synthesis of emerging theory, recent research, and available evidence.

The authors whose work and ideas appear in this book introduce and describe this rigor and complexity. First, they define the achievement gaps that exist in poverty and affluence—in urban, suburban, and rural communities—as differences in experiences of sociocultural history, economy, and context, not as deficits and deficiencies in children, their families, and communities. Second, they provide us with a rich set of comprehensive guiding principles and strategies to assist policymakers, districts, communities, and schools in closing achievement gaps among various groups. Attention to the complexities of understanding and addressing the deeper issues identified in these chapters must not be left to chance and intuition. Redefining and integrating current understandings of normal human development, and reframing the reform agenda accordingly, requires explicit attention by the education community to accomplish the following goals:

- Integration of cross-disciplinary knowledge (from biology, sociology, and psychology) of normal human development in varied contexts
- Embedding of the current knowledge of normal human development in comprehensive reform and teacher preparation to focus on teaching and learning
- Transformation of school organization, management, and community and parent resources to support teaching and learning for all students
- Alignment of the political policies (federal, state, district, and school), resources, and accountability measures required to transition from fragmentation and simplicity to complex, comprehensive reform

This concluding chapter summarizes the authors' significant points and guiding principles and offers a framework for reform to close the achievement gaps among groups.

Normal Human Development in Varied Contexts

Strategies to close the achievement gaps among socioeconomic and racial/ethnic groups must be grounded in an understanding of the complexities of normal human development in different historical, sociocultural, and economic contexts. Simplistic, one-dimensional reform proposals that are limited to management solutions, decentralization, standards and accountability, class size reduction, or curriculum and assessment content fail to consider these dynamics.

Monocultural Versus Sociocultural Perspectives

Trumbull, Greenfield, and Quiroz (Chapter 4) invite us to consider how the United States has traditionally assumed that one goal of schools is to create a monocultural society reflecting the majority Eurocentric culture. This assumption, they suggest, has led many educators to ignore or devalue the cultural assets of children who are not part of the majority culture. Educators expect children to leave their cultures (knowledge, abilities, interests, values, etc.) at the schoolhouse door and to function as empty vessels into which teachers pour school knowledge. This unexamined expectation does not acknowledge that students' cultures exert powerful influences over what knowledge is *valued* and what is learned. An appreciation of the role of culture in human development is consistent with a subtle shift in perspective from teaching to learning, and a focus on knowing the learner. This is a move away from the information transmission view of traditional learning (the teacher as knowledge giver) to an understanding of how learning occurs (Bransford, Brown, & Cocking, 1999; Oakes & Lipton, 1999).

Educators currently incorporate culture into school celebrations of heroes, heroines, holidays, and food. However, celebrating Black History Month or Cinco de Mayo and scheduling "Ethnic Foods Night" represent only one component of valuing and incorporating varied cultural identities and experiences. Integrating the implications for teaching and learning from neuroscience, sociocultural experiences, multifaceted ability development, intrinsic motivation, and identity studies enables the education community to promote the view that the cultural context itself mediates learning. The cultural context provides a frame of reference, a lens enabling the learner to value and make meaning of new knowledge.

Intelligence, Ability Identification, and the Role of Effort in Achievement

Stevenson and Stigler (1992), and a recent report prepared by the U.S. Department of Education (1998), describe the Japanese culture and education system. According to these reports, embedded in both of these entities is an assumption that the role of *effort* is the major factor in learning and success. Many Japanese students are confident that the investment of time and effort will lead to mastery of the academic curriculum. In contrast to the Japanese emphasis on effort, Resnick (1995) offers the following observation of the education system in the United States:

> Early in this century, we built an education system around the assumption that aptitude is paramount in learning and that it is largely hereditary. . . . —that effort actually creates ability, that people can become smart by working hard at the right kinds of learning task—has never been taken seriously in America or indeed in any European society, although it is the guiding assumption of education institutions in societies with a Confucian tradition. (p. 56)

Marzano, in Chapter 3, further challenges current assumptions about ability development and intelligence. He points out that "one of the perceived 'truisms' in education has been that a student's intelligence or aptitude accounts for the lion's share of the variation in student achievement" (p. 48), and argues that enhancing a student's background knowledge can directly influence the type of abilities most closely associated with academic achievement. Because a limited vocabulary inhibits one's ability to store experiences in abstract ways, he suggests instruction in language and vocabulary development specific to the teaching and learning of new content. Marzano's six-step process for vocabulary instruction (see Chapter 3) strengthens the learner's ability to make meaning of new knowledge. The process includes building on the learners' existing knowledge and vocabulary by requiring imagery and explanations of new terms in their own words—that is, in the language they bring to school.

The Focus on Meaningful Cognitive and Affective Connections

In addition to research reported by authors in this volume, other research supports powerful outcomes reflecting a focus on meaningful cognitive and affective instructional connections. Knapp, Shields, and Turnbull (1995) identify three important alternatives to traditional instructional practices, recommending instruction that

- Helps students perceive the relationship of parts to wholes,
- Provides students with the tools to construct meaning in their daily lives and the real world, and
- Makes explicit connections between subject areas and what is learned in school and children's home lives.

In addition, Bell (2001) describes high-performing schools, teachers, and classrooms where students and teachers are engaged cognitively and affectively. In these high-poverty schools, teachers require students to interact with people in their families, neighborhoods, and communities. These teachers know students and their communities well enough to integrate assignments with community history, events, conditions, and issues. Knapp and colleagues (1995) conclude, "Low-performing children increase their grasp of advanced skills at least as much as their high-achieving counterparts when both groups experience instruction aimed at meaning. And for both groups, this approach to instruction produces results superior to those of conventional practices" (p. 774).

Trumbull, Greenfield, and Quiroz (Chapter 4) and Zeichner (Chapter 5) emphasize the importance of the teacher's knowledge of the role of culture in normal human development and outline the implications for teacher preparation. According to these authors, efforts to make schooling more responsive to students' varied cultural backgrounds have been limited, as previously indicated, to curriculum content (heroes, heroines, holidays, and food) and the perspectives, contributions, and histories of minority groups (group identity). Trumbull, Greenfield, and Quiroz define culture as "a group's knowledge and expectations about appropriate modes of interaction and the patterns of activities that are common to that group." They point out that "developmental psychology has undergone something of a paradigm shift in the last two decades"—from an understanding of development as an individual matter to an understanding of the role of social interactions. According to these authors, "A broader understanding of the cultural value systems in which children grow up is necessary to improve the education of minority students. If school reforms are to close the achievement gap, they must recognize the role of culture in schooling and the relationships between home culture views of child development and those implicit in schooling practices" (p. 68).

The Integration of Neuroscience, Cognition, and Sociocultural Theory

Figure 9.1 outlines agreements among emerging neuroscience and cognitive theory supported and cited by the authors represented here and in other studies. A definition of learning as *the ability of the learner to make meaning of new knowledge by making connections with existing knowledge* is supported by much 20th-century research (Caine & Caine, 1991; Dewey, 1916, 1938; Piaget, 1969; Vygotsky, 1981). The behaviorists, such as Skinner, offer the concept of "reinforcement" to describe the dynamics of learning—what gets learned is what is valued and rewarded in the learner's experiences. Gardner (1999) summarizes the contribution of cognitive psychologists to the understanding of learning and/or the development of intelligence, "I now conceptualize an intelligence as a biopsychological potential to process information that can be activated in a cultural setting to solve problems or create products that are of value in a culture" (pp. 33–34).

Good teaching is enhanced when instruction engages the learner's knowledge gained from cultural and daily experiences, and values the interest of the learner (intrinsic motivation) in acquiring particular new knowledge. Engaging the learners' intrinsic motivation is a powerful strategy. Researchers observed this prerequisite, according to Bell (2001), in high-performing, high-poverty schools, described as "dynamic learning environment[s] that built upon students' prior knowledge and individual interests."

FIGURE 9.1

Normal Human Development in Varied Contexts: Emerging Theory and Evidence

---

Neuroscience/Brain Research

Learning occurs as the brain searches for familiar patterns (Caine & Caine, 1991).

Psychology

Learning occurs when the brain responds to new experiences by changing schemas or structures in the brain that code experience (Piaget, 1969).

Abilities are developed by the learner's cultural experiences, such as what is learned and valued in the culture (Gardner, 1999).

Learning occurs when the learner is able to connect existing meaning to make meaning of new knowledge (Vygotsky, 1981).

Teaching and learning must integrate what is worthwhile in the learner's daily experiences (Dewey, 1916/1938).

Behaviorism

What is learned is what gets reinforced in the learner's environment and experiences (Skinner, 1974).

Sociology

Culture

Changing social relationships defined by a group's shared historical and social experiences that influence knowledge acquisition, behaviors, developed abilities, values and beliefs and interests (Ogbu, 1994)

Resilience

The ability to recover from adverse experiences in caring environments that communicate high expectations and provide meaningful engagement to develop a sense of autonomy, social competence, problem solving, and a sense of purpose and future (Benard, 1996)

Sociocultural Theory and Literacy

The requirements for learning in general are central to literacy development. Early literacy and reading proficiency are influenced by (1) the ability of students to distinguish the sounds of the language they are reading—the alphabetic principle and phonemic awareness, and (2) the skills required to gain meaning—that is, prior knowledge and vocabulary development—from reading (Bartoli, 1995; Braunger & Lewis, 1997; Crochunis, Erdey, & Swedlow, 2002; Knapp, 1995; Knapp et al., 1995; Ladson-Billings, 1994; Mathes & Torgesen, 2000; Oakes & Lipton, 1999; Osborn & Lehr,

1998; Pikulski, 1998; Snow, Burns, & Griffin, 1998; Taylor, Anderson, Au, & Raphael, 2000). Teachers need both skills in reading instruction and knowledge of their students' cultural experiences to build value into literacy development. According to Oakes and Lipton (1999):

> In the past thirty years, cognitive research has shown that learning is a process of meaning making, and sociocultural studies have shown that social contexts not only influence but also become what students learn. These two areas of research give English language arts educators overwhelming evidence that all students come to school with sociocultural, meaning-making experiences that prepare them for full adult literacy. This includes cultural literacy for rich cultural lives and formal literacy for successful and powerful economic and political participation. . . . Students should engage in literacy activities that allow them to communicate about real things of interest and that have relevance beyond school. (p. 154)

Cultural Knowledge and Accountability

To offer additional insight into the role of culture in human development, Trumbull, Greenfield, and Quiroz (see Chapter 4) describe the cultural differences that value either individualism or collectivism. They illustrate these differences in the way a culture defines and socializes intelligence. For example, children are socialized to be assertive and competitive, or they are socialized to value consideration for others; they learn to acquire knowledge for the sake of knowledge, or they learn to acquire knowledge that has social use. The authors describe these intangible cultural values and differences as "invisible culture." They caution that the invisible cultures of homes and communities, which foster social development, may be in conflict with the invisible culture of the school, which prizes cognitive development. They recommend cultural knowledge as a component of accountability and suggest, "In a culturally sensitive school environment, the teacher both validates the social relationships of children from collectivistic backgrounds by showing interest in their family experiences, and is explicit about her expectations for a topic of study. This approach facilitates a process of bidirectional cultural exchange" (p. 75).

Sociocultural Experience and Resilience

In Chapter 6, Benard introduces another component of the sociocultural experience, *resilience*. Individuals who cope with risks and challenges, such as those from troubled families and poverty, who successfully become competent, confident, and caring, as well as successful, are *resilient*. According to Benard, these resilient individuals exhibit social competence, problem-solving skills, autonomy, and a sense of future.

An Integrated View for Future Reform Measures

Future reform measures, based on an integrated view of human development, might require schools to provide descriptions (in reformatted school improvement plans) of how they will embed attention to emerging brain research, cognitive psychology, knowledge of culture, intrinsic motivation, and resilience in staff development activities and monitor these elements in curriculum, instruction, and assessment practices.

Figure 9.1 outlines the relationships among the bodies of knowledge graphically illustrated in Figure 9.2. The outline and graphic illustration offer the education community a lens through which to organize reform supported by cross-disciplinary knowledge (from biology, psychology, and sociology) and evidence.

Human Development, Teacher Preparation, and a Focus on Teaching and Learning

Education reform to close the gaps among groups must ensure that educators are made aware of emerging theoretical integration. Educators who understand how learning occurs in varied contexts (see Chapters 4 and 5) and who are aware of current conceptions of intelligence and ability development (see Chapter 3) are able to design and introduce instruction that connects new knowledge with learners' knowledge, abilities, values, and interests. We have the tools to create high outcome schools where educators exhibit high expectations and students come first.

Sociocultural Theory, Teacher Preparation, and Instruction

To accomplish what Trumbull, Greenfield, and Quiroz call "bidirectional cultural exchange," Zeichner calls for changes in teacher education and professional development. He challenges assumptions guiding current restructuring proposals: "Changes in the ways in which teachers interact with students in classrooms must be accompanied by or preceded by changes in schools' systemic and structural conditions" (p. 107). In Chapter 5, Zeichner recommends the following seven measures:

1. Having high expectations and the belief that all students can be successful, and communicating this belief instead of making excuses, such as blaming bureaucracies, parents, or communities
2. Making curriculum and instruction responsive to what is important to students in their home cultures
3. Providing peer learning centers and turn-taking in reading groups
4. Integrating community-related themes in writing projects
5. Incorporating the explicit teaching of school formats and principles

FIGURE 9.2

Normal Human Development:
A Framework for Theoretical Integration of Teaching and Learning

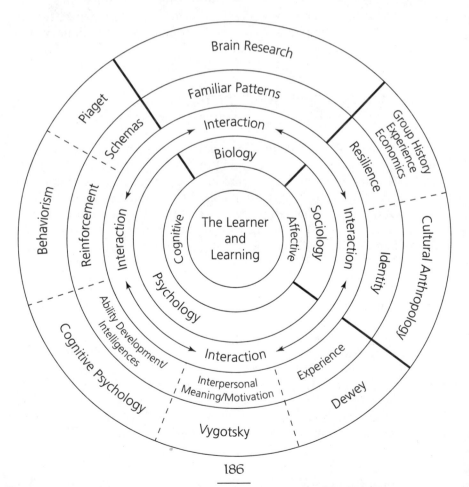

6. Making home visits, conferring with community members, talking with parents, consulting with minority teachers, and observing children in and out of school
7. Ensuring that teachers have a deep understanding of the subjects they teach

In Chapter 7, Stevens points out that "[i]n the United States, much of the educational research has attributed differences among ethnic groups' academic achievement to race and socioeconomic status. In contrast, other countries cite content coverage as the major contributor [to group differences in] achievement" (p. 138).

Stevens's research findings recommend strong educational *leadership* to ensure the following principles of high-quality instruction:

- **Content coverage.** All students have access to the core curriculum and critical subject matter topics, and curriculum content and text content are in alignment.
- **Content exposure.** Teachers organize instruction so there is enough time-on-task for students to cover and learn a specific topic or subject.
- **Content emphasis.** Teachers select instructional content from the core curriculum; selection includes both a dominant level of instruction and skills that will be emphasized to *all* students.
- **Quality of instructional delivery.** Lessons are coherent, and instructional activities are connected logically and sequentially with a beginning, middle, and end.

Marzano (see Chapter 3) further underscores the possibilities of instruction. He affirms that the education community already knows instructional interventions can alter aspects of language abilities developed in the students' daily experience that are most closely associated with academic achievement. He points out that these interventions have been "severely underutilized, particularly in the last two decades." He encourages the education community to incorporate the following four guiding principles in instruction:

1. Students should receive direct instruction on words and phrases that are critical to their understanding of content.
2. As part of this instruction, teachers should expose students to new words multiple times—preferably about six times.
3. Teachers should encourage students to represent their understanding of new words using mental images, pictures, and symbols whenever possible.

4. The goal of vocabulary instruction should not necessarily be an in-depth understanding of new words, but rather an accurate, albeit surface, knowledge of new words that will form the basis for greater understanding of content.

Resiliency and the Power of "No-Excuses" Schools and Teachers

In Chapter 6, Benard describes the power and practices of "turnaround teachers and schools," that is, those "no-excuses" teachers and schools to which Zeichner referred that establish caring relationships and refuse to let students fail. She paints a picture of caring teachers and schools, and offers self-assessment tools that define and identify teachers who

- Demonstrate caring and support, offer positive/nonjudgmental feed-back, express interest, and so forth.
- Communicate high expectations, recognize strengths, and offer pos-itive feedback.
- Provide opportunities for student participation, choice, and contri-butions.

Benard concludes that changing beliefs about the untapped potential of students requires schools and leadership that provide for teachers what students need—provisions for personal reflection, staff dialogue, and resi-liency study groups.

A focus on the *how* of learning offers the education community a framework for enhancing and integrating current reform proposals and strategies (see Figure 9.3) and reforming pre- and inservice teacher prepa-ration programs.

Transforming Schools to Support Teaching and Learning

The same mix of historical, sociocultural, and economic conditions and con-texts that create the macroecology of urban communities (Lee, 2002; Wil-liams, 1996) is responsible for the nature of achievement gaps in suburban, rural, and affluent schools. However, members of the education community, including politicians as well as educators themselves, demonstrate limited perceptions of learning and of understanding achievement gaps. Many still attribute achievement patterns solely to the attributes of students, their par-ents, and/or their schools. Manning and Kovach (Chapter 2), Stevens (Chap-ter 7), and Marzano (Chapter 3) argue that this misguided perception con-tinues to shape and limit research agendas, policy decisions, and practices.

FIGURE 9.3

Human Development: A Focus for Teaching and Learning

- Introducing literacy standards through meaningful instruction and language and vocabulary development
- Extending the school day or school year to provide additional meaningful instructional time on aligned curriculum and assessment content and standards
- Enhancing instruction in smaller classes with staff development that ensures meaningful, challenging instruction and caring relationships
- Prioritizing goals, objectives, strategies, and program decisions in comprehensive school plans to support whole school reform
- Scheduling and focusing teacher preparation time on content knowledge and meaningful instruction
- Strengthening cognitive and affective student-teacher relationships
- Coordinating community resources and parent engagement activities to support instruction and assure caring relationships
- Formulating supportive policies and allocating resources informed by understandings and implications of theoretical integration

Manning and Kovach observe that "the content of professional interactions remains largely focused on student—rather than curricular or systemic—deficits. . . . It is necessary, therefore, to provide recommendations on how schools and districts can organize to ensure curricular equity by changing practices in the areas of curriculum and instruction, grouping and tracking, retention and remediation, and district policy" (p. 36). They conclude that schools must achieve a clear focus on challenging curriculum and quality instruction through district-level standards, family, community, and social services connections; and schoolwide organizational support. Five elements specifically needed include the following:

- Strong leadership
- Collaborative decision making
- Personalized environments
- Efficient and effective use of time
- Ongoing data-based professional development

Louis and Ingram (Chapter 8) offer their research defining the organizational conditions that ensure teacher engagement. They describe the following four types of engagement, two of which are affective, focusing on human relationships in the school, and two of which are instrumental, focusing on the goals of teaching and learning:

1. Engagement with the school as a social unit—a sense of community and personal caring among adults within the school and integration between personal life and work life.
2. Engagement with students as unique whole individuals—acknowledging and responding to students' thoughts and knowledge, listening to their ideas, becoming involved in students' personal as well as school lives, and in general being available to students who need support or assistance.
3. Engagement with academic achievement—writing and developing curriculum, sharing ideas and experiences about teaching as a craft with other teachers, making good and creative use of class time, expressing high expectations.
4. Engagement with a body of knowledge needed to carry out effective teaching—expressing one's personal passion for a subject and seeking ways to connect the subject to students' lives.

Attention to this existing and emerging theory and evidence requires support at all levels of the education system. Providing parents and community organizations with knowledge of normal human development in appropriate formats (such as participation with school improvement teams, workshops, literature, and so forth) and identifying and coordinating community agencies and resources strengthens the focus on teaching and learning (see Benard, Chapter 6).

Aligning Policy, Resources, and Accountability

Making use of the impressive body of knowledge and evidence on closing the achievement gap requires policy alignment and accountability at federal, state, and local levels. Research suggests that when schools succeed with culturally diverse and socioeconomically disadvantaged students, there exists a powerful belief system of high expectations that rejects deficit assumptions about children and their cultures, abilities, and life circumstances. In-depth research conducted in two school districts serving culturally diverse and socioeconomically disadvantaged students revealed important dimensions of teacher belief systems:

What we heard and read were differences about where the responsibility for ensuring student success should be lodged. Some respondents said that all students could succeed and it was the teachers' job to ensure that this happened. In other words, they did not want educators to accept any excuses for learning not taking place. We have labeled this a "no excuses" approach.

Others took exception to such an idealistic belief, suggesting that there were limits to what educators could accomplish. One portion maintained that students had to show some effort first; another group stressed that home environments had to be more supportive of education. (Corbett, Wilson, & Williams, 2002, p. 14)

A "no excuses" belief system is identified in recent reviews of education reform summarizing the conditions required for learning. Reform literature extensively describes practices observed in schools that successfully serve culturally diverse and socioeconomically disadvantaged students—that is, schools where achievement gaps are closing between groups (Annenberg Institute for School Reform, 2002; Cohen & Loewenberg Ball, 2001; Education Trust, 1999; Elmore, 2002; Johnson & Asera, 1999; Rossi & Stringfield, 1995). (See Figure 9.4 for a list of such practices.)

FIGURE 9.4

Characteristics of Schools Where Achievement Gaps Are Closing

- Important, visible and attainable goals
- High expectations
- Focus on the learners and on teaching and learning that builds on learners' experiences
- Strong leadership
- Collective sense of responsibility among staff for improvement
- Instruction aligned to standards
- Staff development and scheduled time for teachers to discuss and plan
- Parent and community engagement
- Additional time for instruction
- Frequently monitored individual student progress
- State or district accountability systems
- Adequate resources
- Perseverance

Assessments and Standards

The authors represented in this volume distinguish between the simplistic goals, objectives, programs, and strategies designed to improve achievement and the more complex systems and structures that exist where achievement gaps are actually closing.

Stiggins (1999) comments on the current assumptions concerning assessments and standards. He questions whether standards that use intimidation will lead to productive change and more effective schools. He chronicles the history of large-scale assessment programs that began in the 1930s with the "College Boards," continued in the 1950s and 1960s, with commercially developed, norm-referenced, districtwide standardized testing, and into the 1970s, 1980s, and 1990s, with the implementation of national and international assessment programs for achievement accountability. According to Meier (2002) and Reeves (2000), educators should view standardized tests as merely one tool among many to determine accountability. Reeves says that for an accountability system to be effective, it must determine the following:

- Individual student achievement
- Whole school performance
- Ways to help students learn
- Educational effectiveness

In addition, Stiggins (1999) emphasizes the need to link assessment and student motivation. Echoing Benard (Chapter 6) and the resilience literature, he recommends that educators strive to (1) keep students from losing confidence in themselves as learners, and (2) rekindle confidence among students who have lost that confidence. Stiggins observes that students use the information they receive through classroom assessments to draw conclusions about themselves as learners. He strongly recommends that educators find ways to help students learn to respond to more internal/intrinsic motivation, or in other words, to learn to take responsibility for their own academic success.

To accomplish the challenges outlined to close achievement gaps, there must be major shifts in assumptions designed to improve achievement—concerning the knowledge base, focus of instruction, strategies, and accountability systems (see Figure 9.5).

To accomplish the challenges outlined requires the commitment of the following individuals and groups:

- **Researchers and theorists** to outline a comprehensive framework for understanding human development that reflects the complexity of all of the available knowledge
- **Higher education and teacher preparation institutions** to develop and introduce pedagogy and experiences that build on this framework
- **Governments (federal, state, and district) and policy agencies** to craft policies and procedures requiring and monitoring the implications of the framework and providing necessary resources and support

FIGURE 9.5

Improving Achievement and Closing the Gap: Theory and the Broad Differences

	Improving Achievement	Closing the Achievement Gap
Knowledge Base	Individual psychology	Sociocultural development
Focus of Intervention	Curriculum, instruction, and assessment	The learner, teaching and learning, and supports for learners
Strategies	Decentralization, class size reduction, standards or programs, charters, and vouchers	Cross-disciplinary integration, whole school reform, structures, and alignment
Accountability	Schools, administrators, teachers, and students	Shared across institutions and the education community
Evidence	Improved achievement	Emerging consensus of theory, evidence and research confirming the conditions required for closing achievement gaps

- **Knowledgeable communities and parents** to provide the necessary caring and supports for learning
- **Districts and schools** to design and implement structures (for example, increased time for integrated, relevant instruction and standards) and environments (caring interpersonal relationships and high expectations) that ensure student success

It is clear that the complexities of closing the achievement gaps among groups mandates accountability across the education community. The need to revisit commonly held assumptions bears repeating. Simply reducing class size assumes that all teachers are prepared to implement a "no-excuses" agenda. Transitioning to site-based management assumes educators will focus on teaching, learning, and service to students differently than when management is directed by central office staff. Introducing standards assumes all educators in the district and school have the will to ensure that all students will learn them. Cole (1996) thoughtfully outlines what, in the end, must be done by every segment of the education community and every individual in education (researcher, college professor, policymaker, educator, parent, and so forth) in the following statement:

> Adopt some form of cultural-historical psychology as your theoretical framework. Create a methodology, a systematic way of relating theory to data that draws upon both the natural sciences and the cultural sciences, as befits its hybrid object, human beings. Find an activity setting where you can be both participant and analyst, enter into the process of helping things grow in the activity system you have entered by bringing to bear all the knowledge gained from both the cultural and natural sciences sides of psychology and allied disciplines. Take your ability to create and sustain effective systems as evidence of your theory's adequacy. (pp. 349–350)

A final comment on the importance of implementing change using this integrated knowledge base from Stephen J. Gould's *The Mismeasure of Man* (1981):

> We pass through this world but once. Few tragedies can be more extensive than the stunting of a life, few injustices deeper than the denial of opportunity to strive or even to hope by a limit imposed from without, but falsely identified as lying within. (pp. 28–29)

References

Annenberg Institute for School Reform. (2002). *School communities that work: A National Task Force on the future of urban districts* [Online]. Providence, RI: Brown University. Available: http://www.schoolcommunities.org/gaptl.html

Bartoli, J. S. (1995). *Unequal opportunity: Learning to read in the U.S.A.* New York: Teachers College Press.

Bell, J. A. (2001). High-performing poverty schools. *Leadership Magazine*, Association of California School Administrators. 8–11 [Online]. Available: http://www.acsa.org/publications/

Benard, B. (1996). *Environmental strategies for tapping resilience checklist.* Berkeley, CA: Resiliency Associates.

Bransford, J. D., Brown, A. L., & Cocking, R. R. (Eds.). (1999). *How people learn: Brain, mind, experience, and school.* Washington, DC: National Academy Press.

Braunger, J., & Lewis, J. P. (1997). *Building a knowledge base in reading.* Portland, OR: Northwest Regional Educational Laboratory.

Caine, R. N., & Caine, G. (1991). *Making connections: Teaching and the human brain*. Menlo Park, CA: Addison-Wesley.

Cohen, D. & Loewenberg Ball, D. (2001). Making change: Instruction and its improvement. *Phi Delta Kappan, 83*(1), 73–77.

Cole, M. (1996). *Cultural psychology*. Boston: Harvard University Press.

Corbett, D., Wilson, B., & Williams, B. (2002). *Effort and excellence in urban classrooms: Expecting—and getting—success with all students*. New York: Teachers College Press, Columbia University, & Washington, DC: National Education Association.

Crochunis, T., Erdey, S., & Swedlow, J. (Eds.). (2002). *The diversity kit: An introductory resource for social change in education—Part III: Language*. Providence, RI: LAB at Brown University.

Dewey, J. (1916). *Democracy and education*. New York: Free Press.

Dewey, J. (1938). *Experience and education*. New York: Collier Books.

The Education Trust. (1999). *Dispelling the myth: High poverty schools exceeding expectations*. Washington, DC: Author.

Elmore, R. (2002). *Bridging the gap between standards and achievement*. Washington, DC: Albert Shanker Institute.

Fullan, M. (1999). *Change forces: The sequel*. New York: The Falmer Press.

Gardner, H. (1999). *Intelligence reframed: Multiple intelligences for the 21st century*. New York: Basic Books.

Gould, S. J. (1981). *The mismeasure of man*. New York: W. W. Norton & Company.

Johnson, J., & Asera, R. (1999). *Hope for urban education: A study of nine high-performing, high-poverty urban elementary schools*. Austin, TX: Charles A. Dana Center, University of Texas at Austin.

Knapp, M. S. (1995). *Teaching for meaning in high-poverty classrooms*. New York: Teachers College Press.

Knapp, M. S., Shields, P. M., & Turnbull, B. J. (1995). Academic challenge in high poverty classrooms. *Phi Delta Kappan, 76*(10), 770–776.

Ladson-Billings, G. (1994). *The dreamkeepers: Successful teachers of African American children*. San Francisco: Jossey-Bass.

Lee, J. (2002). Racial and ethnic achievement gap trends: Reversing the progress toward equity? *Educational Researcher, 31*(1), 3–12.

Mathes, P. G., & Torgesen, J. K. (2000). A call for equity in reading instruction for all students: A response to Allington and Woodside-Jiron. *Educational Researcher, 29*(6), 4–14.

Meier, D. (2002). Standardization versus standards. *Phi Delta Kappan, 84*(3), 190–198.

Oakes, J., & Lipton, M. (1999). *Teaching to change the world*. New York: McGraw-Hill College.

Ogbu, J. U. (1994). Culture and intelligence. In R. J. Sternberg (Ed.), *Encyclopedia of human intelligence: Vol. 2* (pp. 328–338). New York: Macmillan.

Osborn. J., & Lehr, F. (Eds.). (1998). *Literacy for all: Issues in teaching and learning*. New York: Guilford.

Piaget, J. (1969). *The mechanisms of perception*. New York: Basic Books, Inc.

Pikulski, J. J. (1998). *Teaching word-identification skills and strategies: A balanced approach*. Boston: Houghton Mifflin.

Reeves, D. B. (2000). *Accountability in action: A blueprint for learning organizations*. Denver, CO: Advanced Learning Press.

Resnick, L. (1995). From aptitude to effort: A new foundation for our schools. *Daedalus, 124*(4), 55–62.

Rossi, R. J., & Stringfield, S. (1995). What we must do for students placed at risk. *Phi Delta Kappan, 77*(1), 73–76.

Skinner, B. F. (1974). *About behaviorism*. New York: Alfred A. Knopf.

Snow, C. E., Burns, S., & Griffin, P. (Eds.). (1998). *Preventing reading difficulties in young children*. Washington, DC: National Research Council.

Stevenson, H. W., & Stigler, J. W. (1992). *The learning gap: Why our schools are failing and what we can learn from Japanese and Chinese education*. New York: Simon and Schuster.

Stiggins, R. (1999). Assessment, student confidence, and school success. *Phi Delta Kappan, 81*(3), 191–198.

Taylor, B. M., Anderson, R. C., Au, K. H., & Raphael, T. E. (2000). Discretion in the translation of research to policy: A case from beginning reading. *Educational Researcher, 29*(6), 16–26.

U.S. Department of Education. (1998). *The education system in Japan: Case study findings: Individual differences and the Japanese Education System* [Online]. Available: http://www.ed.gov/pubs/JapanCaseStudy/chapter3a.html

Vygotsky, L. S. (1981). The development of higher forms of attention in childhood. In J. V. Wertsch (Ed.), *The concept of activity in Soviet psychology* (pp. 198–240). Armonk, NY: M. E. Sharpe.

Williams. B. (1996). *Closing the achievement gap: A vision for changing beliefs and practices*. Alexandria, VA: Association for Supervision and Curriculum Development.

Index

f indicates material appearing in a figure.

About the Authors

Bonnie Benard is an internationally known figure in the field of prevention and youth development theory, policy, and practice, particularly for introducing and conceptualizing resiliency theory and application in her 1991 monograph, *Fostering Resiliency in Kids: Protective Factors in the Family, School, and Community.* She holds an M.A. in social work and is currently a Senior Program Associate with the Health and Human Development Program at WestEd in Oakland, California, where she has led the development of a statewide resilience and youth development assessment for the California Department of Education. She has received numerous awards, including most recently WestEd's 2002 Award for Distinguished Contribution to the Field.

Patricia Marks Greenfield received her doctorate from Harvard University and is currently Professor of Psychology at the University of California, Los Angeles (UCLA), where she is a member of the developmental psychology group. Her central theoretical and research interest is the relationship between culture and human development. She is a past recipient of the American Association for the Advancement of Science Award for Behavioral Science Research, and has received teaching awards from UCLA and the American Psychological Association. Her books include *Mind and Media: The Effects of Television, Video Games, and Computers* (1984), which has been translated into nine languages. More recently, Greenfield and R. R. Cocking coedited the books *Interacting with Video* (1996) and *Cross-Cultural Roots of Minority Child Development* (1994).

Since 1969, Greenfield has done field research on child development and socialization in Chiapas, Mexico. She is currently involved with a research project in Los Angeles that investigates how cultural values influence relationships on multiethnic high school sports teams, and is also engaged in the Bridging Cultures teacher-research and professional development project.

John A. Kovach is the Associate Director of Field Services at the Laboratory for Student Success at the Mid-Atlantic Regional Educational

Laboratory, Temple University. His training is in sociology. He has both research and applied experience related to educational programming and evaluation in minority and adult education, and has taught at the Pennsylvania State University and the Kutztown University of Pennsylvania. In addition, he has been a Senior Research Associate with the Adult Learning Project in Washington, DC; directed the National Indian Adult Education Needs Survey for the Office of Indian Education; and written articles and book chapters dealing with poverty and education, Native American education policy, and adolescent drug use. His current research and writing focus is on urban education policy, educational segregation, and teacher quality. Kovach can be reached at the Laboratory for Student Success (LSS), Temple University, 1301 Cecil B. Moore Avenue, Philadelphia, PA 19122-6091. Telephone: (215) 204-3016.

Karen Seashore Louis is Professor of Educational Policy and Administration at the University of Minnesota. She received her doctorate in sociology at Columbia University; her major areas of specialization include organizational behavior, knowledge utilization, sociology of education, and research methods. She has authored many books and articles in her areas of interest and is active as a reviewer of professional publications, most recently exploring the topics of school improvement and change, quality of teacher work life, democracy and educational systems, and academic-industry relations in science. She has conducted comparative studies of the educational system in countries ranging from the Netherlands to Azerbaijan.

JoAnn B. Manning is the Executive Director of the Laboratory for Student Success at the Mid-Atlantic Regional Educational Laboratory, Temple University, where she provides the intellectual and administrative leadership to support interdisciplinary teams of researchers and practitioners addressing emerging problems in education. She has served in many roles during her career of over 30 years in education, including teacher, supervisor, director of special education programs, and principal for the School District of Philadelphia. She is also a former assistant superintendent and a former superintendent for school districts in the state of Pennsylvania. Her research focuses on building family, school, and community partnerships and turning around low-performing schools. Over the course of the past decade, Manning has contributed to edited volumes on successful reading instruction, school choice, linking collaborative services with school reform, urban education, teacher education, and adaptive education strategies. She is also active on several professional boards, including the National Advisory Board for *The School Community Journal*, published by the Academic Development Institute; the Leadership Team for the Collaborative for Academic, Social, and Emotional Learning at the University of Illinois at Chicago; and the Board of Directors for the Philadelphia Chapter of the Black Alliance for Educational Options (BAEO). She can be reached at the Laboratory for Student Success (LSS), Temple University, 1301 Cecil B. Moore Avenue, Philadelphia, PA 19122-6091. Telephone: (215) 204-3007.

Robert J. Marzano currently works as a senior scholar at Mid-Continent Research for Education and Learning in Aurora, Colorado; an associate professor at Cardinal Stritch University in Milwaukee, Wisconsin; and a Colorado-based private consultant. He is the coauthor of several books, most recently *Classroom Management That Works: Research-Based Strategies for Every Teacher* (with Jana S. Marzano and Debra J. Pickering, 2003); *Classroom Instruction That Works: Research Strategies for Increasing Student Achievement* (with Debra J. Pickering and Jane E. Pollock, 2001); and *A Handbook for Classroom Instruction That Works* (with Jennifer S. Norford, Diane E. Paynter, Debra J. Pickering, and Barbara B. Gaddy, 2001). In addition, Marzano was head developer of the *Dimensions of Learning* and *Tactics for Thinking* programs for the Association for Supervision and Curriculum Development.

An internationally known trainer and speaker, Marzano received his B.A. in English from Iona College in New York; an M.Ed. in reading/language arts from Seattle University, Seattle, Washington; and a Ph.D. in curriculum and instruction from the University of Washington, Seattle. He may be contacted at 7127 S. Danube Court, Centennial, CO 80016. Telephone: (303) 796-7683. E-mail: robertjmarzano@aol.com.

Blanca Quiroz is a doctoral student of human development and psychology specializing in issues of language and culture in education. A former teacher, Quiroz is currently a Research Assistant at the Center for Applied Linguistics' Early Childhood Study of Language and Literacy Development of Spanish-Speaking Children. She has conducted research on cross-cultural communication and values in California urban schools, and recently conducted research on the transference of literacy skills between languages among bilingual elementary students. A participant in the Bridging Cultures Project since its beginning in 1996, Quiroz is the author of *Bridging Cultures Between Home and School: A Guide for Teachers* (2001) and edited the Fall 2001 "Immigration and Education" issue of the *Harvard Educational Review*. She is now working on a dissertation about the study of early language and literacy skills among Spanish-speaking families in Boston.

Floraline I. Stevens has worked as an independent evaluation consultant since retiring in 1994 from the Los Angeles Unified School District, where she served as director of Program Evaluation and Assessment. Between 1992 and 1994, she served as Program Director at the National Science Foundation (NSF) in the Division of Research, Evaluation, and Dissemination of the Directorate for Education and Human Resources. She continues to work with the NSF on the meta-evaluation of the Ventures in Education Program and nationwide project evaluation workshops. As a Senior Fellow at the National Center for Education Statistics, Stevens researched the topic of opportunity-to-learn programs in relation to equity for poor and minority students; her work on the topic has been published by the Office of Educational Research and Improvement and the *Journal of Negro Education*. Currently active on the national advisory boards of numerous educational institutions, projects, associations, and publications, Stevens earned her doctorate in educational psychology, research, and evaluation at the University of California at Los Angeles.

Elise Trumbull is an applied psycholinguist specializing in issues of language and culture in education. A former teacher and school assessment specialist, she has conducted research on assessment in settings from California to Micronesia. She has directed the Bridging Cultures Project since its inception in 1996 and is Research Coordinator for "New Perspectives on the Assessment of English Language Learners," a new project on the assessment of English-language learners sponsored by the National Science Foundation. Trumbull is coauthor with Beverly Farr of *Assessment Alternatives for Diverse Classrooms* (1997), and coeditor with Farr of *Grading and Reporting Student Progress in an Age of Standards* (2000) and *Bridging Cultures Between Home and School: A Guide for Teachers* (2001).

Belinda Williams is a cognitive psychologist with more than 30 years of experience studying the academic achievement patterns of culturally and socioeconomically disadvantaged students. She has held senior research and development positions at the University of Pennsylvania, the Northeast and Islands Regional Educational Laboratory at Brown University, and Research for Better Schools. Her research focuses on the impact of cultural environments on cognitive development. In addition to her work with the National Education Association's *Priority Schools Initiative*, state departments, universities, national associations, and school districts, she is the editor of *Closing the Achievement Gap: A Vision for Changing Beliefs and Practices* (1996) and coauthor of *Effort and Excellence in Urban Classrooms: Expecting—and Getting—Success from All Students* (2002). She received her doctorate in psychology from Rutgers University.

Kenneth M. Zeichner is the Hoefs-Bascom Professor of Teacher Education and Associate Dean of the School of Education at the University of Wisconsin–Madison. In his current position as a professor in the Department of Curriculum and Instruction, he coordinates a professional development school partnership involving six schools in Madison and teaches graduate courses in the study of teacher education. He has recently written about such topics as preparing teachers for cultural diversity, action research, reflective teaching, and teacher education reform. In 2002, Zeichner received the American Association of Colleges for Teacher Education's Margaret B. Lindsay Award for Distinguished Research in Teacher Education.

Related ASCD Resources

At the time of publication, the following ASCD resources were available; for the most up-to-date information about ASCD resources, go to www.ascd.org. ASCD stock numbers are noted in parentheses.

Audiotapes

Alternatives to Retention and Social Promotion: Personalizing the Learning Environment for At-Risk Students, by Leslie S. Kaplan and William A. Owings (#201203)

Building a Learning Community by Welcoming Every Student, by Richard Curwin (#203186)

Creating a Climate for Learning: Essential Strategies for the Urban Classroom, by Helen Maniates (#203156)

Books

Beyond Islands of Excellence: What Districts Can Do to Improve Instruction and Achievement in All Schools, by Wendy Togneri (#303368)

Creating and Inclusive School, by Jacqueline S. Thousand and Richard A. Villa (#195210)

How to Involve Parents in a Multicultural School, by Bruce McDonnell Davis (#195081)

Videos

Educating Everybody's Children (six videos with two facilitator's guides) by Robert W. Cole (#400228)

Multicultural Education (40-minute program and facilitator's guide) by James Banks and Carlos Cortes (#494033)

For more information, visit us on the World Wide Web (http://www.ascd.org), send an e-mail message to member@ascd.org, call the ASCD Service Center (1-800-933-ASCD or 703-578-9600, then press 2), send a fax to 703-575-5400, or write to Information Services, ASCD, 1703 N. Beauregard St., Alexandria, VA 22311-1714 USA.